HEROES

BEHIND BARBED WIRE

HEROES
BEHIND BARBED WIRE

by KENNETH K. HANSEN
Colonel, Infantry, USA

D. VAN NOSTRAND COMPANY, INC.
PRINCETON, NEW JERSEY
Toronto · London · New York

D. VAN NOSTRAND COMPANY, INC.

120 Alexander St., Princeton, New Jersey
257 Fourth Avenue, New York 10, New York
25 Hollinger Rd., Toronto 16, Canada

*All correspondence should be addressed to the
principal office of the company at Princeton, N. J.*

COPYRIGHT, 1957, BY
D. VAN NOSTRAND COMPANY, INC.

Library of Congress Catalogue Card No. 57-11591

Published simultaneously in Canada by
D. VAN NOSTRAND COMPANY (Canada), LTD.

Preface

This is the story of the program, in conjunction with the conflict with communism in Korea, on which former President Truman and General MacArthur saw eye to eye. Its inception is a tribute to their foresight, for their program was one which, in any future war between the free world and the communist complex, we shall be obliged to apply again.

If it is made plain that we will again apply it, and that we will carry it to its logical conclusion, the next time—that we will not merely free anti-communist prisoners of war but will arm them to fight for the liberation of their nations—it is entirely possible that future communist aggression may be curbed. Such a program, fully implemented, can be as great a deterrent to small wars as the H-bomb is to great wars, and can rank next to the intercontinental ballistic missile as a deterrent to world war.

The success of the Truman-MacArthur program was due to two more genuinely great leaders, General Mark W. Clark, who needs no identification, and the late Major General Robert A. McClure, former Chief of Psychological Warfare, U. S.

Army—and to many hundreds of their able associates and assistants. I have mentioned as many of these as possible in connection with their efforts; I only wish it were feasible to name them all. I do want to express my appreciation, in particular, to Commander Edgar H. Forrest, USN, and Lieutenant Colonels Frederick W. Hess and Vaughn F. Meisling, USA, for their assistance in recalling details of the valiant and victorious struggle of the anti-communist heroes in Korea.

KENNETH K. HANSEN

The Joint Staff,
Washington, D. C.
August, 1957

vi

Contents

1

A New Principle of Freedom

"The armistice in Korea," said President Dwight D. Eisenhower in his 1954 Memorial Day speech, "inaugurated a new principle of freedom—that prisoners of war are entitled to choose the side to which they wish to be released. In its impact on history, that one principle may weigh more than any battle of our time."

The battle for the establishment of this principle began on V-E Day in 1945, although few recognized it for what it was at the time. It is not entirely ended.

The first skirmishes were won by the side opposing the principle of free choice. With the capitulation of Germany, it became extremely important to the U. S. S. R. to round up the ex-members of the Red Army and the civilians who had defected to the Nazis, no matter what their status—in German uniform as members of the Vlassov Army, prisoners of war, forced laborers, displaced persons, political refugees. For of all the allies, only the U. S. S. R. at that time grasped the significance of the Red Army defections, by regiment, division, even army, as the panzers rolled eastward in the initial invasion of

Russia. Had Hitler understood it and had he fully employed ex-Red soldiers against Red soldiers, the outcome in the east might have been different. Unlike the Napoleonic debacle, this march on Moscow might have been triumphant. But the Nazis, mistrusting these men who had rallied even to them against the Red regime, and quickly alienating the civilian population which had welcomed them as liberators, lost their big opportunity.

With the Nazi surrender, Soviet teams began to scour Europe, reclaiming any and everyone for whom there was any semblance of an excuse for repatriation to Russia, and many for whom there was none.

No onus need attach to the non-communist allies for agreeing to this procedure. Each nation had its own problems in repatriating its nationals. Cooperation seemed to be the only answer in meeting the problem of the displaced persons, a problem which still has not been solved. In the flush of victory, with the Reds yet to doff the mask of ally, with every other nation busy with its own concerns, with overworked officers and enlisted ranks rotating home too rapidly, few had time to concern themselves with the question of whether Latvians, Lithuanians, or Estonians, for instance, really were Russians or independent nationals.

But once the repatriation operation got under way, strange stories began to circulate about the singular lack of joy with which the displaced easterners faced the prospect of returning to the bosom of Mother Russia. American officers coming back from Italy told of repatriates embarking from Bari who jumped into the sea and drowned rather than return to Russia. Others returning from Austria told of cattle cars which had to be locked and festooned with barbed wire to keep their passengers from leaping into ravines. And a British merchant marine captain told of delivering a shipload of repatriates to Murmansk, only to see them marched behind the nearest warehouse and to hear a long, ominous rattle of machine-gun fire.

In short, those who had lived under the Soviet system knew that anyone who had escaped from it, even under the most horrible of wartime conditions, was suspect, and that immediate death of one's own choosing was preferable to having no choice, upon one's return, between execution or the alternative of a lingering death in a slave labor camp.

In the four years which followed V-E Day, another shocking fact became evident to the world. Communist concern over Soviet prisoners of war and displaced persons did not extend to captured Axis personnel. Post-war repatriation had been woefully one-sided. Hundreds of thousands of Germans and Japanese were still being held by the U. S. S. R. Lesser numbers but a substantial total of Italians, Spaniards, and others who had fought for the Axis, either out of conviction or compulsion, were also missing.

It had also become painfully apparent that the U. S. S. R. was no longer an ally, but would be the enemy in the event of World War III. The cold war was on, and it was hot in spots—in China, in Greece, in Indochina, and in Malaya. The Iron Curtain had been christened and lowered, and it had moved westward in Europe to shadow Czechoslovakia. More than 25,000 Greeks had been added to the total of prisoners of war and displaced persons behind it.

3

Under these circumstances, it was not surprising that one of the major concerns of the free world delegates meeting in Switzerland in 1949 for the post World War II revision of the Geneva conventions on prisoners of war was repatriation, after any future war, of their nationals, as well as prevention of mass repossession of refugees and ugly communist retaliation upon them.

One revision in the 1949 Convention for which the United States contended successfully was an obligation to carry out the release and repatriation of prisoners of war immediately following the cessation of active hostilities, rather than upon the conclusion of peace—a useful clause when one considers that the U. S. S. R. has thus far blocked a peace treaty with Germany for all concerned, and waited eleven years to conclude their inconclusive peace treaty with Japan. And in Korea there is only an armistice, not peace.

Every possible safeguard, for both prisoners of war and civilians, was included in the convention. The language in some sections was broad, but it had to be. It was essential to secure Soviet acceptance. This was accomplished, and ratification or accession by the satellites, with the exception of North Korea and Red China, followed as a matter of course.

Before the United States Senate could consummate ratification, communist aggression erupted in Korea. But General MacArthur immediately announced that the United Nations Command (UNC) would adhere to the humanitarian provisions of the conventions, and Secretary of State Acheson reaffirmed this to the International Committee of the Red Cross. Belatedly, the Foreign Minister of North Korea, in a message

4

to the Secretary General of the United Nations, said that the North Korean forces would observe the "principles" of the Geneva conventions.

The communist forces attacked the Republic of Korea on the 25th of June, 1950. Before the Communist onslaught, Seoul fell three days later.

The United Nations intervened, and by the Fourth of July, the governments of forty-four member nations announced support of such intervention. Suwon was lost the same day. Two months later, the Republic of Korea (ROK) Army and the U. N. forces—United States and British only, at that stage—had been compressed into the famous Pusan perimeter, just a heel-hold on the Korean peninsula.

On the 15th of September, General MacArthur landed his memorable left hook—United States and British naval units, American air and two U. S. divisions—at Inchon. This time the Pusan perimeter erupted. Seoul was retaken on the 28th of September, three months to the day from its capture.

By late October, U. N. forces—the Sixth ROKA Division first—reached the Yalu. And in late October, Chinese Communist "Volunteers," first feinting and then flanking the U. N. troops in force, proceeded to chew them up.

By the end of December, the U. N. forces—now including Australian, Belgian, Dutch, French, Greek, Luxembourgeoise, Filipino, Thai and Turkish units—were pushed back to the 38th Parallel, the imaginary line at which the war had started. On January 4, 1951, Seoul again fell to the communists. But this time, the U. N. forces held south of Seoul, and in the same month General Ridgway began to grind his way north.

5

During February and March, the Chinese Communist Forces were crushed, as the North Korean Army had been destroyed the fall before. Seoul was liberated for the final time on March 14. On March 24, General MacArthur, pointing out to the enemy that communist aggression, first North Korean, then Chinese, had twice failed, offered to meet the enemy commander to arrange a cease fire.

The communists answered with an April offensive. The U. N. forces—Canadians and New Zealanders now among them too—rolled with the punch, then held with a ten to one advantage in casualties. A second offensive in May only brought the Reds twenty times the U. N. casualties, and restored the April battle line. The United Nations Command now held one hundred thousand Chinese and Korean prisoners of war, and its forces were pressing into North Korea for the third time.

On the 23rd of June, 1951, Jacob Malik, chief Soviet delegate to the United Nations, proposed a cease-fire and an armistice. Armistice negotiations began on the 10th of July: there was no cease-fire.

2

POWs as a Psychological Warfare Weapon

The use of prisoners of war as a psychological warfare weapon is as old as history, but it has remained for world communism to perfect and advance it to a leading place in the Red arsenal. As the Chinese communist forces in 1948 spread out across China from Yenan, it became standard practice to seize upon a group of Nationalist prisoners, bind their wounds, treat them solicitously, and feed them well. Those who responded "righteously" to such treatment and indicated a desire to change sides could be accommodated. Those who remained recalcitrant could be taken to the nearest ravine and shot. The remainder were turned loose, to go back to their own lines, tell of the excellent treatment they had received, and lower the resistance of their fellows to capture.

At the same time, in Europe, with an election approaching in France and the Communist Party in need of an assist, a dozen Alsatians could be repatriated from a Soviet slave labor camp and an infinite amount of propaganda reaped for the "kind communists." Such token repatriations—of Germans, Japanese, Italians, Spaniards—have been employed profitably

7

by the Soviet Union for the last ten years, with never a word of the thousands of similar unfortunates still languishing behind the Iron Curtain.

There is a long-range psychological warfare advantage to these delayed repatriations, too, fitting in neatly with the over-all communist exploitation of mankind. Psychology in the Soviet Union has been empirical rather than scientific. All advances stopped in 1917; modern psychiatry could cure many, on both sides of the Iron Curtain, of the disease of communism, and modern psychiatry was therefore banned for good communists on both sides of the curtain.

But the conditioned reflex was discovered by Pavlov in 1890, one of the few legitimate Russian firsts, and the communists know it well. Apply a certain stimulus, and you get a certain response. Give a dog a bowl of food and ring a bell at the same time, and the dog slavers. Before long he slavers at the sound of the bell alone—no food is necessary. In communist economies, this may have certain advantages.

Apply this, now, to unrepatriated prisoners of war in a slave labor camp. They are overworked and underfed, and when it is too dark to work they are subjected to endless, repetitious lectures . . . indoctrination . . . brainwashing. With their resistance low, inevitably they absorb some of the indoctrination and begin to give the desired answers. Some give them because they are really conditioned; others to mitigate the relentless pressure.

These, then, are transferred to slightly lighter work and given slightly better food. They confess their bourgeois "sins," and they feel better. They are not expert calorie counters and

8

may be forgiven if they think they feel better because of good marks in Marx rather than because of diminishing danger of death from starvation. Now they may be worked even a little less, fattened up so that they will not photograph so shockingly, and put on the lists of prospective repatriates.

They are still screened carefully, because there is always the risk that some are shamming conversion, but eventually they may become part of a token repatriation. Home they go, to sow doubt and dissension wittingly or unwittingly. And their nations relax hopefully at this new evidence of Soviet good will at last—for they too have been conditioned to slaver at the sound of a bell.

Exploitation of prisoners of war by communist nations was so thoroughly developed by the time of the Korean conflict that it can be said that they had worked out a definite policy with respect to prisoners. That policy, in short, was to retain as many free world prisoners as was possible—for brainwashing, blackmail, and bargaining—and to get back every communist prisoner. This would seem to call for carrying water on both shoulders, but that is standard operating procedure in the communist system. The communist propagandist has a different story for each audience, secure in the knowledge that exposure of his contradictions will rarely if ever have the widespread effect of his initial lies.

At any rate, when the Korean armistice negotiations began the first agenda item proposed by the communists was the matter of the prisoners of war. The United Nations Command negotiators and UNC headquarters in Tokyo recognized this as one of the stickiest problems in conjunction with an armistice

9

in Korea, and one on which the talks might hang up for all time. Consequently they moved to place it last on the agenda.

It was a sticky problem for several reasons. There was, first, the question of who had won the inconclusive war. The communists had taken more than 60,000 prisoners of war; the UNC, more than 160,000. But 50,000 of the communists' prisoners had been Koreans whom they had "released at the front," that is, press-ganged into slave-labor battalions and prisoner of war guard units. So the proportion of prisoners of war, to the uninitiated eye, seemed to be on the order of 15 to 1.

Second, both sides were aware of the fact that a proportion of the prisoners of war in the hands of the United Nations Command did not wish to return to communist control. How large a proportion neither side knew—the UNC because its intelligence said the proportion was greater than the communists expected it to be and verification of that fact would not help to get an armistice, and the communist side because its intelligence said the proportion was very low. The Korean conflict was more than a civil war, but it was a civil war too, and as always in such situations the intelligence task is made easier by the fact that an agent of one side can pass himself off as a farmer—a few yards from a prisoner of war stockade on the other side—and vice versa.

Even a low percentage of prisoners of war not wanting to return to communist control was unpalatable to the enemy, however, and it was probably due to the steps the communists took to reduce that percentage, and the fact that those steps took time, that the UNC negotiators were successful in getting the question of the prisoners of war moved down on the

10

agenda to the next-to-the-last item. By the time the truce talks reached it, the communists were ready with their exploitation of the prisoners for psychological purposes.

The first part of their general policy on prisoners of war—retention of as many as possible of the UNC prisoners—had already been implemented. When Lieutenant General W. K. Harrison, Jr., who had succeeded Admiral C. Turner Joy as the chief UNC truce negotiator, taxed Nam Il, the chief communist negotiator, with the disappearance of five-sixths of the Korean prisoners in communist hands, Nam blandly replied that "your question does not exist at all. Our policy of releasing (sic) prisoners at the front is well known."

The next step, to regain a maximum of the Red Chinese and North Korean POWs, presented more difficulties. Their position with respect to the prisoners who did not wish to return to them was that the UNC was, by "persecution" and "terror," forcibly detaining them. The obvious contradiction that persecution and terror would hardly persuade even an anti-communist to throw in with the UNC bothered them not at all. And the kidnapping of Brigadier General Francis T. Dodd, head of the UNC POW Command, was the opening gun in the campaign to "prove" this persecution and terrorization. General Dodd, responding to a request of the leaders of a huge communist compound for a consultation, was seized, dragged to a hidden "command post" in the center of the enclosure, and held hostage. The price of his release was to have been a promise from the UNC to "stop" persecuting and terrorizing the communist POWs, implying that the command actually had been conducting such a campaign.

As is so often the case in communist propaganda, the enemy was guilty of the very crimes with which the United Nations were charged. When word was received in North Korea that even a few of the Chinese and Koreans in UNC hands did not plan to return, the communist espionage and propaganda machine went into action. A detailed CINCUNC—"Commander in Chief United Nations Command"—study published by General Mark W. Clark early in 1953, and presented in the U. N. General Assembly by U. S. Ambassador Henry Cabot Lodge, blueprinted the organization by means of which Nam Il piously deplored American "savagery" with respect to the prisoners of war, in the armistice negotiations, and on the other hand directed agitation among the prisoners to bolster his specious charges.

Those who would criticize the U. S. Army for permitting a situation to develop in which a brigadier general could be kidnapped by his own prisoners should consider some of the problems faced by the successive Commanders in Chief in the Far East. The logistical problems alone of feeding, clothing, and housing an ever-mounting total of POWs were enormous. The security problems presented by such a disproportionate number of former enemy troops in the Eighth Army rear were as serious. There never were enough U. S. soldiers in Korea from the beginning to the end of the conflict to guard them properly, and the other nations participating in the U. N. action were averse to having their troops used for this purpose, as witness the Canadian clamor when their troops were called upon for assistance in the post-Koje period. Every ROK soldier who could be trained was needed for combat, too, and the end arrangement was a system in which, with minimum U. S. assistance, the prisoners of war were guarded by Korean security forces under the ROK Provost Marshal General.

They were placed on Koje Island, to the south of the Korean peninsula, so that in the event of UNC reverses and organized action on the prisoners' part there would be at least a stretch of water between them and the Eighth's rear. Grouped in compounds of up to 8,000 men each, they presented to the Prisoner of War Command a problem quite unlike that encountered by U. S. military police in World Wars I and II.

Unlike German and Italian prisoners who would move tractably to the rear under the command of their own officers, and Japanese who considered themselves dead in the eyes of the Emperor and needed only to be protected from their Korean fellow-prisoners, the hard-core communist Chinese and North Korean POWs organized themselves into military forces as formidable as the regiments they had left in the north. The supposed minority of anti-communists were kept in subjection by precisely the terror and torture of which their American custodians were being accused, not stopping short of brutal and bloody murder.

This was the explosive situation when the armistice talks progressed to the prisoner of war agenda item—and all progress ground to a halt. The communists were adamant in their insistence upon regaining all of their personnel. The United Nations Command was equally insistent on the principle that no genuine anti-communists among them should be returned—that the UNC should not be guilty of the inhumanity of which

13

the non-communist allies of World War II had unintentionally been culpable.

Nothing inhibited forceful presentation of the communist position. The UNC, on the other hand, was embarrassed on several counts.

First of all, there was the matter of the prisoners of war from sixteen United Nations and the Republic of Korea, in communist hands. Nothing that might prevent regaining an absolute maximum of these men, if and when an armistice was signed, could be risked.

Then there was the problem of what to do with and how to take care of the undetermined proportion of anti-communist POWs. While President Rhee might be disposed to accept the North Koreans, it was not expected that he would welcome the Chinese within the Republic of Korea. The United Nations Command was a multinational organization with its base in Japan, a neutral non-member—at that time—of the U.N. Japan might take the Chinese, but feels that it already has too many Koreans. None of the other fifteen U. N. members was offering sanctuary, and, since all the prisoners were without valid passports, the McCarran act effectively barred them from the United States.

Finally, there was the fact already cited—the conviction that revelation to the communists of the number who would actually choose to renounce repatriation would not be helpful in securing an armistice at all. The possibility also had to be considered that the communists might decide to fight their way the length of the Korean peninsula and on to Koje to regain all of the prisoners by force, rather than admit defection on such a scale.

The POWs, in short, were an embarrassment to the United Nations Command. One Eighth Army wag suggested, at about this time, that the communist forces could win the war promptly by ordering a few hundred thousand more hard-core, recalcitrant Reds to surrender. On the basis of one U. S. soldier to guard each prisoner, the remainder of the Red forces could roll on south with only scattered U. N. opposition.

But the prisoners were still a weapon to the communists. That they could obtain from them a fair amount of intelligence out of the compounds has already been noted. The way they got intelligence, orders, and instructions into the camps was by ordering surrenders on a small scale. Among the steady stream of surrenderees were private soldiers who passed every test which might have revealed them as agents, often as officers. Off they went to Koje, there to deliver Nam Il's latest instructions to the communist compound leaders, frequently to assume command of compounds and bear down even more heavily on the anti-communist elements.

In such a deadlock, it was inevitable that the question of exactly how many prisoners of war did not wish to return should be asked at Panmunjom.

3

The "Screenings"

The United Nations Command knew the proportion of prisoners of war who had freely surrendered in Korea, in distinction to being forcibly, physically captured, but that was an item of intelligence it was not, and still is not, about to give the communists. However, it did not know what percentage of the surrenderees were so anti-communist that they would renounce their homes and families, and what percentage had surrendered to escape, simply, the prospect of probable death. Nor did it know what proportion of captives, released from overt communist domination in the prisoner of war camps and given decent treatment at UNC hands, might decide against repatriation.

There was, of course, a way to find out: ask them. The communist negotiators at Panmunjom, secure in the knowledge that Nam Il had passed instructions to the communist compound leaders to vote their compounds as units, against repatriation, and to resist any attempt to screen the prisoners of war individually, gave tacit assent to a proposal to do just that. Further, they furnished the UNC with a declaration of amnesty, signed by General Kim Il Sung, Commander of the "Korean People's Army," and General Peng Teh-huai, Commander of the "Chinese People's Volunteers." This promised both the Korean and the Chinese prisoners that they would be fully forgiven for their crime of having been captured by the UNC. That a declaration of amnesty should have seemed logical to the communist commanders is in itself a devastating commentary on the repressiveness of their regimes.

Over loudspeakers installed in the compounds, and from loudspeaker trucks, the amnesty declaration was broadcast to the prisoners of war on Koje for two successive days in April, 1952. It was prefaced by the following UNC announcement:

"All prisoners of war will be individually interviewed in the next few days. This interview is being conducted for the purpose of determining which prisoners of war desire to be repatriated to the Korean People's Army or to the Chinese People's Volunteers, and which ones have compelling reasons which they feel would make it impossible for them to return to their own side. This determination will speed up the rate of repatriation at the time prisoners of war are exchanged.

"At this time I must caution you that the decision you make is a most important one, possibly the most vital one you will ever be called upon to make. You must most carefully consider each aspect of the matter. You must make your own decision and for your own safety it is essential that you do not discuss this matter with others and above all that you let no other person, even your best friend, know what your decision will be prior to the time you are asked for it by the interviewer.

"To those prisoners of war who are not violently opposed to

17

repatriation, the United Nations Command will guarantee return to your authorities at the time prisoners of war are exchanged. Your decision in this matter will be considered final. The UNC can make no guarantee whatever as to the ultimate fate of those who refuse to go back to their own people.

"Before any of you, for any reason which you think may be compelling, decides irrevocably to reject repatriation, you must consider the effect of your decision on your family. The fact that you are a POW has been reported to your authorities and they know that you are alive and well. If you fail to return, the communists will undoubtedly consider your family suspect. You may well never see your family again. You must consider this matter from every angle.

"If your final decision is that you are violently opposed to repatriation, you may undoubtedly be held in custody here on Koje-do for many long months. However, the UNC cannot house and feed you forever. The United Nations Command can make no promises regarding your future. In particular, the UNC cannot and will not guarantee to send you to any certain place. This is a matter which you should consider most carefully.

"Interviews will be conducted in each compound to prepare rolls of the prisoners of war to be repatriated. Rosters by battalion have already been prepared.

"Within a few days interview points will be established near the sally port in each compound. At the appointed hour prisoners of war will be formed by battalion according to roster. Unarmed UNC clerks and U. S. MPs will enter the compound to conduct the interviews. Prisoners of war will move to the

18

interview point when called by the clerks, where they will be asked to express their decisions. They will carry their equipment and clothing with them.

"Depending upon each individual's decision, he will remain in his present compound or be moved immediately.

"After individual interview, prisoners of war who are to be repatriated will be housed in compounds separate from those prisoners of war who strongly oppose repatriation.

"You are reminded that quiet and good order must be maintained within the compound during the conduct of these interviews."

Faithfully obeying Nam Il's instructions, a majority of the Korean compound leaders refused the screening teams entry to their compounds, and no reliable figure could be obtained of the North Koreans who would refuse repatriation. It may seem strange that U. S. officers and men were unable to enter compounds holding prisoners of war who were in their custody, but to anyone familiar with the scene and the situation, it is quite understandable. Koje is a rugged island, and rocks as big as grapefruit were everywhere at hand as elementary weapons. These were supplemented by spears made from tent poles or tool handles, often with tips of nails or steel shanks from Army shoes, and three-foot flails of barbed wire from the enclosures themselves.

To have forced entrance to and complete control of a compound of 5,000 recalcitrant North Korean communists, by manhandling them, would have required a minimum of 10,000 U. S. troops, and it could not have been accomplished even then without a great deal of bloodshed on both sides.

Of the Chinese compounds on Koje the two larger were believed to be largely anti-communist, and the two smaller pro-communist. The former two had been expected to agree to screening; the latter two to refuse. But, surprisingly, the leaders of all four consented to individual interrogation of their men—the communist leaders, in all probability, because the orders to do otherwise had come from a Korean source.

Actual screening began on the morning of April 8, 1952, the date of the first victory for the free world in the battle for voluntary repatriation. The largest Chinese compound, with approximately 8100 prisoners of war, was the scene. Each man was queried separately and given a personal and private interview in an inclosed booth, safe from any possibility of coercion or intimidation at the hands of either his anti-communist or pro-communist fellows.

Seven questions were asked each man, to determine definitely his true and uninfluenced choice, which would be noted by the interrogator on his identification papers. Since this compound was reputed to be predominantly anti-communist and against repatriation, if the prisoner elected repatriation he was taken immediately to a waiting truck for relocation in another compound. If he did not wish repatriation, he was taken, via the walkway between the two barbed-wire fences skirting the enclosure, back to his original quarters.

It will be noted that the questions were weighted as strongly as possible toward repatriation: this was going to be as fair a test of the wishes of the prisoners of war as the United Nations Command could devise. Each man was reminded of his family, of the fact that he might remain at Koje long after those

20

electing repatriation had gone home, and of the fact that his future could be guaranteed in no way. The full set of questions follows:

1. Will you voluntarily be repatriated to Communist China?
2. Will you forcibly resist repatriation?
3. Have you carefully considered the impact of such actions on your family?
4. Do you realize that you may remain here at Koje-do long after those electing repatriation have returned home?
5. Do you realize that the United Nations cannot promise that you will be sent to any certain place?
6. Are you still determined that you would violently resist repatriation?
7. What would you do if you are repatriated in spite of this decision?

The questions were asked one at a time, and a reply was insisted upon before proceeding to the next question. However, if at any time or at any stage of the interview the POW expressed a desire for repatriation, the questioning stopped and he went out to the waiting truck. But even if his answer to the second question might be that he would kill himself rather than return to Red China, that he would fight to the death rather than return, or that he would risk death to escape before he would return, he was still asked the succeeding questions so that he would realize the implications of his choice of non-repatriation.

The fifth question was included because the more extreme anti-communist elements in the compound had circulated a rumor that anyone opposing repatriation would be sent to Formosa to join the Nationalists. At that stage of the armistice negotiations it was impossible for the UNC to make such a commitment; in fact, as is evident in the questions, it was even impossible for the UNC to promise non-repatriation at all. Every precaution, consequently, was taken to make the men realize the gravity of their choice.

While it had been expected that more than half of the men in this compound would reject repatriation, it had also been expected that at least a third would elect repatriation, for personal considerations of home and family, if not political considerations. But the bleak prospect of an unending life behind barbed wire, the only alternative to repatriation which could be offered at that time, did not deter them.

The results were confounding. The victory for voluntary repatriation was a smashing one. Six thousand nine hundred men, eighty-five per cent, forswore their homes and families under communism; only fifteen per cent decided for Red China. And with many of these, it was evident that they reached their decision not because it was Red, but because it was China.

In the next compound, with more than six thousand occupants, the victory was even more startling. Less than ten per cent voted to go home.

The third compound was a different story. It held only 253 prisoners. They said they were communists, they were well-organized, and they proved to be communists. As a man, they elected individually to go to Red China.

The fourth compound, predominantly communist but less

well organized, could score only 85% repatriates out of approximately 1500 men.

The over-all results were four to one, four Chinese who would forcibly resist return to Red China out of each five Chinese prisoners of war. The percentage among the North Koreans only could be estimated, because of the compounds which resisted screening, but in two of the compounds which consented to be screened, the results again exceeded all expectations. In the first, known as the "Anti-Communist Youth League" Compound, only 18% chose to return to North Korea. The second, the "Christian Compound," divided almost equally between repatriation and non-repatriation.

PICTORIAL SUPPLEMENT

The following pages present, in pictorial form, glimpses into the lives of the Chinese and Korean prisoners-of-war during their internment by the United Nations Command and their subsequent release. These pictures have been generously supplied by the Signal Corps, U. S. Army, and many of them are reproduced here for the first time.

The narrative continues immediately after these pictures with Chapter 4 of the book.

The first convoy of Chinese POWs released under terms of Operation Recovery enters the gate of Ascom City, Korea. The story culminating in this event is told pictorially in the following pages.

Capture and Processing

The story begins with the capture of the enemy in Korea. The hard-core communist Chinese and North Korean POWs presented the UNC with a new kind of problem. Unlike the German and Italian prisoners of World War II who had moved tractably to the rear under the command of their own officers, nor like the Japanese who had considered themselves dead in the eyes of the emperor, the communist breed organized themselves in military forces as formidable as the units they had left in the North.

But there were others, too—those who chose the barbed-wire compounds of the United Nations Command in preference to the intolerable confinement they had suffered behind the Bamboo Curtain.

. . . some were captured. This is Pfc. Robert M. McClaves of Grayson, Ky., 25th Infantry Division, and a POW who had hidden under pine boughs.

. . . some surrendered. The leader of these men, pictured in the act of giving themselves up, is waving a surrender-safe conduct psychological warfare leaflet.

. . . some were recalcitrant, hard-core communists. This man became a leading agitator and trouble-fomenter on Koje.

... some were anti-communists and simply happy to be alive and out of the fighting. This man was the 20,000th POW taken by the 25th Infantry Division.

... some were frightened children.

Good treatment started with capture. That is a can of pineapple, from a 10-in-1 ration, in the POW's left hand.

The interrogator reads from this POW's diary: "July 18, 1950. I went home to my boarding house from my work in the bank. North Korea is building a big army. I am drafted. Today is very hot and I am tired from training; maybe tomorrow I can rest. I am very lonesome, I miss my sweetheart very much."

The "screening" on Koje Island. The men were interviewed singly and in private booths.

Even as prosaic an event as the issue of new shoes is an occasion for celebration to the anti-communist Chinese POWs.

New fatigues, blankets and individual rice bowls were issued to the POWs.

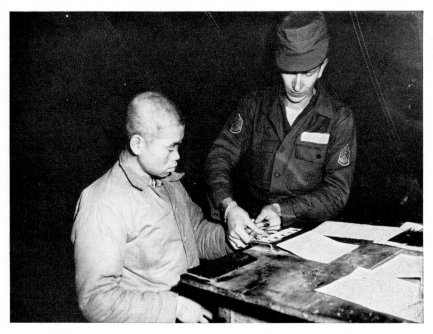

Each POW was photographed and fingerprinted.

Rehabilitation

The ingenuity of man, whatever his beliefs or color, is a remarkable thing, and it displays itself in many ways. The rehabilitation program provided a fertile field in which beer cans developed into stoves, tooth powder into actor's make-up, tin cans and rubber ponchos into drums, atabrine tablets and blood into yellow and red dyes, C-rations into gourmet's delights. But, above all, the thirst for untainted knowledge and spiritual guidance remained the primary needs of the prisoners of war, needs which in their fulfillment insured the success of the program.

This smith's apprentice is hidden behind him, tending the fire. Knowing how to make horseshoes will come in handy after release, and in the meantime the POWs played the American game of horseshoes with them.

Father John F. Coffey, Department of the Army civilian Catholic chaplain to Korean POWs, conducts a discussion group.

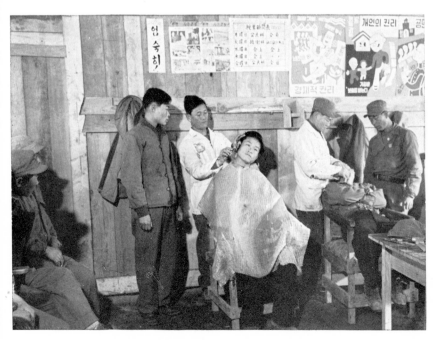

Barber College, with attentive apprentice.

A tailor shop. The steam iron came from the blacksmith shop, the table and tailor's yardstick from the carpentry shop and the shade on the light from the tinsmiths.

Carpentry shop. Note the two-edged Asian saw and the use of the plane toward the carpenter, not away from him.

Cobbler and apprentice, cutting GI shoes down to Chinese and Korean sizes.

Welding Class, with apprentice and American instructor.

Beer-can production line in a tin-smithing shop, with finished stove-pipe
sections. The conical sections are the first stove-pipe joint, for oil-drum
stoves.

POW potter and some of his products.

Drama: Dewy-eyed daughter, mother and villainous landlord; in this play
he is probably a communist cadre. A swing is an essential feature of every
Korean courtyard or stage setting.

A POW compound band broadcasts to the entire camp from the enclosure radio studio.

A corner of the sculpture studio in one of the anti-communist Korean camps.

Chinese POW: Good news in the camp newspaper.

Korean Folk Dance: "Farmer's Band" in background supplies a clashing, clanging rhythm.

Boy Scout Parade: drum corps passing in review. The caps are surplus Army Nurse caps, the drums old drums and tin cans covered with rubber ponchos and canvas shelter halves.

High-bar exhibition at an athletic festival.

Ordeal by "Explanation"

The explanations to the Korean and Chinese prisoners-of-war became the supreme test of their anti-communism. Theirs was a decision made in the face of stark and elemental alternatives—the prospect of reunion with loved ones or final separation, homeland or exile, slavery or freedom, death or life.

The explanations were replete with drama and pathos, and yet not without flashes of humor and comedy. Laughter often was a staunch reed in support of one's anti-communism.

The tattoos on the back of Chao King-chung are within an outline map of China. The top line reads "Oppose Communism Resist Russia." The hand points to the line, "Erase our humiliation and recover our country."

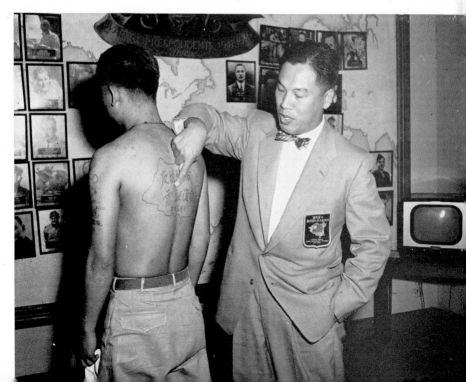

Sitting left to right, Lt. Gen. K. S. Thimayya, Chairman, Neutral Nations Repatriation Commission; I. J. Bahadur Singh, Political Advisor; Major General Thorat, Commander, Custodial Forces India; and Lt. Col. R. Streenavasan, Chief Public Information Officer. In rear, left to right: Brigadier B. M. Kaul, Chief of Staff; Major Makhan Singh, a Public Information Officer; during Lt. General Thimayya's first open press conference at the Neutral Nations Repatriation Commission, Headquarters, 6 October, 1953.

A. Col. Peter Straumann, *Swiss, Alternate Delegate;* B. Armin Daen Iker, *Swiss, Chief of Delegation;* C. Col. Pavel Winkler, *Czech, Alternate Delegate;* D. Col. Ladislaw Simovic, *Czech, Chief of Delegation;* E. B. N. Chakravarty, *India, Alternate Chairman;* F. Lt. Gen. K. S. Thimayya, *Chairman, NNRC;* G. Jan Stenstrom, *Sweden, Chief of Delegation;* H. Maj. C. Hamilton, *Sweden, Staff Assistant;* J. Stanislaw Gajewske, *Poland, Chief of Delegation;* K. Col. M. Graniowski, *Poland, Alternate Delegate;* L. W. S. Anand, *India, Advisor;* M. P. N. Haksar, *India, Advisor;* N. Bahadur Singh, *India, Advisor;* O. Maj. Y. Munshi, *India, Military Assistant;* P. Capt. S. K. Bahri, *India, ADC to Chairman;* S. Lt. Col. R. Streenavasan, *India, PIO;* T. Brig. B. M. Kaul, *India, Chief of Staff.*

Two Indian officers, with unidentified Chinese communist "explainers."

Incident and argument at Tent 12, Explanation Area "A".

The Chief UNC Observer talks to American, Chinese and Korean representatives at an explanations "prep school" at Minsan-ni.

A smuggled photograph—cameras were forbidden in the explanation area—of Explanation Compound "A".

Joe E. Chung (right), leader of Chinese Compound 27, talks with an assistant in the DZ while his compound mates go through calisthenics in the
background.

The seven "murderers" of Compound 28--actually the compound leaders—
after their release by an Indian court martial.

Major Puri of the Custodian Force, India, and the leader and assistant leader of Chinese Compound 24.

Chinese compound play: Joseph Stalin accepts, from a "communist cadre," a neatly packaged "Communist China."

Chinese compound play: Joseph Stalin is condemned by the devil, and dragged to his fate by irate Chinese and assisting evil spirits.

The tattoos on Hu Ah-Kang, flanking the flags of the Republic of China, say "I devote myself to my country."

Release

In the final test, free world ideas and ideals worsted communist brainwashing by a score of one thousand to one. Nearly half of the Korean and some three-fourths of the Chinese prisoners-of-war chose freedom in South Korea and in Taiwan rather than repatriation. Thus voluntary repatriation has become, in the words of General Mark W. Clark, "a beacon to guide others now suffering under Communist tyranny to the sanctuary of freedom and human dignity."

Maj. Gen. Wm. S. Lawton, commander of the Korean Communications Zone, talks to two Chinese POW leaders on the day of their release.

Anti-communist Chinese heroes board LST's at Inchon, bound for Taiwan and freedom. Their pets participate in the emancipation of these "American Agents," leading fierce police dogs," as the communist ra-

Anti-communist Korean heroes, loaded down with their
not inconsiderable possessions, board a train at Munsan-
ni for freedom in the Republic of Korea.

Anti-communist Korean heroes are wildly welcomed as their freedom
train reaches Seoul. But the woman at the left holds a hand-lettered sign
with the name of her husband, anxiously seeking news of him.

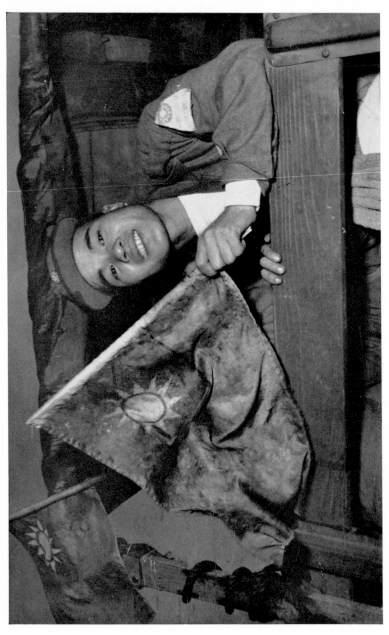

The flag this released anti-communist Chinese hero waves was stained red with his own blood.

4

The Big Deterrent to Little Wars

The shattering significance of the anti-communist score on Koje made the communists at Panmunjom exceedingly sorry that they had ever brought up the question of how many non-repatriates there might be—and they took immediate steps to suppress the answer. Their propaganda line, of course, was already set—"persecution," "terrorization," and "forcible retention"—despite the fact that its contradictions were now more obvious than ever before. A smashing propaganda blow was necessary to obfuscate the issue, and the orders came down from Nam Il to agitate to the utmost, to kidnap a senior U. S. officer if possible, and, as the price of his release alive, exact a "confession" from the Prisoner of War Command that it had done a lot of things it had not done, and a promise to stop doing one that it had—the polling of the prisoners of war. From that point on, the term "screening" was anathema to the Red side.

The kidnapping of General Dodd resulted, a bigger prize than Nam Il could possibly have anticipated. But it was so big a blow to the United Nations Command that, in the end, it backfired against the communists. It was a challenge to the authority of the UNC in the POW camps which could not be, and was not, ignored. It resulted in the breaking up of the compounds holding thousands of men into manageable compounds of not more than five hundred men each, in the complete screening of all of the POWs on the basis of their choice for or against repatriation, and in the relocation of all of the Chinese on Cheju-do and all of the Korean anti-communists on the mainland. And it definitely established the fact that not only four out of five Chinese but three out of five of the North Korean prisoners would forcibly resist return to communist domination. The free world had won a major engagement in the battle for the right of men to choose freedom and reject Red slavery.

A solid majority of these men, for all they knew, had opted for death or a life behind barbed wire rather than return to communism. They had been promised nothing more than continued imprisonment, the most hopeless existence a man can face, one which many of them had already lived, by that time, for almost two years. But they had lived under communism, too, and they knew that death or imprisonment was vastly to be preferred.

The ratio of those who chose non-repatriation over those who chose communism was so overwhelming that an impression became current that the United Nations Command, to influence surrender in Korea, had promised asylum and sanctuary to prisoners of war. Demaree Bess, writing of the POWs in the *Saturday Evening Post* the November before, had made that erroneous assumption.

But the rulers in Moscow, Peiping, and Pyongyang knew that no such commitment had been made before the surrender of these men, and that no such commitment had yet been made to them. UNC psychological warfare leaflets and radio broadcasts had promised only good treatment, nothing more, as an inducement to surrender. Since their surrender, the men had been given nothing more than good treatment—and nothing less.

In the Red capitals the communists knew that asylum and sanctuary had not been promised. If sixty per cent of their Korean victims and eighty per cent of the Chinese whom they had callously condemned to death in human sea attacks had sworn to die rather than return for further Red exploitation, what would the percentages have been if they had been promised asylum?

What would the total prisoner of war bag have been if they had been promised an opportunity to fight against communism in Korea, in Free Chinese and Free Korean brigades? Although there were many more communist Chinese than Korean troops in Korea—though it now seemed a misnomer to refer to them as communist—there were far more Korean POWs in UNC hands. The great deterrent to surrender on the part of the Chinese was the language barrier, and the very good chance that a man eager to surrender would be shot before he could get the idea across.

And the final question, which must have been asked time and time again all the way from Moscow to Panmunjom and Panmunjom back to East Berlin, was this: if the communists renewed their defeated aggression in Korea, and the war

26

spread, from North Korea into Manchuria, from Formosa and Vietnam into China, and, perhaps, from Western Europe into Eastern Europe—what percentages of Asians and Europeans, troops and civilians alike, would rally to freedom and turn their guns toward Moscow?

The POWs were men of military age, Chinese who had known in their lifetime only civil war, invasion, civil war again, and now external aggression; Koreans who had known only foreign domination, first Japanese and then communist. Neither had ever had a chance to enjoy a life of peace under a truly democratic government.

If these poor, buffeted men still had the spirit and determination to strike out against communism, one might assume that their families and fellow soldiers in Red China and North Korea would make the same choice in the same proportion. In fact, were it not for their families and homes, perhaps these men would have chosen freedom in even greater number.

And if these peoples of the Orient who had never been given a chance to live in both peace and freedom would choose against communism in such overwhelming numbers, what would be the percentage of Europeans, who know peace and democracy, to turn against communism if they were given the opportunity?

What would be the percentage of Karelians, Latvians, Estonians, Lithuanians, Poles, Czechs, Slovaks, East Germans, Rumanians, Albanians and Bulgarians? Or, for that matter, the percentage of Ukrainians, of White Russians—even Great Russians?

We know, today, the percentage of Hungarians.

The satellites, if one includes Red China as a satellite—and one should, because it makes the Red Chinese furious and contributes to independence on their part—lie across the Kremlin's lines of communication in three of the six possible directions of future aggression: to the west in Europe, to the southwest in the Balkans, and to the southeast in Asia. Moscow can mount an attack only to the northwest against Finland and Norway, to the east against Japan and Alaska, and to the south against the soft underbelly of Asia, without crossing the territory of a satellite. Soviet strategy must therefore presuppose the spearheading of communist aggression with satellite troops—if only to push them forward out of their own nations. But suppose Polish troops were given the order to march west on Germany?

Hungary has given us an answer to this, too.

If the free world adheres to the principle established in Korea, and states and re-states its determination to return no one to communism against his will, those Polish troops would turn their guns to the east.

The principle of non-forcible repatriation, particularly if it is coupled in any future instance of communist aggression with the formation of free brigades, divisions and armies to fight back for freedom, against communism, places an impossible inhibition upon the Kremlin in any war plans it may have.

How fully, for instance, can the Kremlin arm the satellites? Polish infantry, of course, may have its full complement of infantry weapons, even light and medium artillery for support. But heavy artillery? Tanks? Aircraft? These supporting weapons which make a force self-sufficient and self-sustaining

28

cannot be built to point and threaten and fight in but one direction.

Token artillery, tanks and airplanes the satellites must have, of course, for prestige, and there is an obvious solution to the problem of making them useless if they are turned toward Moscow. The artillery and tanks are worthless without ammunition, and the continuing source of that ammunition may be another satellite or the U. S. S. R. itself. Airplanes must have parts and provender, too, and if the MIGs of the proud Red Chinese air force do not get Rumanian fuel in Polish tankers for their Czech engines, they will not fly. But this in itself imposes an again impossible logistics burden on the communist complex. In time of general war with sea lanes contested and land lines interdicted, it would be beyond solution.

This is as big a deterrent to little wars as the H-bomb is to big wars.

5

Psychological Warfare

Although the chief communist spokesman in the armistice negotiations at Panmunjom, Nam Il, was a Korean—a Soviet citizen, but still a Korean—it became clear as the talks dragged on over the question of the POWs that the Korean anti-communists were expendable. Naked communist aggression in Korea had pretty well demonstrated Korean feelings about communism. More than two million North Koreans, by the communists' own reckoning, had fled to the Republic of Korea in the fall and winter of 1950-51, to escape the advancing Red Chinese "volunteers." Communist charges that they had been "abducted" and "kidnapped" could not eclipse this fact, perhaps because the free world could not grasp *why* the U. N. forces should kidnap two million civilians, or for that matter *how* their relatively few retreating troops managed to do it.

With two million or more civilian refugees testifying against communism in Korea, a hundred thousand troops more or less who also preferred freedom in the Republic of Korea could be written off.

Korea was a communist mistake in Asia, the least profitable

of the way-stations on the timetable of communist conquest. It would have come in handy in a double envelopment of Japan, and it had been announced as being outside the United States defense perimeter in the Pacific. But the United States "double-crossed" the U. S. S. R.—from the communist viewpoint —and came to the Republic's defense. Worse than that, the United States took advantage of incredible short-sightedness in Soviet statesmanship, their concurrent boycott of the Security Council, to rally the United Nations in reacting to communist aggression and publicizing it painfully all over the world. No doubt about it, Korea was unprofitable, and, once the northern half with which the adventure had started was regained, could and should be liquidated. Japan could still be penetrated militarily from the direction of Sakhalin or politically from the direction of Shanghai. Once Japan was a proper satellite, Korea would be in a powerful pincers. The Korean POWs could be dismissed without further dramatizing their anti-communism.

Not so with the Chinese anti-communist POWs.

With an armistice, the Korean situation is pretty much of a stand-off. The communists cannot renew their aggression without again coming into unprofitable conflict with the United Nations and, this time, risking World War III. The United States and the United Nations have made it plain that their interest in Korea was and is simply the stopping of aggression. With huge Chinese communist armies in North Korea dwarfing the North Korean armed forces, with reinforcements across the Yalu, and with the few million remaining miserable, bruised, battered North Korean people more concerned with simply staying alive than with rebellion against impossible odds, North Korea is no threat to the communist complex.

But China under communism is something else. One of the oldest and wisest of the civilizations of this earth, it has known every shade of government under the sun, but never so vicious a government as communism. Communism, striking at the Chinese family system, infinitely boring with its endless political meetings, horrendously embarrassing with its public confessionals, cannot but be abhorrent to the Chinese.

Four out of five soldiers from a tightly disciplined army, brainwashed daily, chose a life behind barbed wire over a return to communism. In the civilian population, reached less regularly with Mao's mouthings, one only can conjecture at the proportion which would rise in rebellion if there were the slightest chance of success.

The truism that a man with a pitchfork does not rise in rebellion against troops with tanks and machine guns may not apply to a country with six hundred million people. "East" Germans attacked Soviet tanks with cobblestones in 1953. "Communist" Hungarians attacked Soviet tanks with Molotov cocktails in 1956. "Red" Chinese soldiers might turn U. S. S. R.-supplied machine guns on their Soviet "advisors" by 1959.

The Red overlords of mainland China do not have to guess at the degree of disaffection which exists there. They chronicle almost daily, over Radio Peiping, sabotage in factories, depredations of "wild beasts"—the communist euphemism for peasants-turned-bandit—in the fields, executions of supposed

32

Chiang and U. S. "agents" who were probably no more than poor Formosan fishermen.

And these same Red overlords know that so long as President Chiang Kai-shek or any successor flies the flag of Free China on Taiwan there exists a rallying point for rebellion— rebellion which might spread like a flash fire across China and the Soviet Union itself to the European satellites.

There simply are not enough tanks, cannon, and machine guns in the world to suppress rebellion among nearly a billion people, particularly if the men who man the tanks and guns are themselves in the forefront of the fight.

The Chinese communists at Panmunjom thought of all this, and renewed their efforts to get their hands on the Chinese prisoners of war. They could not, they simply could not, let these men go free, to go to Taiwan or anywhere else in the world to testify to the thin veneer of communism in China.

So the communist negotiators remained adamant on the POW question. On the 8th of September, 1952, General Harrison made three propositions to them. They were couched in the most palatable terms possible, but the essential feature of all three was that all of the prisoners of war would be brought to the demilitarized zone and permitted to go north or south, as they chose.

Even this the communists could not risk, and the United Nations Command thereupon unilaterally recessed the truce talks on October 8.

At this time the UNC held, in round figures, 170,000 POWs. The screenings had revealed, among the communist Koreans, 38,000 who might better be classified as civilian internees than

33

as prisoners of war. In their initial sweep south, the communists had forcibly impressèd into their ranks every superficially fit South Korean male who fell into their hands. They had no military training, no combatant status—simply a rifle or a shovel thrust upon them. They were "soldiers" only as long as it took them to find a means of surrendering to the U. N. forces.

Consequently, in the fall of 1952, the U. N. Command, in Operations "Homecoming" and "Thanksgiving," released these 38,000 civilian internees in the Republic of Korea, reducing the total number of POWs to around 130,000 and bringing the total of those who had opted repatriation above the remaining number who had said they would forcibly resist repatriation. But even this face-saving circumstance failed to bring the communists back to the truce table.

In November, the Indian delegation to the current General Assembly of the United Nations introduced a suggested solution to the prisoner of war problem in Korea, providing for a neutral nations commission to sort out the Chinese and Korean recalcitrants according to ideology. Although it paralleled in every important respect the eventual plan adopted at Panmunjom, the Russian delegation angrily rejected it, and the stalemate continued.

It was not until the following spring that the communist position weakened, in an unexpected direction. The League of Red Cross Societies, meeting in Geneva in December, had called attention to the fact that the provisions of the Geneva Conventions with respect to the exchange of sick and wounded prisoners of war had not been carried out in Korea. The com-

34

munists had carried out none of the provisions of the conventions, and had refused access to North Korea on the part of representatives of the International Commission of the Red Cross, but the Geneva resolution tactfully concentrated on the problem of the sick and wounded. General Mark W. Clark acted quickly, suggesting staff talks on the matter at Panmunjom. In the static military situation, he reinforced this with aggressive psychological warfare, the only weapon he could use to the hilt.

Early in March, Stalin died, and late in March, the communists not only acceded to an exchange of sick and wounded but also proposed resumption of the armistice negotiations.

The immediate result was "Little Switch" in April, in which 6,000 communist POWs were repatriated in exchange for barely a tenth as many UNC sick and wounded. But, again, the total of Chinese and North Korean POWs in United Nations Command hands was reduced, and the question of who had won the war in terms of prisoners taken became a little less embarrassing to the communists.

The truce talks re-opened on a Sunday, the 26th of April, and General Clark waited to assess the communist attitude before increasing his psychological pressure on them. They were as intransigent as ever, and he issued the order for the next step. A flight of U. S. Far East Air Force B-29's roared up and down the Korean side of the Yalu on an extraordinary bombing mission.

Their bombs were set to explode at a maximum altitude, and as each bomber reached a point directly downwind from its assigned MIG fighter base across the Yalu in the Manchurian sanctuary, it released its load. Thousands of wind-borne psychological warfare leaflets, in Russian, Chinese and Korean, carried to the pilots of those MIGs General Clark's offer of $100,000 to the first pilot to bring an operable Soviet-built jet plane to Kimpo Air Base near Seoul, and $50,000 to any succeeding pilot. Simultaneously, the Voice of the United Nations Command (VUNC) radio network started broadcasting the same offer.

One objective of the offer, General Clark announced to the world press, was to procure one or more Soviet jets for intelligence purposes. But bearing in mind the fact that many a Chinese and North Korean soldier had been killed in attempting to surrender on the ground, either by fire from his own side or U. N. cross-fire, he announced a second objective, his real one. Without dwelling on the fact that any one of the aggressive pilots of the Fifth Air Force in Korea might be as anxious as any infantryman to score his first or fifth or tenth victory, he also announced that he intended to inhibit the combat effectiveness of the enemy's air arm in the same manner in which psychological warfare had limited the combat potential of the enemy's ground forces.

The communists began jamming the Russian portion of the VUNC broadcasts, grounded their MIGs for eight days of superb spring flying weather while they screened their pilots to be sure they had hostages for each one, and applied themselves to the truce talks with extraordinary vigor. When the MIGs reappeared over North Korea, in reduced numbers, Fifth Air Force kills doubled. Per MIG sighted, they tripled.

6

And More Psychological Warfare

The basis upon which the communists were willing to re-open the truce talks had been revealed in a cable from Chinese premier Chou En-lai to the U. N. General Assembly. Although he disputed the assertion of the United Nations Command that there were among the Chinese and North Korean prisoners of war many who did not wish to be repatriated, he went so far as to say that if, after an armistice, there were indeed such, they should be turned over to a "neutral state," there to receive "explanations" which would allay their fears and persuade them to return home.

With the resumption of the talks themselves, it developed that what the communists meant was that the POWs who re-fused immediate repatriation should be physically shipped out of Korea to an unnamed "neutral Asian nation," there to re-ceive these reassuring explanations for six months.

The United Nations Command—perhaps in this instance its United States component—demurred immediately. The ex-pense of shipping fifty thousand men a minimum of twenty-five hundred miles to Indonesia, the nearest neutral Asian nation possibly willing to accept them temporarily, would un-questionably devolve upon the United States, as would their accommodations and support. It might even be necessary to send them four thousand miles or more, to Burma or India. "Explanations" sounded suspiciously like brainwashing, and six months of unalloyed access to the men under the benign eyes of neutrals who understood neither the Chinese nor Ko-rean languages was simply too much, however neutral they were. Besides, President Rhee was already making unhappy sounds and would never have consented to the removal from Korea of the North Korean POWs. He holds the position, and rightly, that his is the only duly constituted government of Korea. The communists refused to let the North Koreans participate in the elections which fleshed it out, but Mr. Rhee held open their quota of seats in his legislative assembly.

General Harrison told the communist negotiators that the prisoners would remain in Korea, that while the UNC was not opposed to neutral custody, the question of who was to do it and how had to be settled first, and that two months were long enough for "explanations."

The communists countered with a proposition which paral-leled, with one or two exceptions, the Indian plan that the U. S. S. R. had so angrily rejected the preceding December. On the Indian plan they grafted their concept of explanations, but reduced the period they wished to devote to brainwashing to four months. The POWs could remain in Korea and would be guarded by troops from each of five neutral nations. Instead of referring the prisoners who refused repatriation after four months to the United Nations for disposition, as in the Indian plan, the peace conference provided by the draft armistice agreement was to determine their fate, without time limit.

The Republic of Korea voiced immediate objection to the stationing of communist guard troops on Korean soil. Counting perhaps a little too much on predicted communist concentration on the Chinese POWs, the UNC proposed, in a solution still paralleling the Indian plan, release of the Korean anti-communist prisoners on the day the armistice would become effective. Although the communists had offered only token disapproval, for the record, of the successive releases of 28,000 and 10,000 Korean civilian internees the fall before, the proposed release of 35,000 more Koreans at one swoop was too much for them to agree to in advance of the event, and they firmly rejected this feature.

The suggestion that the Korean POWs be released immediately upon signature of the armistice was made on April 30th. Three days later, in a relatively unpublicized address which was not followed by an official action but which certainly received the attention it deserved from the communist side, Mr. O. K. Armstrong, a former U. S. Congressman who had been active in behalf of the anti-communist POWs, introduced a new idea.

He stated that one of the U. S. Government's cold war policies, which he expected to be announced in the next few days, would be "the immediate release of all our Korean prisoners of war and all Chinese prisoners who desire to fight for the United Nations." He argued that "it would be a rank injustice to turn these prisoners over to a so-called neutral nation. . . . The Korean prisoners are in their own homeland. In simple justice they should be released. . . ." He went on to say

39

that if the fiction that the Chinese are "merely volunteers" were accepted, then these "volunteers" should be assisted to "go to Formosa voluntarily to fight for their nation's freedom."

Both sides went into huddles, from which they emerged on May 25 to enter negotiations in secret sessions secluded from criticism by the Republic of Korea, on the one hand, and the rest of the world, on the other. By the 8th of June, agreement had been reached on the POW issue. Communist concessions included provisions for turning over the custody of the prisoners to Indian troops only, limiting explanations to ninety days, and allowing the "Neutral Nations Repatriation Commission" to "declare the relief from the prisoner of war status to civilian status" of prisoners remaining after thirty more days, in the event the political conference had not disposed of them otherwise. UNC concessions included dropping the proposal to release all Korean POWs, and leaving the term "Repatriation" in the name of the commission.

President Rhee made no concessions, and on June 18 and the three days which followed the Republic of Korea guards at mainland anti-communist Korean POW camps released nearly 27,000 men. From the Pusan hospital camp they even released sixty-four happy Chinese, who disappeared as completely into the Korean landscape as their fellows.

The communists dutifully broke off the truce talks, but after waiting exactly the nine days it took General Clark to reply to their letter signalling the break, resumed them and worked as hard as ever toward the armistice. After all, a defeat in the explanations by 22,000 anti-communist POWs would not be nearly so bad as a defeat by 49,000. Twenty-two thousand was a nicer, rounder, *smaller* number. They would get 76,000 men back with the signing of the armistice; the proportion of anticommunist prisoners on whom the world's attention would be focussed was far more in their favor after Mr. Rhee's action. That more than half of the original total of prisoners of war in UNC hands had chosen freedom might even be forgotten, in time.

7

The Pilot Rehabilitation Project

Both sides took a long chance in their final agreement on the disposition of the problem of the POWs.

The communists, insistent to the last that the anti-communist prisoners had been intimidated, "tortured," "persecuted," and "terrorized" by the United States—always the Americans, never the United Nations—were running the risk that the POWs really were anti-communist, that communism would be spectacularly repudiated in Asia for the first time, as it was daily being repudiated in Europe. The final figure of 22,604 prisoners who were to be put to the test in the explanations was puny compared to the cumulative figures of refugees from the Reds in Europe, but if they withstood the explanations to the end and went over to the free world en masse, it would be a dramatic setback to communism.

The risk the United Nations Command ran in accepting the explanation procedure was equally dangerous. If any significant majority of the remaining 22,604 POWs succumbed to the communist explanations, doubt would be cast upon the anti-communism of the 65,000 non-repatriates already released.

And domestic repercussions within the United States and international criticism among the cooperating United Nations would have been both loud and bitter.

The conflict in Korea had been prolonged almost beyond human patience over the issue of the POWs, for more than a year and a half, a year and a half in which thousands of casualties had been incurred despite the relative stalemate. The impatience of the American people had been strikingly demonstrated in the election of 1952, and none of the U. N. allies, except President Rhee, had any more appetite for continuing the fighting than the United States had.

The fine, the historic action of the United States and the United Nations in halting naked communist aggression in Korea would have been eclipsed completely by recrimination and backbiting.

How then could the United Nations Command, or more properly the United States, since the overriding decision in this matter was made in Washington, take such a chance?

The United States authorities concerned had been convinced, months before the armistice negotiations had been proposed, more than a year before the decision was made to keep on fighting until the prisoner of war question could be resolved, of the dedicated anti-communism of an astounding proportion of the Korean prisoners. This was before there were any Chinese prisoners. And when these came along, evidence of their militant anti-communism was even more convincing.

In October-November, 1950, after the Inchon landing and just before the Chinese "volunteers" were thrust into the Korean fighting, the North Korean POW bag increased from

43

40,000 to 80,000. These men were tractable and cooperative, and moved to the rear in great groups, virtually unguarded. The question they asked most frequently was when they were going to be armed and permitted to fight the communists. There were, of course, communists among them, biding their time, but the general air was that of men who had escaped to freedom.

Impressed by this attitude, and by the then current successes of the Government of Greece in the rehabilitation of communist guerrillas, the U. S. Department of the Army, with the personal approval of President Truman, ordered the initiation of a pilot rehabilitation program for the Korean prisoners of war. Lieutenant Colonel Donald R. Nugent, USMC, who had been an American educator in Japan before and after World War II, was named to head the program.

Five hundred North Koreans were selected for the project, without questioning as to their political convictions. They were picked, however, to be as representative as possible of the educational level of the total prisoner of war population, and to represent civilian occupations among the POWs as accurately as possible. They were also a cross-section as to age and marital status, and were un-representative in only one respect, the fact that one-fifth of them were officers, a necessary concession to making them average otherwise.

The first thing the five hundred were told, at the outset of the program, was that their participation was purely voluntary. The program would be that required of a detaining power under Articles 34-38 of the Geneva Convention on prisoners of war, which imposes the provision of religious, intellectual and

44

recreational facilities for POWs. If any or all of the features of the project were not to their liking, they could retire to their quarters and there would be no reprisal of any nature. It was hoped that the schedule would be sufficiently interesting to induce them to attend all sessions, but if they were not interested, they were under no compulsion whatever to be present. If they had any suggestions toward making the sessions more interesting, their ideas would be welcomed.

The organizer, chief instructor, and final head of the project, Mr. Monta L. Osborne—later to be attacked viciously by Radios Peiping and Pyongyang as "the notorious Colonel Osman"—pointed out to the POWs that, as North Koreans of military age, they had never in their lives received wholly objective information. Until 1945 they had been under Japanese domination, and everything they had been told had been what the Japanese chose for them to hear. During the last four years of this period, during World War II, the censorship and distortions to which they had been subjected had been extraordinarily severe. Then, coming under Soviet rule, they had entered a period in which the information which reached them was even less reliable, and a period in which belief in that information, nevertheless, was mandatory.

They were now to receive, for the first time in their lives, he told them, completely objective information. They did not have to believe it unless they wished to. They could ask questions, discuss it among themselves, and make up their own minds.

It had not been expected that many questions from the POWs would be forthcoming at the very start of the program,

45

but there was an unusual response, perhaps because of the extraordinary appeal of the principal lecturer. He was Lieutenant Colonel, then Captain, Ryong C. Hahm of the U. S. Army, who holds a law degree from the University of Seoul, a divinity degree from Vanderbilt, and a Ph.D. in international law from Yale. Before World War II, he was an instructor in international law at Harvard; he is now on the staff of the Federal Bureau of Investigation. His talk on the background and beginnings of the conflict in Korea developed acute interest on the part of the POWs, who had no knowledge whatever, for instance, of United Nations attempts to unify Korea peaceably.

The Army had no printed materials in the Korean language other than psychological warfare leaflets and newssheets, but the United States Information Service (USIS) supported the project with pamphlets, with a weekly news sheet, with the magazine "America" in Korean, and with motion pictures. The UNC in Tokyo broadcast daily psychological warfare news programs and commentaries, truthful and factual, the same programs sufficing for both North and South Korea, and these were re-broadcast to the five hundred over loudspeakers, for them to hear or not as they wished.

These broadcasts were not "Big Brother" repetitions, insistent and inescapable. As with the lectures and other features of the project, the POWs could retire to their quarters if they did not wish to hear them. But repeated checks of the quarters throughout the program never revealed a higher count of absentees than fifteen, despite the cold, colds, and discomfort of a rainy Korean autumn.

At the end of the first day's sessions, the five hundred were asked if they desired religious services. None wanted Buddhist services, quite a few asked for Catholic services, and a surprising number asked for Protestant services. The first service, attended by 120 of the men, was non-denominational; the following Sunday, 45 men attended a Catholic service and 165 a Protestant service.

Film supplied for the program by USIS had Korean sound tracks, and films which had been used in the civil information and education program in Japan, during the occupation, had Japanese sound tracks. Although all Koreans more than six years old understood Japanese at that time (Japanese had been the language of oppression in Korea for two generations), it was nevertheless decided to project Japanese-language films without sound. Captain Hahm would preview the film, make notes, and then accompany it with a running verbal commentary in Korean. This soon gave rise to an opportunity for a discussion among the five hundred on the role of majority and minority views in a democratic system.

Inexpertness on the part of the projectionist—the one POW whose profession that had been in civilian life—soon revealed to the audience that the film which had been shown to them without sound had, in fact, Japanese dialogue and commentary, music and sound effects. After one showing there were requests that it be shown again, this time with sound. Mr. Osborne explained why the Japanese sound tracks were not being used. He suggested that the men discuss this viewpoint, then take a vote on whether or not they wished to exclude the Japanese language from the program. After much discussion, a vote showed 95% of the men in favor of hearing the Japanese sound tracks.

The men were then asked what should be done, in a democratic system, about the 5% who did not want to hear the Japanese language. More discussion ensued. Some thought that they should be forced to listen to it, since the majority had voted that way. Others believed the minority had certain rights. It was finally agreed that in matters of law, majority rule should prevail, although the minority might still work to get the law changed or repealed. But in entertainment or education, no one should be forced to see or hear something he did not wish to see or hear.

It was announced that since the majority had no objection to the Japanese sound track, the film would be shown again with sound. The minority need not attend unless they wished. In the future, film in Japanese would be shown first with sound, and the minority would be excused. They could see the picture at a later showing, with a Korean explanation.

The five per cent stayed for the second showing, and there were no future requests for separate screenings. The Japanese language edition of "Reader's Digest" was added to their slender store of reading materials.

The ROK Government cooperated in the pilot rehabilitation program by making nationally known Koreans available as lecturers. Their talks, as well as the pamphlets distributed to the five hundred, were used as a basis for group discussions, and the avidity with which the men seized on the first oppor-

48

tunity in their lives for self-expression was remarkable. Their whole-hearted participation in the project did not stop with the formal sessions. The more literate were observed, during the first week-end they were gathered together, reading the pamphlets to the less well-educated and then discussing them.

At the end of the first week, twenty men of varying educational levels were selected to make three-minute talks to the entire group on "My Part in This War." They were asked to explain the circumstances under which they came into the North Korean Army, what they had been told they were fighting for, and how they felt about the whole thing at the present time.

Although these speakers were really volunteers, they were, for the most part, exceedingly shy, afraid of the microphone and acutely embarrassed. But when they heard their voices coming back over the loudspeakers, they gained courage, and after the first seminar the problem was not in obtaining volunteers but in picking twenty men from five hundred volunteers.

One of the first to speak began his remarks with a rather eloquent preface.

"First of all," he said, "I must express my gratitude at this opportunity. You, chief educator and other instructors, are so kind and good as to give us, the very captives, many books and newspapers in behalf of our education, and to permit us to explain our opinions freely. This kind of thing we could hardly dream of even a few days ago. We are now very much delighted and hopeful.

"On June 25th we were driven down by the puppet leadership from North Korea with the object of the so-called liberation of our fatherland. The communist leaders always advocated that only we, the North Koreans, were on the side of justice, and, therefore, had the righteous urge to liberate Southern Korea at the risk of our lives. We were thus misled by such propaganda, and in sheer ignorance of truth. But now we view the matter in its true light."

A second said:

"We are already convinced that we were misled and deceived by the communist party. Now that we know, why can't we join the ROK Army now, instead of spending a few months in this camp? I have talked to many, and many of us want to join the ROK Army."

It was to be more than "a few months," more than three years, in fact, before these men were to have an opportunity to join the ROK Army—three years in which they underwent so bitter an ordeal that it is a wonder that their determination never wavered, and that their number swelled from five hundred to many thousands.

Their personal histories revealed the ruthlessness of the Red regime in shocking monotony. One 18-year old, a middle school graduate employed in a factory, said that just one month before the invasion of South Korea, "inspectors" came to the factory to persuade him to "enlist" in the army. When he still demurred after several visits, he was informed that he would be discharged from the factory and deprived of his rations. He "enlisted," and with no military training whatever participated in the 25 June attack.

A miner and a student similarly demurred until they were thrown into jail. Seven other students, finding that graduation day in early June was conscription day, fled their homes, only to be pursued by the police and caught. Two other students were given no opportunity to flee. A carpenter who was the sole support of his mother fled successfully; the police simply jailed his mother, and he returned to secure her release. One farmer, with several friends from his village, hid out in the mountains for 25 days, but they all came back, too, when they heard what was happening to their families. Three brothers, farmers, fled just before their harvest, but came back in two weeks for the same reason. Few had had more than a day or two of military training. None wanted to return to such a system—and small wonder.

Entry of the Chinese into the Korean conflict and their thrust south forced evacuation of the five hundred and abandonment of the pilot rehabilitation project in December, 1950, but not before a number of valuable lessons had been learned.

While the POWs were being moved from Seoul and Inchon to Pusan and Koje-do, plans went forward swiftly for resumption of the rehabilitation program as soon as they were re-settled. Not for just five hundred men this time, but for all of the thousands of North Koreans in hand, the Chinese who were beginning to accumulate behind barbed wire, and thousands who were still to come.

The months between the ending of the pilot rehabilitation project and its resumption for all of the prisoners of war taken by the United Nations Command in Korea were momentous.

They encompassed the re-conquest of Seoul by the communists, its re-taking by the forces of the United Nations, and the relief of General MacArthur. But General MacArthur had recommended the expanded program to the Department of the Army, and General Ridgway, his successor, gave it his full support.

8

Full-Scale Rehabilitation on Koje

By the time the rehabilitation program was resumed, in June, 1951, the total number of POWs had grown appreciably, and there were now many Chinese among them, for whom a parallel project had to be prepared. Five months had elapsed, but in that time more than 150,000 men had to be transported to Koje-do—Koje Island, in Korean, in which the suffix -to or -do has now replaced the Japanese -jima or -shima, "island." Barracks, compounds, kitchens, latrines, and hospitals had to be erected on barren Koje, and the pressing needs of so many men had to be taken into account before the UNC could indulge in the luxury of an educational and recreational program.

It had been necessary to write, translate and print study materials in two languages. Instructors had been trained. In the pilot project it had been found that the available Korean teachers were woefully lacking in the training necessary to conduct such a program—not in enthusiasm or ability, but in

53

simple pedagogical means and methods. During the Japanese occupation the Korean language had been banned and most of the school-teachers had been Japanese. During the Soviet occupation, most of the instructors in North Korea had been communist "Soviet Koreans," Koreans of Soviet nationality who were more at home with Russian than with Korean. The instructors in South Korea, with brief American training, were now too busy training the growing ROK Army for General Van Fleet. New teachers had to be found and trained from the ground up.

Mandarin and Cantonese-speaking instructors were recruited, the latter principally from the United States, where ninety-nine of one hundred Chinese-speaking Chinese-Americans speak Cantonese. The requirement for Chinese teachers on Koje was principally for Mandarin-speaking instructors, who were sought among students in the United States, the comparatively small Chinese colonies in Japan and Korea, and finally in Hongkong and Singapore. Recruiting on Formosa among the Nationalist Chinese was avoided, to rob the enemy of any opportunity to charge that these essential language assistants were "Chiang agents" and "Nationalist spies." This precaution need not have been taken, for the Peiping propagandists blithely began to make exactly that charge, and not only that, to make the same charge with respect to the anti-communist leaders who developed among the POWs themselves. Notwithstanding the fact that prior to their surrender they had been "Chinese People's Volunteers," they were now "Chiang Kai-shek agents." If the instructors and prisoner-leaders really had been Chiang agents, no better ones could have been recruited. They

54

were to assist in delivering to the Generalissimo, in the end, an entire division of young, aggressive, militantly anti-communist troops.

The greatest handicap of the rehabilitation program among the Chinese and North Korean prisoners of war in United Nations Command custody was at the same time one of the principal reasons for its success. This was the high rate of illiteracy among the prisoners.

Of the Chinese, 43% were completely illiterate. Two-thirds of the Koreans, reflecting certainly one benefit of Japanese occupation but also their own determination to keep their own language alive, were literate. For many of them, this meant literate in Japanese as well as Korean. Until 1945, the Korean language had been banned in the Japanese-run schools, but the Koreans, in North and South Korea alike, bootlegged their "Hangul," an extremely advanced phonetic alphabet much easier to learn than Japanese and Chinese ideographs.

By educational level, the Chinese and Korean prisoners of war compared thusly:

Years of Education	Chinese %	Korean %
None	43.0	18.9
1-3 years	39.0	18.3
4-6 years	12.9	45.8
7-9 years	4.0	11.5
10-12 years	1.0	5.0
Over 12 years	0.1	0.5

Because of the differing difficulty of Chinese ideographs as compared to Korean phonetics, many of the Chinese with 4 to

6 years of education still had to be classed as not completely literate, while many of the Koreans, on the other hand, could read comic strips or ordinary correspondence with 1 to 3 years of formal education plus home study of the Korean language.

This made the number one project of the rehabilitation course a literacy program, and was one of several features of the endeavor which had fully as much appeal for even the die-hard communists among the prisoners of war as it did for the anti-communists. A thirst for knowledge knows no ideology, and if there is one thing which transcends political barriers in Asia it is such a thirst. Illiterate many of the prisoners of war, communist and anti-communist alike, may have been, but they were not stupid. Far from it. The success of the literacy program was astounding by educational standards, East or West.

Fond of the literacy program as the Chinese repatriates were, their actual or pretended communism kept them from cooperating in an evaluation of its effects. Since their enthusiasm equalled or exceeded that of the anti-communists, however, it may be presumed that it did as much for the communists as for the anti-communists, if not more. One reason may have been that it was a continuation of one program to which they had been subjected under communist control as members of the People's Liberation Army or "volunteers."

The communists, in the consolidation of their conquest of mainland China, had recognized the high rate of illiteracy as one of their handicaps, just as it was recognized in the rehabilitation project. One aspect of the ceaseless indoctrination to which soldiers in the Red Chinese armies were subjected, pos-

56

sibly the only aspect to which they did not object, was literacy training.

At the time of capture or surrender, all prisoners of war were given a literacy test, and grouped in five categories. These were complete illiterate, low illiterate (recognizes a few characters and sometimes sentences, but unable to read comic strips or ordinary correspondence); partial illiterate (able to read comic strips or correspondence, but unable to read newspapers); literate (able to read newspapers), and high literate—able to read and write well.

The table which follows shows the improvement in literacy level of 14,020 anti-communist non-repatriate Chinese, between the time of their surrender or capture and May, 1953, when the survey was made.

	Time of Surrender or capture		Time of Survey	
Complete illiterate	5,905	(42.1%)	712	(05.1%)
Low illiterate	3,696	(26.4%)	5,275	(37.6%)
Partial illiterate	2,292	(16.3%)	3,945	(28.1%)
Literate	1,243	(08.9%)	2,427	(17.3%)
High literate	884	(06.3%)	1,661	(11.9%)
	14,020	(100%)	14,020	(100%)

When one considers that the rehabilitation project did not begin until June, 1951, and that this survey was made in May, 1953, two years interrupted by the Koje disturbances and the move of the Chinese prisoners of war to Cheju-do, the results are all the more remarkable. Whereas the complete illiterates comprised the largest group at the time of surrender, this group two years later was the smallest.

57

Such progress—accompanied by equal progress in other fields as well, in many instances—was an important morale factor for the anti-communist prisoners of war. Perhaps it was an important morale factor for the communists as well. Both groups certainly needed sustenance during the two years and more of armistice negotiations.

It is probable that the Korean prisoners of war, with their less difficult alphabet, made even greater progress than the Chinese. But President Rhee's release of 27,000 anti-communist Koreans, in June, 1953, interrupted the parallel survey among the Koreans. Before it and they could be reorganized, the armistice had been signed, and the subject was, well, academic.

Textbooks for the Korean prisoners of war were the Laubach "Literacy Primer," "First Language Reader" and "Second Language Reader." The students were considered to have completed the literacy training course successfully when they were able to read, with reasonable speed and comprehension, the materials in the second language reader and in other publications written at the same language level, and to write the Korean language at the same level.

For the Chinese prisoners of war, literacy training consisted of study of the four volumes of James Yen's "Thousand Character Text." Successful completion here called for reading and writing on the level of the fourth volume, but this was so markedly a "basic Chinese" and interest on the part of many of the prisoners of war was so great that a special 1400-character dictionary was developed from which special materials were prepared.

58

These extra characters were necessary for communication of the social, economic and political ideas required for a basic educational program. The final list included nine hundred characters from the Yen list, and five hundred selected from other published sources or added because a specific need for them had become evident.

Romanization of the "List of 1400 Most Frequently Used Chinese Characters" was based upon that of Mathew's Chinese-English dictionary, published by Harvard University Press in 1952, and a new index was compiled alphabetically according to the romanization of each character.

Other sources utilized in the final compilation included an article by J. R. Moncrief in "The Chinese Recorder," Volume 65, 1938; "Two Thousand Chinese Characters," as corrected and added to by Father W. Grootaers; the "Word Frequency List, Colloquial Chinese," of the Institute of Chinese Studies, from a 1945-48 study of texts of conversational Chinese, and "The Five Thousand Dictionary" by C. H. Fenn, Harvard University Press 1944.

Communist sources included the list of the Department of Education of the "Chinese People's Government" of 1952, of 1500 characters divided into 1011 most frequently used and 489 less frequently used, and an Osaka (Japan) Foreign Language College reprint of the list of the Chinese Central Ministry of Education of the "People's Republic" of 1952, of 1997 characters divided into 1015 most frequently used, 487 frequently used and 495 less frequently used.

This most exacting academic achievement was supervised by James H. Pott, M.A., University of Michigan, former president of St. John's University in Shanghai and now on the faculty of Chung Chi University, Hongkong. He was assisted by Z. T. Wong, M.A., M.I.T., Sgt. Harry C. Milholland, Jr., B.A., Yale, and Ting T. Ssutu, A.B., Chung Shan.

Classes were composed of 25 to 50 students, and an instructor selected from among the prisoners of war themselves was assigned to each class. As with all aspects of the rehabilitation project, attendance was voluntary, but classes were generally kept below the upper limit of 50 so that there were always vacancies for diffident students. Teaching methods were sufficiently diverse and interesting to build student attention to a high level and keep it there. In addition to normal blackboard-textbook methods, literacy training charts were employed, and classes conducted for six to ten hours a week so that students would make sufficient progress to remain interested.

Next in priority were orientation classes—in effect, current events classes. The pilot project the fall before in Seoul had clearly demonstrated the hunger of the prisoners of war for unbiased, factual presentations of what was going on in the world, and where and why, and who were the personalities involved—the things which had been kept from them completely by communist censorship.

Attendance at these classes too was voluntary. In anti-communist compounds they were crowded. In compounds in which the ideological struggle had not yet been resolved, attendance was limited to anti-communists and communist leaders, the latter picking up names of articulate anti-communists for later liquidation, and arguments for use in the inevitable brainwashing sessions to follow. After the screenings and clear-cut separation of communist and anti-communist compounds in 1952, the orientation classes were dropped entirely as far as the communists were concerned.

Orientation was a better name for these classes than current events, particularly for the North Koreans, who had to be up-dated to the twentieth century historically before any attempt could be made to brief them on the problems of Korea as it entered the second half of that century. Men of military age, their concepts had been formed under an increasing barrage of Japanese propaganda culminating in an almost complete absence of information during World War II. Then, suddenly, they had become targets of the usual flood of communist misinformation.

None of them had any inkling of the post-war attempts of the United Nations to unify Korea, and the fact that these attempts had been thwarted by Soviet Russia. All of the officers knew that North Korea had invaded the Republic of Korea at Soviet instigation, but many of the common soldiers quite genuinely believed that their thrust into South Korea had been made in repelling an attack upon North Korea by the "American imperialists."

The Chinese did not have to be led by the hand through two generations of modern history, but there was a tremendous gap in their knowledge, too, from the date on which their units of the Nationalist Army or their provinces had been swallowed by the communists up to the present.

To have compelled these men to attend these classes would have been futile, and nothing whatever would have been accomplished. The time they had spent in interminable communist classes, forced to listen, to confess, to parrot in chorus, had rendered them almost immune to indoctrination. But the orientation classes were voluntary. They were interesting and informative, and the eagerness of these men to learn was pathetic. The communist version of recent history was noted, and the free world version presented. The instructors gave them the facts, and left it up to them to make up their own minds. There were among them sufficient officers and natural leaders who knew the communist versions to be false, and their own shrewdness had often told them that communist insistence on certain points pointed to their untruth. In their own discussions they arrived at sound conclusions quite penetratingly.

Orientation was scheduled for a minimum of two two-hour blocks of instruction per week, and a maximum of four two-hour blocks. As in the literacy program, methods used in presenting the materials were diverse, interesting and stimulating. Instructional procedures were varied from period to period and day to day.

Lectures, talks and explanations were kept as brief as possible, and accompanied by the use of visual aids. Motion pictures were utilized as frequently as possible, preceded always by an explanation of what the men were going to see, and followed by a discussion in which they themselves were encouraged to take part.

Opaque materials projectors, "balopticons," were used to blow up magazine illustrations and one-of-a-kind materials for all to see, and slide and film-strip projectors were used to the utmost. When a subject would lend itself to dramatization,

62

skits and playlets or puppet shows were presented, by the instructors, instructors and students, or the students themselves.

Exhibits and poster displays were contrived in conjunction with instruction, and then left as semi-permanent displays in the instruction centers, where the men could inspect and discuss them at their leisure. Panel discussions, forums, symposiums and similar methods were employed to tie the students in with the instruction and stimulate them to positive thinking.

Radio broadcasts were simulated, and the Chinese prisoners of war took to the microphone even more readily than the Koreans in the pilot project. Quiz shows, general discussions, question and answer periods and speeches and dialogues by students were employed. Compositions and themes written by the prisoners of war were read and discussed in class meetings, and talks and oral reports by the students were regular features. Recorded radio programs were played, and followed by discussion.

The methods used were those of the U. S. Army, which can cram an ordinary year of college level work into thirteen weeks. These were amplified by the efforts of some of the best educational brains it was possible to recruit from civilian sources in the U. S. The qualifications of Major R. C. Hahm have already been noted. Assisting him on the Korean side were William C. Kerr of the University of California and Princeton, who had long experience as a missionary in Korea, and Dexter Lutz, who was in charge of the agricultural aspects of the project and who had also had long experience in Korea, and spoke Korean.

Chinese-speaking educators in addition to Mr. Pott, already mentioned in connection with the special Chinese dictionary, included Dr. Henry Gilbert White of the University of Minnesota, now on the faculty of the U. S. Air Force Academy, and William D. Stout, M. A., Kentucky.

Other "educationists"—the U. S. Army term—included Dr. Billie Hollingshead, U. S. C.; Dr. John Benben of Northwestern, Edmund Cross of Columbia, Richard P. Harris of California and David R. Hoshimiya of Brigham Young.

But because the program was conducted first in a dozen and finally in scores of individual compounds and in two languages, these educators had to be backed up by other American personnel, Chinese and Korean educators, teachers, interpreters and translators, and finally by prisoner of war instructors on the individual class level. These were rarely trained teachers, and if they were, they were certainly untrained in the intensive American methods being employed. So teacher training classes, workshops, lesson outlines, lesson plans and lesson programs were all necessary, and it mounted into a formidable undertaking.

A number of techniques would be used even during one two-hour period of instruction. For example, a period might begin with a short lecture by the instructor, in which he emphasized the most significant points of the subject for the period. This would be followed by a general discussion, of about the same length as the lecture. After the discussion an appropriate film would be shown, preceded by an orientation and followed by another discussion. The period would end

64

with a review by the instructor of the significant items taught during the two hours.

During each week of the program all methods, media and materials were concentrated around one theme. If that theme were "The Farmer in Democratic Nations," the pamphlet material, motion pictures, visual aids and all other materials would fit that theme.

The program began out-of-doors during the summer of 1951 but moved indoors as quickly as possible, for shelter first from rain and that winter from snow, and because blackout facilities were necessary for motion pictures, slides and film-strips. Beginning in tents, it moved through prisoner-constructed huts to really adequate Quonset classrooms by the time the armistice was signed. Whenever possible, instructional centers were built in each compound, with a stage and wings, offices, lighting, a projector and a public address system. Such a center could be employed for classes in the daytime, for prisoner of war plays and their beloved Oriental operas in the evenings. In the later segregated anti-communist camps it became possible to build camp instructional centers, with indoor and open-air theaters, libraries, classrooms and shops. Seating progressed from straw mats to benches, and a first row of amazingly comfortable chairs in which the camp commander and his staff could be honored guests at opera premieres, with tea and cigarettes during the intermissions.

Walls of the centers were used for exhibit space, and they were made as attractive and comfortable as possible under the circumstances. The walls of the offices of the principal class-

65

room theater at Pusan Camp #9, for anti-communist North Koreans, used as dressing rooms when it was fulfilling its theater function, were neatly whitewashed at a time when there was no whitewash to be had in Korea. The prisoners of war had donated three months' supply of tooth-powder.

9

News and Entertainment

Third priority in the rehabilitation project was given to radio-type broadcasting. This involved a central control room at each camp, and later, in the anti-communist camps, one or two sound-proofed studios and loudspeakers in all compounds.

The control rooms were equipped with monitoring receivers, amplifiers, record and transcription turntables and tape-reproducers, so that programs might be re-broadcast directly off the air or recorded and re-broadcast later. Live-microphone pickups were possible, from studio or control room and from individual compounds, so that a play or a band concert in one compound might be broadcast to others. Individual amplifiers in each compound could broadcast independently, or be cut into the camp system.

Broadcasting was emphasized both as a means of information and as an aid to control, and its recreational and entertainment aspects came a distinct third.

United Nations Command psychological warfare radio broadcasts during the Korean conflict were unusual in that the same Korean-language programs were heard in both South and

67

North Korea. So, as a matter of fact, were communist programs from North Korea. As countries go, Korea is small, and radio waves will not drop dead at a battle-line or a geographical parallel. The communist distortions of Radio Pyongyang in the north were so obvious, so blatant and so self-defeating that no measures whatever were taken by the Republic of Korea or the UNC to prevent them from being heard, either by jamming or by restrictions on listening.

In North Korea, on the contrary, severe restrictions were placed upon listening to either the Voice of the United Nations Command or the Korean Broadcasting System, and VUNC was consistently but unsuccessfully jammed. VUNC and KBS cooperated amiably and effectively, carrying each other's programs to both South and North Korea, and concentrating on honest, factual Korean and world news.

These programs were piped to the North Korean POWs morning, noon and night, and VUNC Chinese language news and commentary programs were provided to the Chinese POWs. As the armistice approached, and after it was signed, news programs of special interest to the prisoners were also broadcast within the camps, but the principal radio diet in the POW camps was the Voice of the United Nations Command. As with the literacy program, the communist compounds raised no objections to the broadcasting program, although they would occasionally organize demonstrations to drown out news they considered bad and better unheard.

When the anti-communist POWs were moved to the demilitarized zone after the armistice, they brought the educational features of the rehabilitation project right along with them, under their own instructors. To assist them in keeping the program going, the Eighth Army installed amplifiers and loudspeakers in all of the new compounds. The communist "explainers" construed the terms of reference with respect to the POWs to permit broadcasting to the compounds by loudspeaker. The Neutral Nations Repatriation Commission saw no objection, providing the broadcasts were supervised by an NNRC sub-committee, and broadcasts began.

They began and ended on the same day, except for a few feeble attempts with portable amplifiers and loudspeakers. The anti-communist prisoners climbed the compound poles, pulled down the loudspeakers and reeled in the wires. These they used to rig still-higher staffs flying the Nationalist Chinese and ROK flags.

The communist POWs on Koje and Cheju could have done the same to stop the broadcasting there, but they didn't. They were just as interested in truthful news as the anti-communists.

Again, as with the pilot project in Seoul, this was not Big Brother type broadcasting. There was, it is true, a captive audience, but the loudspeakers were at the corners of the compounds and not in the huts. If anyone didn't wish to listen to the programs, he could go into his hutment and shut the door. In the communist compounds many did, but more listened. During cold weather the number who congregated outdoors, particularly for news, was remarkable.

The loudspeaker system was used for supplemental teaching and fill-ins for compounds which had missed classes because of work details or for other reasons. It was useful for announcements, and when it was not occupied otherwise it broadcast Chinese or Korean music and VUNC, Voice of America or Radio Free Asia commentaries. Special programs were designed to popularize and stimulate interest in various phases of the rehabilitation effort other than orientation, such as literacy and vocational training, work projects, physical education and athletics, juvenile education, health and sanitation, and recreation. Holidays and anniversaries received special attention.

The anti-communist POWs themselves were a prolific source of broadcast material. They would write, rehearse and broadcast plays, skits and operas to the limit of the time which could be made available to them, and each compound would strive to outdo the others.

And finally, in the communist compounds, the broadcasting system was used as a control measure. It was very difficult to organize a sullen, chanting, marching demonstration with the loudspeakers blaring a bright waltz.

Broadcasts were scheduled from 5:00 to 8:00 a.m., 11:00 a.m. to 1:00 p.m., and 5:00 to 9:30 p.m., so that they would not interfere with organized classes or work details. A special survey of all Korean anti-communist POW camps conducted in the spring of 1953 ranked news, Korean music and drama at the top of the preference scale, and sports reports and audience participation programs at the bottom.

No U. S. radio broadcasts ever achieved such high Crossley, Hooper or Nielsen ratings. The rehabilitation project programs regularly received the careful attention of 60% of the available audience, and some particularly favored broadcasts such as news reports ranked as high as 95%.

In order of popularity, Korean POW program preferences

were for straight news programs, commentaries, modern Korean music, traditional Korean instrumental music, traditional Korean folk songs, dramas about famous people, dramas about world events, poetry and music, variety programs, dramatized stories, discussions, western music, sports programs and audience participation shows.

POW requests for special programs were of interest, and were taken into account in subsequent programming. They included "Bae Beng Gud," a Korean witch who symbolizes amusement, singing and dancing; serial reading of Korean and foreign novels, western folk songs, religious music, sermons, and stories about how modern conveniences were invented. Neither the Chinese nor the Koreans were taken in to the slightest degree, incidentally, by Soviet claims to first invention of all that is modern in this world; they derived, in fact, great amusement from them.

Requests for educational programs ranged through sociology, economics, agriculture, sanitation, science, mathematics, English, the Bible, and sex. Only the last request was ignored.

10

Democracy in Action

Compound 65 on Koje Island—the fifth compound in Enclosure 6—was not a representative compound. It was the only compound on Koje which never, at any time, came under communist control. But Compound 65 furnishes an effective answer to those who say that dictatorship, either of the right or the left, is inevitable in the Orient.

Compound 65, Korean POWs, started out in May, 1951, with approximately 8,000 men. They built their own compound. The camps on Koje were on hillsides and even hilltops as often as possible, to keep from taking any arable land away from the islanders. The area of Compound 65 included the site, in 1592, of the historic but long-crumbled castle that Admiral Soon Sin built to repel the Japanese in the Korea-Japan war at the end of the sixteenth century.

Rehabilitation project personnel arrived with the POWs from Pusan, and the first permanent building was the school house, completed on the 5th of July.

Communist cells had arrived among the other POWs, however, and they had not been idle, either. After an abortive ef-

72

fort to seize control of the compound on May 20, they instigated a full-scale riot on the 16th of August. Two thousand additional POWs had been added to the compound, for a total of 10,000, and to preserve internal order among so many men 105 "compound monitors" had been elected. The compound monitors put down the riot without having to call on the UNC authorities for assistance, and arrested and turned over to the camp command the 22 communist ringleaders. A flare-up of rioting at reveille the next morning was also suppressed, and 78 additional communists arrested. The compound monitors' intelligence system, getting wind of a planned third riot, twice intercepted orders for it, again arrested the ringleaders, and prevented it completely.

The strength of the compound went up and down as men were moved to newly completed compounds to relieve the overcrowded situation, as communist elements were removed to communist compounds, and as anti-communist elements were received from other compounds. On the 10th of January, 1952, it stood at 6163 men, and after a week of active campaigning Lee Dong Ju, the chief compound monitor, was formally elected compound leader. He received 3689 votes; Hyun Dong Sun 1231, and Lee Sung Jin 1155. There were 84 men who abstained from voting, and 4 voided ballots—a democratic election in which 99.93% of the eligible voters participated. Lee Sung Baek, who had been elected temporary compound leader the previous May, stood aside and did not run for re-election, to be sure that the process would be wholly democratic. He had attempted to schedule the election of his successor the early part of the preceding summer, but the August riots had prevented an orderly campaign and election at that time.

A "Sunday meeting," with commanders of platoons, companies and battalions in attendance, served as a legislature for the compound.

Having failed to secure control of the compound by force, the diminished communist element turned to a standard Red device—assassination—with Lee Dong Ju and Lee Sung Baek as their principal targets. Communist agent Lyu In Soon pretended illness and was admitted to the headquarters hospital. There, fellow agent Kim Hong Tae passed him a small quantity of poison which he had procured from a North Korean communist medical officer on duty in the hospital. A third agent, Han Man Sik, who was a member of the kitchen police, was to put this poison in the leaders' soup as he served the evening meal.

But surveillance by the compound monitors of the security of the leaders was so strict that Han had no opportunity to poison the soup unobserved. He buried the poison near the latrine—and was caught in the act. That was the last gasp of communism in Compound 65.

In the meantime, the rehabilitation programs proceeded apace. Compound 65 had everything every other compound had, and some features others did not have.

They had, for instance, their own newspaper, named simply "Our Newspaper." They had English classes as well. These started out slowly, until Sgt. William J. Paolucci, their rehabilitation chief, volunteered to conduct after-hours seminars, an hour every night except Sunday, in English conversation. With

74

this encouragement, the class increased to more than 75 members.

While all of the anti-communist compounds went in heavily for dramatics, Compound 65 had an extraordinarily successful Culture department. Ranging from one-actors to productions in four acts and six scenes, the titles of some of their plays are especially engaging.

"Bloodstained Sword," "A Day in Seoul," "Mr. Park Visits Seoul" and "Dear Free Land" give an idea of some of their preoccupations. Romance was not neglected, as witness "Love at the Port," "Son-in-law Wanted," "Princess Bell-Flower," and "White Pearl."

They built stage-settings out of cardboard and kraft paper boxes, hemp bags, poster paper, paper bags, tin cans and wooden ration boxes, dyed with tooth powder, clay, grass, lime and DDT! Hemp and rice bags made costumes, and tooth powder, soot, clay and pine resin were used for make-up.

Culture departments of the individual battalions were also active, and some of their productions, played to appreciative audiences in other battalions, included "Quack's Hospital," "Sword of Wrath," "Leaders," "Cigarette Butts," "Naivete," "Justice," "My Homeland Where the Flowers Bloom," "For the Cause of My Fatherland," "Reef in Life," "Love in a Pawnshop," "Sons of the Republic of Korea," "Going Home," "Prop of the Republic of Korea," and "Land of Passion."

Comedies included "Physical Exercise in the Moonlight"—the title is a Korean saying which is the equivalent of "crazy!"—and "Self-Styled Guitar Virtuoso," put on at Christmas but with a bathing beach locale. "Shanghai Typhoon" and "Foggy

Shanghai" were devoted to the struggles of political exiles during the Japanese occupation of Korea.

A music department regularly scheduled Korean operas, variety shows and concerts ranging from jazz to classics and folk and religious music. Since they had no "sing-sing girls," they made do with "sing-sing boys." In one singing meet, a chorus of 20 singing "Return to Sorrento" competed with a chorus of 40 in "A Night at the Silla Ruins." Silla was one of the three ancient Korean Kingdoms. Silla won easily over Sorrento, but they were not taking any chances.

Each battalion had a "farmer's band," costumed and equipped with hand drums, gourd-shaped tom-toms, bass drums and gongs—Korean hillbillies, with cocked hats, colored sashes, and, for their comedy numbers, farmers' hats.

There was an Art Department, too, and Compound 65 had five art exhibitions, with from one to two hundred paintings, wood-carvings and sculptures in each. A special boys' exhibition had 120 entries.

"Our Newspaper" had almost as many contributors as readers, and to use up excess articles the "School Weekly" came into being.

A Protestant Church in Compound 65, organized in July, 1951, outgrew the tent assigned to it and graduated by the next March to two tents side by side. It had 300 members, despite the fact that in November Deacon Yum Dong Sik and a Christian cadre—how different from a communist cadre!—moved to Compound 69 and founded a church there. In December, Park In Whan and another cadre founded a church in Compound 95, and Yun Chi Duk and a third cadre were dispatched to the

76

newly founded church in Compound 62. This third mission required a high order of courage, for Compound 62 had been and still was heavily infiltrated with communists, and the issue of communist or anti-communist control had not been settled there.

In addition to Sunday School, Sunday church services and a Wednesday prayer meeting, the Protestant Church conducted a Bible course every evening except Sunday and Wednesday, with five church workers and 250 students. Korean missionary Kim Ah Ryol conducted a Bible class in English every Thursday afternoon, for 80 students.

The Catholic Church was founded in the compound in September, 1951, when Maryknoll missionary Father Pachi, with the cooperation of the camp authorities, helped all of the Catholics in Compounds 61, 62, 63, and 64 to gather together in Compound 65, where they could be free from the communist persecution they had suffered in the other compounds. This consolidation brought together 126 Catholics and 260 converts.

For the Catholics, there was a mass and a Bible class each Sunday, and prayer meetings every morning and every evening with an average attendance of eighty. Christian doctrine classes were conducted for two hours daily, secular studies one hour daily, and hymn recitals three times weekly. At Christmas, the Catholic congregation presented "The Rebirth," an adaptation from "Les Miserables," in one act and two scenes.

The Catholic Church had its missionary program, too. Kim Young Il and three others went back to Compound 63, Kim Kwan Ok and five to 64, and Shin Sang Chul and three to Compound 68.

This religious activity in Compound 65 was not exceptional. Chinese- and Korean-speaking Protestant and Catholic chaplains of the United Nations Command ministered to all of the anti-communist POWs, and on Cheju there was a Buddhist chaplain as well for the Buddhist Chinese.

The Anti-Communist Youth League, in Compound 65, was known as the "Daihan (Korean) Youth Corps." It was in charge of all patriotic celebrations and ceremonies, and its organization pointed the way to success for just about any similar organization. Practically everyone in it was an officer.

The headquarters provided twenty-three responsible jobs. Each battalion group had sixty-three officers—and there were five battalions. The figure rose geometrically when it came to companies, and there were still platoons and squads to be reckoned with.

Compound 65 had the best of all of the Boy Scout programs, too, with five troops, 170 scouts, and Sergeant Paolucci as Scoutmaster. While life within a POW compound restricted them somewhat in the merit badges for which they could qualify, they made up for this in other ways.

As POWs, each Scout received a cigarette ration, but on March 4, 1952, all of the Scouts forswore smoking. The following week was "Good Conduct Week," during which they presented cigarettes to the "old people"—their term—as an expression of respect. Other tasks which they set for themselves during Good Conduct Week were the relief of the sick and wounded, the reformation of bad habits and abstention from indiscreet remarks or acts, and reformation of manners toward the older leaders.

During "Clean-up Week," they policed up every vestige of trash in the compound, and swept the athletic field and parade ground to get rid of all the stones, a mammoth undertaking.

They sent out a cadre, too, to get the Boy Scout movement going in Compound 69, and Education Minister Pak of the Republic of Korea attended the activation ceremony. They also presented a well-deserved medal of merit and letter of appreciation to Sergeant Paolucci. Perhaps you saw the pictures of Sergeant Paolucci in the press, with the orphaned Korean boy he adopted despite the fact that he is a bachelor. Sergeant Paolucci came back after the war for a second tour in Korea, an ambassador of democracy with the Korea Civil Assistance Command.

Paolucci's Compound 65 was democracy in action—and so was every other anti-communist compound.

11

Vocational Training

To the hard-bitten military men who commanded the POW camps, the rehabilitation project in its beginnings was often an exasperation. Driven first to get the camps of Koje built to house the prisoners, then getting the hutments winterized, they were impatient with anything which might interfere with work details. It was difficult for them to see any sense in teaching arithmetic to an adult Korean or calligraphy to a Chinese. Often they resented even the little theater activities of the POWs, despite the fact that these were conducted outside of the eight hours a day which is all the Geneva Conventions say you may work a prisoner of war.

They rebelled even more when the vocational training program got under way, until they discovered that this could help them accomplish their own missions. The POW camps were at the end of the supply lines in Korea. There was the usual argument there between the combat troops and the communications zone, the zone piously insisting that when it came to supplies the troops came first, and the troops profanely accusing the zone of skimming off the cream. (For cream, read beer.) But there could be no question but that the POW camps got their supplies last.

Blacksmith shops were generally the first vocational training facilities established, and each forge spawned others as fast as tools could be turned out. There was plenty of scrap iron in Korea—it sometimes seemed as though the only kind of iron there was in Korea was barely salvageable junk—and iron was what it took to make tools. With the tools, more blacksmiths could be trained, and these blacksmiths could make hutment stoves out of oil drums, and tools for the other shops.

Western and Eastern social systems clashed head-on immediately. Neither the Chinese nor the Koreans employ anything remotely resembling the European apprentice system or the American vocational school. The few blacksmiths among the POWs cheerfully made forges and tools and stoves, but they objected strenuously to making more blacksmiths. Theirs was an ancient and an honored skill, one to be handed down only with the greatest circumspection, from father to oldest son; if there was no son, to some fortunate lad who would be adopted and treated thenceforth as a son.

They were not about to teach blacksmithing to ragtag, bobtail prisoners of war. And every other skilled artisan in the camps felt exactly the same way about passing on his specialty.

Breaking down this attitude took some doing and was generally accomplished in this wise. The blacksmith was, of course, a prisoner of war and subject to military discipline. If the stubborn Americans insisted on permitting half a dozen men to watch him work, there was nothing he could do about it. If the Americans then ordered him away from his anvil, and let one of those men take his place, there was nothing he could do about that, either. But if the man who took his place miserably botched his attempt to imitate the blacksmith, as he usually did, pride of profession had the blacksmith in there showing him how to do it right, with the Americans and the class applauding. Suddenly he had a new status, one even more honorable than blacksmithing. He was a teacher. By the time the directors of the rehabilitation project could equip him with a textbook on blacksmithing, something they did as quickly as possible, he was practically a scholar. If he could not read the manual, he could at least understand and appreciate and point to the illustrations.

Tinsmithing came next, for there were plenty of empty beer cans in Korea and the oil drum stoves needed stovepipes. The tinsmiths devised and the blacksmiths built machines which demonstrated genuine ingenuity, for clipping off the tops and bottoms of beer cans—a can-opener will do this, too, but not on a mass-production basis—slitting them, rolling them flat and crimping them together into sheets of really useful tin. One tinsmith even designed an iron wringer which poured forth sheets of tin corrugated like galvanized iron.

A big side-line in tin souvenirs developed in virtually every camp, and the POWs produced toy tanks, planes and ships and other gew-gaws in which they conducted a lively trade with camp personnel and visitors. The blacksmiths went in for highly polished brass belt buckles and the like, made from expended artillery shell cases, and for more substantial ash trays.

When the carpenters had finished fixing up their own hutments, their shops were busy with furniture manufacture. While some of their efforts were pretty primitive the bulk of their work was surprisingly accomplished, particularly in view of the salvaged lumber and home-made tools they were using. On the side, they carved picture frames. Every camp had an art studio producing training charts, stage settings, and portraits in oil (from snapshots) of the camp commander's wife and children.

Shoe repair and tailor shops were two more vocational projects with which the camp commanders never quarreled. The POWs were clothed in salvaged U. S. shoes and fatigues, which come in two well-known sizes, too large and too small. As far as the generally smaller Chinese and Korean POWs were concerned, they were usually too large and had to be cut down. This did not present too much of a tailoring problem, but cutting down shoes was a major cobbling operation which involved almost complete remanufacture.

In the spring of 1951, while the men were still being held behind scanty barbed wire on Koje and the compounds were by no means escape-proof, the POW uniform gave rise to one major set-back in relations between the U. S. camp authorities and the Korean POWs. As the Koje hills greened with spring vegetation, a POW in green U. S. fatigues could fade away from a working party or through the wire and simply melt into the landscape.

More distinctive uniforms seemed to be the answer, and with a new issue coming up, it was decided to dye them red. Red would stand out fine against the green hills. It was warm enough in the spring sunshine to line the men up, have them

83

divest themselves of their greens and then move along the enclosure to the issue point in their underwear, there to receive bright new red uniforms.

To a man, anti-communist or communist, they refused the red uniforms, and in a contest of wills with the camp command they held out for green uniforms, in their shorts and T-shirts, for ten days. It was the same story in every compound. The Koreans would not accept red uniforms, period.

The relatively few Chinese then in custody accepted them readily enough; red is a good, gay color in China.

The Koreans would not even say why. Communication was difficult at best, but this was one of the worst situations yet encountered. To repeated questioning, all the camp commander and his men got were the whites of the men's eyes.

At the end of the ten days the commander belatedly resorted to an old military solution: he consulted the chaplain. This chaplain was not an Army officer, or perhaps he would have come to the commander with the answer he was seeking. He was a missionary with long experience in Korea, and as puzzled as the prisoners at the commander's insistence that the men wear red uniforms.

"I wish that you had asked me that before you dyed the uniforms red," he replied mildly. "During the Japanese occupation, when a criminal was condemned to death he was given a red uniform. These men think you have decided to shoot them."

The green uniforms were re-issued, and the anti-communist Koreans accepted the commander's apologies readily enough.

84

The damage was done, however, as far as the communist POWs were concerned. They had learned that a completely united compound could defy the U. S. command, and a year later they put that knowledge to use.

All camps had, in addition to the foregoing vocational projects, straw-weaving and welding shops. Then, depending on the natural resources in the vicinity of the particular camp—and the camps were finally spread all across the south end of the Korean peninsula, in addition to Koje and Cheju islands—other vocational activities were organized. One camp had clay near by, ideal for making brick, and developed a busy brick factory. Another, near a source of stone, trained stone-cutters and stone-masons, and its buildings were handsomely and warmly faced with stone. Several were near or incorporated within their boundaries sources of potter's clay and had ceramic shops and kilns which produced really attractive ware. Still another, with an Air Force dump near by, constructed a miniature factory which made rice bowls out of damaged aluminum wing tanks, for all of the camps in Korea.

In general, however, the rehabilitation project did not go in for production for production's sake, but adhered to the principle that only those work projects which could be utilized for vocational training would be selected. The purpose of the vocational program was the development of manual skills among the POWs that would aid in their self-support and in the reconstruction of their countries after their eventual release. It was assumed that providing opportunities to develop work skills would tend to develop favorable attitudes toward the

85

agency which provided the opportunity, the United Nations, and this assumption proved to be correct.

Even the communist POWs, fearful of the educational aspects of the program lest they be weaned away from their careful dialecticism, welcomed the vocational projects. After the screenings and the Dodd incident, every V.I.P. who visited Koje insisted on touring the communist shops, so that he could boast later of having stood unarmed and unharmed within sledge-hammer reach of a communist blacksmith. General Clark finally had to issue an order that no one would be permitted in the communist compounds without his personal permission—and he never gave his personal permission. One unsympathetic POW command colonel attempted to include rehabilitation project personnel in this ruling, but found himself replaced by an infantry brigadier general, so sympathetic and successful that he quickly made major general.

It was the men who were not adapted mentally for the literacy, orientation, or adult continuation programs who particularly benefited from the vocational training. The very Asian reluctance to accept apprentices made the attainment of any skill at any of the useful trades being taught an opportunity which would ordinarily have been hard come by for these Chinese and Koreans, and they appreciated it. Although many of them returned to Red China and North Korea, there can be no question but that with their new-found ability to earn a better-than-average living even under the communist system, they are less dedicated communists today because the United Nations gave them a leg up.

86

As the vocational program settled down, the apprentices were divided into classes, three to a class. Each class would receive 16 hours of instruction a week, two full eight-hour days. One hour in each eight would consist of classroom theory, with the chief instructor, a skilled artisan, in charge. In the other seven hours, each member of the class would receive on-the-job training, with an opportunity to observe, assist, and eventually participate in the work being done.

No deadlines or production schedules were laid down—the training was the important thing. An apt apprentice would be promoted as quickly as possible to an instructor's job, and the slower students given as much time as they needed.

Every camp had one additional vocational activity—a barber college. The American G. I.'s assigned to the rehabilitation project, ingenious as they themselves were, never ceased to marvel at the ingenuity of the Chinese and Korean artisans they superintended. With scissors, combs and even razors made by the blacksmiths, the barbers did a remarkably good job and never lacked for customers, even if their handiwork did excite a suspicion that they had also used locally-made rice bowls.

Under the spreading acacia trees, the blacksmiths even turned out carpenter's saws. An Asian saw, Japanese, Korean or Chinese, is built along the general lines of a butcher's cleaver, a bit elongated; some of them like a double cleaver, with two cutting edges. The carpenter holds his work with his bare feet, and does the neatest work imaginable.

The Korean vocational instructors in Compound 65 on Koje kept a record of what their shops produced. Their blacksmiths

87

made, in addition to the items already listed, honey buckets, shovels, hinges, sieves, hangers, fire pots, frying pans, spits, wrenches, fire buckets, fire alarm bells, sand cans, blades for carpenter's planes, bits, chisels, rakes, hammers, pawls, punches, knives, tin snips, drills and screwdrivers.

12

Night Soil versus Phosphates

When the armistice was signed, the U. S. personnel and some visiting Belgian and Ethiopian liaison officers on Cheju Island had had no mail and no fresh vegetables for three weeks. Their Chinese cooks, expert as they were, were hard put to make anything but C-rations out of the C-rations which were all they had to work with. With no proper harbor for anything bigger than a fishing boat, Cheju was supplied by tank landing ships, and the one LST assigned to the Cheju run had been beached too high for retreat by an extraordinarily high tide three weeks before. It was still beached, waiting for the next full moon.

The C-47 which landed that day on the grass air field which served the big anti-communist camp on Cheju was flown by a Royal Hellenic Air Force crew, mustachioed and magnificent. Nobody but the Greeks had nerve enough to attempt Cheju in that kind of weather, with the tail end of the rainy season overlapping the beginning of typhoon time. It was the first plane in more than a week, gnawing at a big backlog of passengers and mail. For every passenger who showed up with a top priority at K-9, the Pusan air field from which it took off, the pilot kicked off a sack of mail, until he had no more parachutes or Mae West life preservers. He saw that each passenger was wearing one of each, then shouted "Figeh!", which is Greek for "get the hell out of here," to his crew.

It was a sorry camp staff which boarded the plane after its sixth bounce on the Cheju air field, to find no mail and too many passengers to be able to simulate hospitality successfully. The Greek crew declined an invitation to lunch. With luck, they could make it back to Pusan in time for dinner. If they hadn't had luck they couldn't have let down through the murk right over the Mosulp'o air strip, just short of Sanbang-San, the thousand-foot volcanic chimney that seems to lean over one end of the strip, and not too far from Halla-San, the mile-high mountain that centers Cheju.

The nineteen thousand Chinese prisoners on Cheju, fifteen thousand anti-communists and four thousand-odd communists alike, had quite a nice lunch that day, and a better dinner. They had the basic POW ration of rice and dried squid, plus the C-rations the camp staff just picked at, plus.

It was that final plus that broke the hearts of the camp complement. The mostly-beef C-ration component had been cooked up with green peppers. For side dishes there were pickled radishes and fresh onions and tomatoes. Not every man had an egg, but those whose turn it was to have a fresh egg had a fresh raw egg. In some of the compounds, the upper echelons of the POW hierarchy had chicken-and-peanuts or rabbit-and-peanuts, either of which is just as tasty as chicken and walnuts. The dried squid had been soaked out and stewed with Chinese cabbage and leeks. There was a choice between rice, sweet potatoes and Irish potatoes. Many of the anti-communist POWs, permitted to go fishing and sea-weed gathering in reasonable numbers, had fish and nori—dried sea-weed—to vary their diet.

For the camp command it was water, water everywhere, and not a drop to drink. The vegetables had been raised by the POWs, and whether they had used commercial chemical fertilizer or resorted to the use of "night soil," human ordure, the ground in which they had raised them was contaminated by use of night soil for generations and centuries. If any of the American or European officers in the camp command had eaten so much as one fresh tomato, for which they would have given their right arms at that point, they would certainly have dysentery and would be lucky to escape amoebic dysentery, a worm infestation, or both.

The POW gardens had started as the agricultural education portion of the rehabilitation project. No mass production of produce for use in the POW's subsistence messes had been contemplated at the outset, and it had been intended to limit the program to classroom-type activities, demonstrations and experiments within the compounds, and demonstrations and experiments on adjacent land. Nor had it been intended to develop any large-scale work projects for numbers of the POWs, or to take up more than five hours a week of the crowded rehabilitation schedule.

The simple purpose of the program had been to provide an opportunity for prisoners with rural backgrounds to improve their knowledge of efficient farming. It was proposed to permit the few POWs who were already graduates of schools of agriculture to study, plan, write, and teach workable solutions to some of Korea's and China's pressing agricultural problems, and to encourage and train as many as possible to take a part in the rebuilding of Korea and China through improvements in agriculture, conservation of natural resources, and reforestation. Through teaching and demonstration, it was hoped that the POWs could be shown how Asian agriculture could be improved through introduction of new or little known crops and methods and the use of legumes and fertilizers, and to train them in the techniques for such improvement. It was proposed to set aside one to two acres of ground near each compound for use as an experimental demonstration area, dividing it into small plots and planting these to potatoes, vegetables, and other crops selected for their actual or potential value.

The agricultural project got away to a late start in 1951, but there was time to plant late crops and the POWs were set to work gathering lespedeza and kudzu seed for demonstration planting. Lespedeza and kudzu, two of the most useful crops in the southeastern United States for stopping erosion on the one hand and providing forage for beef and dairy cattle on the other, are both native to Korea, but little-exploited, almost forgotten, and completely disregarded for the two purposes for which they were so successfully used by American farmers.

Lespedeza, a low-growing lush legume, was planted in plots heavily treated with commercial fertilizer rich in phosphorus, alongside plots fertilized only with night soil, for comparison planting to the same crops the following spring. Kudzu, with

92

its fast growing vines, was planted in mountainside plots visible from the compounds, to show its usefulness as a groundcover and erosion arrester, and its notable forage potential as well.

In 1952 the spring planting was interrupted by the Koje affair and the relocation of the anti-communist POWs, but not before they had seen barley in legume-phosphorus plots twice as thick and tall as that in night soil plots. In 1953, the anti-communist prisoners, most of them farmers at heart after all and really homesick for their hoes, planted one thousand acres of red Korean clay in truck gardens. The UNC furnished equipment and chemicals for soil testing, seeds and fertilizer, lumber and other materials for hot beds. The blacksmith shops made tools, and the straw-weaving shops supplied bags and baskets. With one notable exception, which will be dwelt on later, there were no draft animals, but there was no dearth of strong backs and willing hands.

U. N. troops in Korea ate fresh vegetables for the first time in military history, vegetables raised on hydroponic, soilless chemical farms in Japan and shipped to Korea. By the time those vegetables got to Korea they were fairly expensive, although no more so than the few less-hygienic vegetables available on the Korean civilian market.

The anti-communist POWS ate fresh vegetables too, the last summer of their internment. And although neighboring Korean civilians harvested nearly three-fifths of the crop—the gardens of the Korean prisoners released by Mr. Rhee in June—and all of the late crops, after the remaining POWs moved to

93

the demilitarized zone in September, the recorded production figures of the agricultural project were still impressive. Had those vegetables been paid for at prevailing civilian market rates, they would have cost more than the entire rehabilitation project for that year.

13

Fun and Festivals

The original compounds on Koje varied in size, housing up to 8,000 prisoners of war. These large Koje compounds were divided by roster, although not physically, into battalions, each approximately the size of the later compounds. After the 1952 spread-out, organization was standardized at up to 500 POWs to a compound, and up to ten compounds in an enclosure.

The physical education and athletics portion of the rehabilitation project was divided into three programs, the first an informal athletic phase of intra-battalion games and activities, then a battalion athletic competition phase. The culmination was a compound athletic festival phase. This program was constant, since it was not dependent on the season as the agricultural program was.

The athletic program was useful in working off any excess animal energy left over after work details, and in teaching democratic methods of choosing leaders. From both standpoints it can definitely be said to have been an absolute failure in the communist compounds, for they always had energy enough left to put on a first class riot and their leaders maintained their command by strong-arm methods which did not stop at murder. But the anti-communist compounds loved it, particularly the festivals.

A festival in a prisoner of war camp enclosure may be hard to imagine, but the Chinese and Korean anti-communists could manage a classy one any day it did not rain, complete with floats. They could not summon the automotive underpinnings of a Pasadena Rose Bowl parade, but they had floats with flowers nevertheless. The flowers were made of toilet paper, of which the Korean prisoners, especially, always had a surplus. They preferred for its more prosaic purpose a rag, washed scrupulously clean and tucked in the waist-band.

Green dye could be had by boiling new fatigues in very little water, and atabrine made a dandy yellow. Blood was the standard red for everything from flags to flowers to signing petitions, and gallons of it must have flowed for each purpose.

A man on horseback with a gaily caparisoned mount attached to the waist of the "rider" was the favorite float, but there were elephants and camels, too, and boats and pagodas, all built on the same general principle.

Each compound athletic area had as a minimum a combination volley-ball and basketball court, a Korean wrestling pit, a boxing ring and a calisthenics area. The enclosure areas had these and in addition an athletic area large enough for a soccer field, a running track, and space for spectators.

Boxing would have been limited had the POWs been classified according to Western weights, but there were seven classes, starting with junior flyweights, who were under 100 pounds. The flyweight class went up to 112, bantamweight to 118, pettiweight to 126, lightweight to 135, welterweight to 158. Anything over 158 pounds was middleweight, and the occasional North Chinese heavyweight went in for wrestling.

Gymnastics included weight-lifting, parallel and high bars, tumbling and pyramids. Equipment was salvaged, worn-out U. S. Army athletic goods, and even ran to baseballs, bats and mitts for the Koreans, who had learned the game under the Japanese, and basketballs for the Chinese, who had learned and taken to the game during the "cultural aggression" of American missionaries.

Some rather special salvaged items of U. S. Army athletic equipment were seized upon with avidity by the prisoners of war. Ping-pong was not new to them, nor was badminton, but they started pitching horeshoes with the same verve with which they essayed more familiar games.

Lining up these salvaged materials presented certain problems to the officers in Tokyo charged with backing up the program. Such materials come under the Special Services staff section, and special services officers who were charged with getting rid of worn-out equipment were interested in getting rid of everything they had on hand, and not being stuck with material of which they could not legally dispose. Signing it over to the rehabilitation project was a legal channel.

Along with the athletic equipment came wheezy manual organs, tired pianos, and musical instruments of all descriptions. These were welcomed, and by the time the armistice was signed virtually every anti-communist compound had a band. They had orchestras, too, some with prisoner-made violins and cellos, for their theatrical productions.

97

Some of the athletic equipment gave the project directors pause, however. One indignant senior officer turned thumbs down on a shipment of golf clubs. How would it look in the newspapers, he asked, if some correspondent saw that shipment headed for the prisoner of war camps and wrote it up? He was mollified however, when it was explained to him that special services wouldn't release the shipment on anything but a 100% basis, that if the golf clubs were refused none of the material was available, and that previous shipments of worn-out golf clubs had been found most useful, with the heads of the clubs chopped off, as pointers for instructors in the educational aspects of the project. They made nice swagger sticks for the camp command, too. One standard practical joke called for careful preservation, intact, of all left-handed mashies, for presentation to right-handed camp commanders who were afraid of getting rusty in Korea on their chip shots.

For the non-athletes and non-musicians among the prisoners of war—some of the non-musicians did not let that stop them and played in the bands anyway—there were libraries and exhibits in each anti-communist enclosure. In addition to making books completely available, these served as regulated reading rooms and centers for distribution of magazines and newspapers. Well-lighted, and number one on the priority list for stoves when all the hutments were not yet heated, they were enormously popular. Selected prisoners of war were appointed as librarians, and books and magazines checked out via a card system. As in the pilot project, it had been noted that the literate POWs would read to others, and it was desired to encourage this to the utmost.

A list of the books and pamphlets employed in the rehabilitation project, in addition to standard textbooks, will be found in Appendix A; the titles are self-explanatory. The book which enjoyed the greatest circulation, and not just because it was supplied in greater number than other titles, was the Bible. Next was the Sears, Roebuck catalog.

As an extension of the enclosure library, each Korean compound had a bulletin board, on which was posted the USIS daily news bulletin, bi-weekly news pictorial, weekly world news and weekly news cartoon; the current issue of the camp newspaper, and the current issue of the United Nations Command Korean newssheets, "Free World Weekly Digest" and "Rehabilitation News." In addition, suitable Korean language periodicals, special rehabilitation project announcements, radio broadcast schedules and schedules of enclosure events were posted, and posters produced in conjunction with the rehabilitation project or by the prisoners themselves.

Only two USIS publications, one bi-weekly and one weekly, were available for the Chinese, though they also received the Chinese-language edition of the "Free World Weekly Digest." No "Rehabilitation News" was printed in Chinese, since the "rehabilitation" in this case had to do with the rebuilding and rehabilitation of Korea by the U. N. Korean Reconstruction Agency, U. N. Civil Assistance Command, Civilian Relief in Korea, the American-Korean Foundation, and other agencies.

For POWs under 18 who had not completed the equivalent of twelve years of schooling, next priority in the rehabilitation project went to a program of full-time schooling.

The curriculum provided for the juvenile classes was exactly

99

the equivalent of that offered in the elementary and secondary schools of the Republic of Korea. In effect, it was much better, for the ROK school system had been terribly disrupted by the communist invasion, with schools suspended, schoolhouses destroyed, textbooks scattered or burned, and such simple needs as chalk and pencils and paper in extremely short supply. They were in short supply in the prisoner of war camps, too, but the first new Korean textbooks since the invasion were printed for the rehabilitation project, and the proofs and surplus and salvaged copies made available to the ROK Department of Education. For its part, the Education Ministry gave the juveniles formal credit for the POW camp study.

There were not too many surplus and salvaged copies, for the 27,000 North Korean anti-communists released by President Rhee took their rehabilitation project textbooks and tools with them. They cut the barbed wire on that memorable night, one camp commander charged bitterly, with wire-cutters and tin-shears made in their own blacksmith shops.

For the Chinese, the curriculum was the equivalent of that offered in the elementary and secondary schools of China prior to 1949. For both, it was determined as accurately as possible the point at which schooling had stopped or had been interrupted, so that the participants would not be bored by going over too-familiar ground or discouraged by being introduced to work which was too difficult.

As in the pilot project, classes were limited to 25 to 50 men, and instructors were recruited from among the POWs themselves. These instructors were excused from work details in so far as possible, so that they could give a maximum of time to preparation. Being excused from work details had no effect on their prestige. The scholar is highly respected in the Orient, and their appointment as instructors was sufficient to give them a great deal of face.

Wherever feasible, the members of the juvenile classes were quartered together, and they had their own athletic activities and vocational shop schedules. One further activity which made perhaps the greatest impression on the younger prisoners of war than anything else, but which seemed so incongruous to the camp commands and to the older prisoners that it was abandoned after the anti-communist prisoners were moved from Koje, was Boy Scouting.

Boy Scout troops, set up under the age requirements of the National Council of the Boy Scouts of Korea and its pro-communist equivalent in China, were organized in each anti-communist compound on Koje in which there was a sufficient number of lads to make them worth while. This was a new world to these Chinese and Korean boys, and they revelled in it. They took to it with such enthusiasm that it was easy to see why Scouting is anathema to the communists. This was something, too, in which virtually every American soldier assigned to the camps was an expert, and there was no dearth of volunteer scoutmasters and assistants.

The amount of scouting activity which could be carried on inside a barbed wire enclosure was surprising. A Korean language version of the Boy Scout Handbook was available in sufficient quantities to give each Scout a copy, and this was invariably the dearest single possession of each of the Korean boys. Mimeographed translations of a chapter at a time had to do for the Chinese, but since so few of them could read them themselves at that stage of the game, the lack was not keenly felt.

But the boys grew older, and with the screenings and the life-and-death struggle in which they were involved as the armistice talks lagged, they were swept up into the more militant organizations of the older prisoners of war. All of the Chinese anti-communist POWs were a unified organization; among the Koreans, the Anti-Communist Youth League came to the fore as the principal outlet for the universal urge to join, to belong. It is still in being in the Republic of Korea, and a mighty fine organization we members think it is, too, even we older honorary members.

14

Evaluation

The remaining elements of the rehabilitation project were adult continuation education, health education, recreational activities, and reading groups.

The adult continuation education exactly paralleled the juvenile education program, but was set up separately to spare the older prisoners of war the embarrassment of participating in classes in which their juniors might be more apt and able. The same instructors functioned for both, but the adult classes attacked their studies with a determination which surpassed even that of the juveniles.

Health education and instruction in sanitation had a secondary purpose in addition to the fact that it was a much-appreciated subject. It resulted in lowering the incidence of diseases in the compounds and decreasing by that much the enormous problems of the UNC camp commands. Doctors among the prisoners of war were employed in this program, but there were not enough of them and they were already busy in the camp hospitals.

The degree of competence of the doctors among the prisoners of war was not all that could be desired, either, and gave a startling insight into what must have been one of the basic reasons behind the absurd but diabolic communist charges that the United Nations Command waged germ warfare in Korea and against mainland China. There were exceptions, of course, a number of Korean doctors educated in Japan and even in Germany, and a few Chinese doctors educated in the United States. But the average "medical officer" in the Chinese and Korean communist armies is usually a medical student, impressed into service before he has completed his training and with no internship whatever. His patients are fortunate, in that case, for he may be only a former medical aid man, promoted to the status of physician or surgeon after a smattering of pharmaceutical training or after having simply watched a surgeon at work.

Intelligence reports and even the North Korean radio reveal that the same situation is true with respect to civilian medical care in North Korea. Much was made in communist propaganda of Czech and Polish medical teams in North Korea, to counterbalance the Danish, Norwegian, Swedish, Indian, Italian and German hospitals and medical personnel on the United Nations side. But when the Czech members of the Neutral Nations Supervisory Commission in North Korea, after the armistice, found themselves coming down with malaria while the Czechs and Poles stationed in South Korea were protected by chloroquine from U. N. sources, it was to the United Nations Command that they appealed for a drug so easily procured in the free world.

There can be no question that the communist propaganda of

104

germ warfare was intended to shift from the communist regimes to the United Nations Command the blame for the miserable civilian and military health services behind the Bamboo
Curtain. It had a secondary purpose in mobilizing the civilian
population in Red China and North Korea against flies and
mosquitoes, and every fly or mosquito despatched was "evidence."

Communist medicine cannot be so bad that it would accuse
the United Nations of spreading disease through feathers and
spiders, but communist propaganda is good enough to know
that an ignorant farmer, finding a feather or spider which had
always been in his barnyard but to which his attention had
never before been directed, could be expected to summon a
little righteous indignation against the fiendish Americans.
The germ warfare propaganda was always renewed on the
21st or 22d of February, not to enlist George Washington in
attesting to its truth, but to get the spring clean-up campaign
started along with the spring thaw, and cut down on the incidence of spring-time epidemics.

Communist propaganda also made much, after the return of
repatriates in both "Little Switch" and "Big Switch," of the
horrible mutilation by the vile Americans of good communist
prisoners of war, in cold-blooded "experiments" and, again, as
a means of terrorizing them into choosing non-repatriation.
Again, too, they did not bother to explain how cutting off a
man's arm or leg would induce him to remain with the perpe-
trators in deathless friendship. After "Little Switch," while the
fighting continued, it undoubtedly constituted a deterrent to
surrender, and after "Big Switch" it was a counter to the ex-

posure of communist atrocities by Ambassador Lodge in the United Nations.

Many prisoners of war, however, had been wounded and needed surgical treatment, and others who became ill in the camps had to have operations. In the communist and anti-communist camp hospitals alike it was standard operating procedure to have an interpreter carefully explain to the patient why he had to have an amputation or an appendectomy.

The hale and hearty anti-communist prisoners of war—anti-communist despite the fact that the persuasive Americans had not employed amputation or mutilation to influence them against repatriation—startled the Indian officers to whom they were turned over in the demilitarized zone by their high standards of sanitation. Commanding crack Indian troops, the Indian officers found the un-officered prisoners of war as scrupulous in their cleanliness and attention to sanitation as were their own strictly supervised troops.

The recreational program in the camps varied from camp to camp and compound to compound, depending upon the talents and proclivities of the prisoners themselves. A complete list of activities would include arts and crafts classes, drawing, painting, sculpture, wood-carving, poster work and arts and crafts exhibits. In addition to bands and orchestras, and the theatrical productions already mentioned, there was choral singing, and folk dances and music classes. Koreans as a race not only seem to have exceptionally fine voices, but also love to sing, and some of their choruses were quite professional.

The favorite Chinese diversion, which needed little organization on the part of the camp command, was gambling, at cards, chess, checkers or anything else on which a bet could be placed.

Koreans and Chinese alike delighted in movies, and this program, starting with newsreels and documentaries in Japanese, progressed through a long list of better American films, some sound-tracked in Korean and Chinese and others with sub-titles. A list of the documentary and entertainment films employed in the program will be found in Appendix B.

Six American film companies, Columbia, MGM, RKO, 20th Century-Fox, United Artists and Warners, deserve commendation for making nineteen outstanding feature films and twenty cartoons available for the continuation of the film program in the demilitarized zone, for nominal fees which barely paid the cost of insuring the prints against loss or damage. The Indian troops enjoyed them quite as much as did the anti-communist POWs.

The reading groups were nearly as popular as the motion pictures, for the educated prisoners loved to read to the illiterates, and the illiterates loved to listen. They were quick to question the instructors on points they did not fully understand, and it was sometimes difficult to tell the difference between a reading group and a discussion group.

Every feature of the rehabilitation project, however, helped to pass the time, and had it been even less complete and even less well worked out, it would still have been a boon to the POWs. From the first surrenders in July, 1950, until the last anti-communist prisoners were released in January, 1954, three and one-half years elapsed, longer than the period between Pearl Harbor and V-E Day.

A scientifically constructed and administered attitude test was taken by 1296 Chinese and Korean anti-communist prisoners of war early in September, 1953, just before they moved to the demilitarized zone. With the objective of determining their attitudes toward democracy, the United Nations, the rehabilitation project, and communism, it was also designed to measure the influence of their civilian educational background upon these attitudes, the cumulative effect, if any, of the rehabilitation project, the residual effects of communist indoctrination, and any significant differences in attitude between the Chinese and the Koreans.

It was found that positive attitudes toward democracy, the U. N. and the rehabilitation project, and correspondingly negative attitudes toward communism, increased progressively from lower to higher civilian educational levels. These attitudes were similarly influenced favorably by the amount of time the individual prisoners of war had devoted to the educational aspects of the rehabilitation program.

The Koreans as a group were apt to be more articulate, and more detailed in their opinions than the Chinese, but slogans and clichés were singularly lacking in the expressions of all respondents.

Residual effects of communist indoctrination were noted in responses to some of the items dealing with purges of landlords, but these expressions were few in number and did not represent the general attitude of the group surveyed. Contrary to communist dogma, the great majority of the prisoners of war defended landlords and rich men on the principle of protection of private property. Such people were considered as having attained their high economic position by dint of hard work; they were regarded as not only benevolent but necessary to a nation.

There were no suggestions that wealth, aside from tillable land, should be divided. No item was specifically intended to measure their attitude toward land reform, but there were many who, although not believing that landlords should be "struggled" or purged, declared that land should be distributed to the peasantry on a "peaceful" basis.

In this connection, the sham of land reform as practiced by the communists—purging of landlords, distribution of acreage, and reconfiscation by taxes in excess of previous rental shares —was well understood and bitterly resented by the Chinese and North Koreans alike.

The Korean prisoners of war generally blamed only the North Korean red regime for aggression against the Republic of Korea, whereas the Chinese prisoners of war were more apt to blame Soviet Russia and Red China for the start of the Korean conflict.

Both the Chinese and the Korean prisoners of war regarded life in a democracy as infinitely superior to that in a communist state, because of the freedom and equal treatment accorded citizens in a democracy. They considered respect for individual rights, freedom of speech and press, and electoral methods as the most ideal conditions in a democracy. Very few of the men tended to over-idealize life in a democracy.

The greatest difference in attitude was revealed on the question of whether the rehabilitation project had or had not influenced the prisoners of war to reject repatriation. The

Korean prisoners were non-committal; the Chinese prisoners strongly resented any suggestion that the rehabilitation project had had anything whatever to do with their choice of non-repatriation. Their anti-communist attitude was not created in the prisoner of war camps, they insisted, and any suggestion that the rehabilitation project or anything else influenced their decision was an insult to their strong stand against communism.

Many of the respondents noted that the rehabilitation project had been a wholly voluntary, strictly educational program, and in no way resembled "indoctrination."

The honesty of the answers of the prisoners of war in this instance is all the more believable because the Chinese and Koreans, no less than any other Asians, are victims of the Oriental positive, the tendency to ingratiate. In fact, an ingratiation test also administered to the prisoners of war showed that the Chinese tended to ingratiate even more than the Koreans. What this means, simply, is that a Chinese or Korean in replying to a question does his best to give you the answer he thinks you want, out of politeness; and a positive answer is the best of all answers. If one asks, "Is this the road to Seoul?" the answer will be "Yes!", whether it is or is not the right road to Seoul. Honesty or dishonesty does not enter into it; after all, all roads lead to Seoul, if one wanders about a bit. Besides, how distressed the big-nose would be if he found out that he was hopelessly lost!

In framing achievement or attitude tests such as the foregoing, therefore, the purpose of the test had to be concealed if at all possible, and all questions had to be open-ended or multiple choice, to force a decision. Whenever feasible, a standard and scientifically constructed ingratiation test would be administered in advance of evaluation tests in the rehabilitation project, to eliminate high ingratiators from the test group.

The finding that the higher the educational level of the prisoners of war, the greater the tendency to be pro-democratic and anti-communist in attitude, is confirmed by the census of North Korean and Chinese prisoners discussed in Appendix D, which shows that the percentage of repatriates was much greater among those with the least civilian education. These were the prisoners of war who were politically naïve and more interested in the immediate idea of going back, not to communism but "to till their land."

15

The Prisoners Balk

The armistice was signed on the 27th of July, 1953, with one important change in the terms of reference on the prisoners of war which had been agreed to and initialled early in June, before the 27,000 anti-communist North Koreans were released by President Rhee.

The original version of the terms of reference had specified that the Indian custodial forces would take charge of the anti-communist prisoners *in situ* in South Korea, and that the Czech, Polish, Swedish and Swiss members of the Neutral Nations Repatriation Commission, and the communist "explainers," would proceed to the South Korean camps.

Against the entry of communist Czechs, Poles and Chinese and North Korean explainers into the Republic of Korea, President Rhee was adamant, and he was equally opposed to the introduction of Indian troops. In reiterating ROK opposition to any armistice at all short of the Yalu, the foreign minister of the Republic of Korea even threatened that the ROK Army would fire on Indian troops.

India had had in Korea, almost since the start of the U. N.

resistance to the communist aggression, an Army field hospital and the equivalent of a battalion of troops. They were non-combatants, it is true, but they were not only skilled medics but paratroop medics, and they distinguished themselves repeatedly in the Korean conflict. But President Rhee had been disturbed—and in this he was not alone, in or out of Korea—by Mr. Nehru's soft words to communism outside India, in contrast to his harsh words for communism within India.

If in communist North Korea black is white and white is black, in President Rhee's Korea black is black and pink is scarlet. To Mr. Rhee, Japan will always be an imperialist, aggressor nation. With India volunteering really magnificently for an undertaking in which she would inevitably be in the middle, pleasing neither side and often offending both, gaining little and possibly losing a great deal—Mr. Rhee grouped the Indians with the communist camp.

He had not objected strenuously to the Indian armistice formula in the United Nations the preceding November-December because it was Indian, but because it was an armistice formula that did not provide for the unification of Korea and release of the anti-communist prisoners. But now that the communists had reversed themselves and appeared ready to sign an armistice substantially based on the Indian formula, he put his foot down flatly on permitting Indian troops and communist observers and explainers to enter the Republic of Korea.

A trip to Seoul by Assistant Secretary of State Walter S. Robertson to plead with him personally was to no avail, producing only a rather equivocal joint statement of broad agreement on an armistice and mentioning this final objection by President

Rhee not at all. It took another trip to Seoul by General Clark, and a flash of face-saving inspiration on the General's part, to overcome this last objection.

The armistice agreement provided for a demilitarized zone along the final battle line in Korea, five kilometers wide, with each side withdrawing two and one-half kilometers—a distance between one and one-quarter and one and one-half miles. The western end of this zone was wider than this minimum distance by virtue of the fact that it terminated at the Imjin River, which flowed in a few miles into the estuary of the Han River. The widening estuary became the demilitarized zone for the remainder of the distance to the west coast of Korea.

General Clark suggested moving the anti-communist prisoners of war to the demilitarized zone, permitting the communist observers and explainers to enter only the DZ from the north and the Republic of Korea not at all, and bringing the Indian troops up the Han River, technically demilitarized as well. Thus they would never set foot in the Republic of Korea, and Foreign Minister Pyun would not feel called upon to carry out his threat to fire upon them.

This face-saving solution was acceptable to everyone concerned except the U. S. Navy, the Army Engineers and the anti-communist prisoners of war. All flatly refused to go along with it.

The Navy's reasons were cogent. It had been assumed, without study of the problem, that the Indian troops would be trans-shipped to landing craft off the mouth of the Han Estuary, and ferried up to the end of the DZ. It was only forty-odd miles down the winding estuary from the end of the DZ to the Yellow Sea. But the thirty-foot tides in the Yellow Sea, which had so complicated the amphibious envelopment of the North Korean Army at Inchon, complicated this operation to the point of impossibility. There were mud flats and sand bars extending many more miles out to sea from the mouth of the estuary. There were flats and bars all the way up the estuary and the Imjin to the DZ, and still a tide of several feet at that point.

The British transports which were to bring the Indian troops would be forced to anchor many miles from land. Big, blunt-nosed landing craft would be able to make fairly good time up the estuary while the tide was flowing. But while it was ebbing the speed of the tide plus the speed of the combined Han and Imjin Rivers would have brought them to a virtual halt, until they inevitably grounded on a flat or a bar. Even a speedboat would be pressed to make the round-trip between tides.

The mud flats and sand bars of the estuary had been a no man's land for two years. They had been mined and re-mined, by both sides, until they bristled with TNT. Any landing craft which grounded in the estuary might not be blown sky high, but it would certainly be marooned for good, and evacuation of the men in it would still be a problem.

The estuary, in short, was not navigable. Even without the non-concurrence of the Engineers, the Navy's objections would have been valid. The Engineers, for their part, had to find a site in the DZ which would house 22,000 prisoners of war and 5,000 Indian troops, in an area as close as possible to an operable rail line—to get the POWs in—but no more than a mile and a quarter wide.

The only practical site proved to be astride the Seoul-Pyong-yang rail line a few miles south of Panmunjom, where it ran west and a little north from Munsan-ni to Kaesong. Here the DZ, turning below the 38th Parallel briefly, ran almost straight south to the Imjin, falling away through swamps to the river.

This area had to be cleared of mines and a camp constructed within 60 days. To have given the engineers the added responsibility of driving a road south to the river through the marshy, mine-infested demilitarized zone would have been both a physical and financial impossibility.

The U. S. Army Transportation Corps came to the rescue, with a proposal to fly the Indian troops in via helicopter.

The objection on the part of the anti-communist prisoners of war was not to be solved so easily.

Up to the signing of the armistice, the anti-communist POWs had been kept filled-in on the progress of the negotiations as a part of the rehabilitation project. They were already troubled, Chinese and Koreans alike, because they had not been released the month before along with the 27,000 North Koreans. They were not pleased with the prospect of facing the communist "explainers"; call the explanations what you would, they called them "hsi nao"—brainwashing. They were perturbed because, although the prisoners of war who had chosen repatriation would be released at once, they still faced six months behind barbed wire.

The Korean anti-communists did not emphatically share President Rhee's antipathy to the Indians, but the Chinese, sur-

116

prisingly, were enormously disturbed at the prospect of being placed in Indian custody. Those who had been Chinese Nationalist soldiers were anti-Indian to a man because India, formerly friendly to Nationalist China, had recognized the usurper Mao at the first opportunity. Some remembered Sikh police in Shanghai with disfavor. None welcomed the idea of being turned over to the Indians.

With the actual signature of the armistice, anti-communists and communists alike were fully informed of its terms with respect to the prisoners of war, in accordance with the armistice agreement. They were given, one to each man, a reprint of the official Chinese or Korean text, and since this was couched in language generally incomprehensible to them, it was explained endlessly in leaflets, their camp newssheets, by means of posters, and over the camp broadcasting systems.

That it was often incomprehensible was no insult to their intelligence. It was later to prove capable of varying interpretation, depending upon whether one was American, British, Colombian—any of the nationalities on the United Nations side—or neutral Indian, Swedish, or Swiss. Interpretation by the supposedly neutral Czechs and Poles did not vary; it was uniformly communist.

16

"Guardhouse Lawyers"

Stringent measures were definitely necessary, and General Clark took them. He dispatched the two senior officers of the rehabilitation project from his Tokyo headquarters to Korea, to talk to the anti-communist enclosure and compound leaders and as many of the prisoners of war themselves as possible. Simultaneously, the rehabilitation project was converted for the first time into a propaganda project.

Much of the agitation among the anti-communist prisoners of war was undoubtedly spark-plugged by the communist agents who had steadily infiltrated their ranks and had remained undiscovered. With a word here and a worry there, they could keep the men in a ferment which, at this stage, was definitely dangerous to the United Nations Command. The armistice had been delayed for more than a year on this single issue of the anti-communist prisoners of war; thousands of casualties had been incurred by men of seventeen nations to establish the principle of asylum and sanctuary in the free world for anti-communists.

Radios Peiping and Pyongyang were already trumpeting that

27,000 North Koreans released by President Rhee had been "kidnapped" and "press-ganged"—into the "puppet army"—to prevent a test of their anti-communism in the explanation arena. Had the remaining North Korean anti-communist prisoners been tempted to essay a mass breakout—or the Chinese on their single island, where a breakout would have been futile, still tried it and come into conflict with their U. S. guards—the communists would have gained a propaganda weapon with which they would have beaten the UNC about the head and ears until kingdom come.

The first step, therefore, was to remove as many of the communist agents as possible. "Big Switch," the mass exchange of repatriate prisoners, just beginning, provided the opportunity, and once more the anti-communist prisoners were polled to be certain that they were united in their determination to resist repatriation to the death.

The temperature in the camps was exactly right for such a move. It was a time for final decision if one did wish repatriation, for a compound full of rabid anti-communists was not exactly a safe place for a proven or even a suspected communist agent.

The Chinese anti-communists violently objected to this final screening. There were communist agents among them, they admitted, but they had been identified, and they had a plan for disposing of them. At dawn the day after the Indian troops assumed their custody they intended to display the heads of these communists on the posts flanking each compound gate.

It was with difficulty that they were dissuaded from this project. The rehabilitation program chiefs were not entirely out of sympathy with such an idea, but they explained to the more moderate leaders that it would shock the Indians probably beyond repair, and that inasmuch as the world press would be there and would write about it widely, no doubt sensationalizing and exaggerating it, it might cost them the free world sympathy they needed to see them through their ordeal. Despite the possibility that they might not have been talked out of this plan, or perhaps because they had not been entirely dissuaded, you could count the Chinese who decided to be repatriated at the last moment on the fingers of one hand. However, the leaders then identified 85 of their fellows as positively being communist agents. All 85 stoutly denied it, but they were segregated in a separate compound, just in case. They were to be heard from later.

In the Korean camps, on the other hand, some 200 purported anti-communists elected repatriation at the last moment. It would not be fair to say that they were all communist agents, for the choice which faced them was difficult: six months of continued imprisonment in the demilitarized zone, or immediate release to go—they hoped—to their homes and families. Fairly good intelligence says they went straight to Siberia.

Their loss was more than balanced by 500 supposed communists on Koje, who decided at the last moment for non-repatriation. They were to be heard from later, too.

With as many of the communist agents as possible eliminated from the compounds, the rehabilitation project entered its brief propaganda phase.

First of all, of course, the armistice agreement annex containing the terms of reference with respect to the prisoners of war was distributed to each man. The armistice agreement existed in three official versions, English, Korean and Chinese, and the official versions were reproduced in their entirety. It was so important a document to the prisoners that those who could read it memorized it. Those who could not read it participated in so many discussion groups that they thoroughly knew the sense of it, and could point to the numbered paragraph under discussion at any time.

The prisoners, in the end, were more familiar with the agreement as to their fate than many of the Indian officers who had the final say as to its administration. The Swedish and Swiss officers of the Neutral Nations Repatriation Commission studied its positive aspects conscientiously, and the Czechs and Poles scanned it as closely for loopholes and means by which it could be circumvented. In the final application of any paragraph, the Swedes and Swiss voted one way, the Czechs and Poles another, and it was up to the Indian chairman of a subgroup or of the NNRC as a whole to cast the deciding vote.

If ever a group deserved the U. S. Army slang designation of "guardhouse lawyers," it was the prisoners of war. But close on their heels were the United Nations Command representatives and observers in the final explanations, most of them veterans of the rehabilitation project. By the time they had answered the questions of the prisoners, before the move to the demilitarized zone, they were also experts—and a good thing.

The special newspaper published for the anti-communist prisoners of war, "Flash," was stepped up from a weekly to a thrice-weekly schedule, to explain the provisions of the armistice agreement, bring them developments in the situation as quickly as possible, and lay the rumors which swept the camps daily. Some of these rumors were inventions of the remaining communist agitators still masquerading in the compounds. Some were passed in from outside, even on remote Cheju. But nothing knocks a rumor in the head so quickly as the truth, particularly the truth in print. As quickly as rumors were encountered, they were exposed on the loudspeaker systems, then countered in the next issue of the newssheet, a 17 by 22 inch affair printed on both sides, of which one copy was printed for each man and other copies posted front and back on compound bulletin boards where they were the focus of excited discussions.

"Flash" brought the POWs straight news, and aside from its increasing circulation and stepped-up schedule was no different from the newspaper furnished in conjunction with the rehabilitation project.

The first task of the propagandists who were called in was to allay the distrust of the Indians on the part of the prisoners. Their fear of the Indian troops—fear is not the right word, for their fears were of no man or men—was essentially based, as is so often the case, on ignorance. It developed that they knew little more about India than they did about the four other neutral nations.

Accordingly, three small leaflets were prepared, with the Indian, Swedish and Swiss national flags in color on one side and brief descriptions of the three countries and their established reputation as neutrals on the other. In no time at all the POWs were fashioning large Swedish and Swiss flags with which to welcome these members of the NNRC. Acceptance of the Indians did not come so easily.

Three documentary films, "Sweden Looks Ahead," "Switzerland" and "Switzerland Today" simply fascinated the POWs, but none were immediately available on India, so newssheets had to do the job. Five in all were printed, utilizing all the materials available at the Indian Embassy in Tokyo, and a sixth was in preparation when the rehabilitation project heads were advised that the POWs were sold, and any further effort might result in over-selling and a revival of suspicion. As it was, the men were working on Indian flags and planning to surprise the Indians with a mammoth observance of Gandhi's birthday on October 2 in the demilitarized zone.

A final leaflet brought them a photograph of and a reassuring statement from Maj. Gen. S. P. P. Thorat, the commander of the Custodian Forces, India. On the reverse of this leaflet was a reproduction of the insignia of commissioned and other ranks in the Indian Army, and these the POWs learned by heart.

The task was not all that simple, however, and there were still misgivings on the part of the POWs. There was redoubled activity on the part of the remaining communist agitators, too, and other measures of reassurance were still necessary. The POWs were deeply distrustful of the Czechs and Poles, but so was the UNC, and no comfort could be given them on that score. Another film, "Fight For Freedom," was helpful in this instance. It compared Czechoslovakia with the Republic of Korea, showing how one was swallowed up by Soviet Russia and how the other fought with the aid of the free world to avoid a similar fate.

Happily for the propagandists, the terms of reference on the POWs had been agreed upon while explanations in South Korea had been envisioned. Moving the site of the explanations to the demilitarized zone had been incorporated at the last minute in a temporary supplementary agreement. Thus the terms of reference themselves, with which the POWs were by this time fully familiar, furnished material for their reassurance.

One of the principal fears on their part which militated against their willing movement to the demilitarized zone was that they would be kidnapped by the communists. The mutterings in the Republic of Korea against permitting communist Czech and Polish NNRC members and Red Chinese and Korean explainers to enter South Korea had given the communists some pause, themselves, about this feature of the armistice agreement. They had inserted in the terms of reference, therefore, the following stipulation:

"Notwithstanding the provisions of Paragraph 5 above (which provided that the UNC forces would be withdrawn from POW installations and the locations taken over completely by Indian forces), the detaining side (the UNC) shall have the responsibility for maintaining and ensuring security and order in the areas around the locations where the prisoners of war are in custody and for preventing and restraining any armed forces, including irregular armed forces, in the area under its control from any acts of disturbance and intrusion against the locations where the prisoners of war are in custody."

124

This paragraph, making the UNC responsible for preventing any attack upon communist personnel within the Republic of Korea by ROK regular or irregular forces, was not affected by the supplementary agreement. The latter bounded the areas of the demilitarized zone to which non-repatriate POWs would be taken, provided that unarmed troops might build camps for them and then withdraw from the DZ, and that armed troops might deliver them to the DZ and promptly withdraw.

And the armistice agreement itself restricted the communists and the UNC alike to a maximum of one thousand civil police in the DZ.

One thousand civil police armed only with their individual weapons and scattered from one end of the DZ to the other would not have been able to fully protect the POWs from a kidnapping attempt, not even with the assistance of an Indian brigade. Unthinkable as such an attempt was to the UNC, involving as it would a clash between communist and Indian troops, it was a real possibility to the POWs. And, as will be seen later, it was a real possibility to the communists, right up to the final liberation of the men whose fates were at stake.

But such a gross violation of the armistice would inevitably have renewed the conflict in Korea, with UNC troops coming to the rescue of the prisoners, the civil police (who were also UNC troops), and the Indian brigade. The paragraph of the armistice agreement quoted above actually made it the duty of the UNC to take such action. So it was possible to reassure the POWs by means of a widely distributed leaflet which showed the location of the camp in the DZ, snuggled against the boundary on the United Nations side and ringed in by civil police with fixed bayonets pointed toward the enemy. The enlarged map, which had no kilometer scale but was drawn truthfully, showed the camp well below the 38th Parallel, backed up by UNC troops, tanks and artillery.

The map was truthfully drawn as far as the scale was concerned, but it differed from reality in one respect, and the artist who drew it had pangs of conscience as a result. His sketch showed the camp hugging the UN side of the DZ line. Actually, when the engineers went to work at the campsite they found a well-mined marsh along the UNC side of the DZ, and it was necessary to build the camp on the higher ground to the west, right next to the middle demarcation line.

The reverse of the leaflet was also effective with the POWs. For the Koreans, it showed happy POWs proceeding to the DZ on trains from their respective camps in South Korea, then happier civilians returning to Seoul and other Korean cities four months later. The camp was labelled with a Korean pun which could mean either "Camp Freedom" or "Camp Rhee."

For the Chinese, it was simply Camp Freedom, and their route was shown by water to Inchon, rail to the DZ and back to Inchon. Their route as free civilians from Inchon was the clincher, for at the end of it was TAIWAN!

At this point, after the armistice had been signed, it was possible to promise the Chinese that if they survived the explanations, they could go to Taiwan. President Chiang Kai-shek and President Rhee issued statements in which they promised to receive the anti-communist heroes with honor in Formosa and the Republic of Korea respectively, and these messages were circulated and broadcast to the POWs. To top it off, the Nationalist Chinese and the Republic of Korea sent missions to visit the camps, each headed by a high-ranking officer, personally to bring the POWs the assurance of their two leaders, and to encourage them to move to the DZ without protest.

President Eisenhower made a statement which was quickly relayed to the prisoners of war, declaring that no force or coercion to get them to return to communism would be tolerated. The Indian Ambassador to the United States, C. L. Mehta, also made a reassuring statement which was broadcast to them.

Finally, it was possible to point out that by the terms of the armistice agreement the United Nations Command was responsible for the logistic support of the POWs, that it would continue to feed and clothe and house them and provide their medical care. U. S. quartermasters and medics would be either with them or near them throughout the ordeal in the DZ, and they derived great comfort from this.

One additional leaflet made a big hit with the POWs, and to a man each kept it in his possession to the end. The leaflet was a 180-day calendar, beginning the day after the armistice was signed and numbered in reverse so that by crossing off each day the men could tell at a glance how many days remained until "Freedom Day."

The armistice agreement was meticulous, as a result of long insistence by General Harrison at Panmunjom, on what was to happen after the agreement was signed, in point of time. Sixty days were allotted for the exchange of POWs who wished to be repatriated, and for placing non-repatriates in the custody of the Indian forces.

The next 90 days were allotted for "explanations." Then:

127

"At the expiration of ninety (90) days after the transfer of custody of the prisoners of war to the Neutral Nations Repatriation Commission, access of representatives to captured personnel as provided for in Paragraph 8 above shall terminate, and the question of disposition of prisoners of war who have not exercised their right to be repatriated shall be submitted to the Political Conference recommended to be convened in Paragraph 60, Draft Armistice Agreement, which shall endeavor to settle this question within thirty (30) days, during which period the Neutral Nations Repatriation Commission shall continue to retain custody of those prisoners of war. The Neutral Nations Repatriation Commission shall declare the relief from the prisoner of war status to civilian status of any prisoners of war who have not exercised their right to be repatriated and for whom no other disposition has been agreed to by the Political Conference within one hundred and twenty (120) days after the Neutral Nations Repatriation Commission has assumed their custody. Thereafter, according to the application of each individual, those who choose to go to neutral nations shall be assisted by the Neutral Nations Repatriation Commission and the Red Cross Society of India. This operation shall be completed within thirty (30) days, and upon its completion, the Neutral Nations Repatriation Commission shall immediately cease its functions and declare its dissolution. After the dissolution of the Neutral Nations Repatriation Commission, whenever and wherever any of those above-mentioned civilians who have been relieved from the prisoner of war status desire to return to their fatherlands, the authorities of the localities where they are shall be responsible for assisting them in returning to their fatherlands."

Sixty plus ninety plus thirty days added up to one hundred and eighty—January 23d, 1954, "Freedom Day."

A few months after Freedom Day the author visited a crack Chinese Nationalist Army unit, a super Officer Candidate School composed entirely of former Chinese Communist Forces prisoners of war. The men in it, former officers and non-commissioned officers and enclosure and compound leaders, were undergoing intensive training while awaiting commands in the CNA. Many had already graduated and assumed commands as vacancies had opened up.

In the cantonment of this group the first place to which visitors were conducted, after a ceremonial cup of tea in their airy and attractive officers' club, was their Korean museum. In this museum, together with thousands of photographs and hundreds of banners and flags and other souvenirs of their Korean experience, was one display which included several copies of "Flash" and every leaflet distributed to them during this period. In the place of honor in the center was one of the 180-day calendars, with every day checked off. The man who had checked it off had had neither a Parker 51 nor a pencil—he just used one drop of blood for every day.

17

Barbed Wire Fever

The prisoners of war now agreed to move to the demilitarized zone, and the propagandists turned them back to the rehabilitation heads. They had accomplished a formidable mission, and they deserve credit for it. Among the U. S. Army personnel involved were Col. James E. Goodwin, Lt. Col. Elwood F. Saxer, Lt. Col. Robert Lavell, Lt. Col. George Lynch, Maj. Robert B. Bleecker, Maj. Ernest Stewart and Lt. John B. Holway. Civilian employees of the Far East and United Nations Command who also distinguished themselves were Bernarr Cooper, James Gibson, Lloyd Evans, Oliver D. Vogt, Charles Dunn, Donald Newman, K. K. Tsai and John Kim.

There were still, of course, loose ends for the rehabilitation heads to knot up and tie off. One meeting of Chinese enclosure and compound leaders on Cheju typified the sort of questions which plagued the prisoners of war, and with which they in turn plagued the POW Command and rehabilitation authorities.

The anti-communist prisoner of war camp at Mosulp'o on Cheju was made up of three numbered enclosures, each with ten lettered compounds. With approximately 500 men to a compound, that made 15,000 POWs. Present at the meeting were thirty-three leaders, the "dai biaos" of each enclosure and each compound.

Their very presence at the meeting was a testament to the faith they reposed in the United Nations Command. In the early days on Koje, it was virtually impossible to negotiate with a leader, anti-communist or communist. One of the most obvious means of breaking up communist terrorism of a compound would have been, of course, removal and segregation of the leader or leaders of the compound. But the leaders were never identified. There were echelons of spokesmen in each compound, and the real leader might be the inoffensive, inconspicuous prisoner engaged in scrubbing clean the sawed-in-half oil barrels which served as latrine containers—the lowliest job in the compound.

The problem would have been more simple had there been fewer than thirty-three. The questions they had were common to all compounds, but every leader had to bring back a specific answer to his specific question, so that he could personally assure his men that he had what used to be referred to in the U. S. Army as the "poop from group," i.e., the "word" from headquarters.

The first question had to do with a matter of face. In "Flash" and in other publications distributed to them they were invariably referred to as "anti-communist prisoners of war." (They were never called just "prisoners," since that implies criminality, while a prisoner of war has honorable status.) The war was over with the signing of the armistice, and the ordinary prisoners of war were being exchanged. These men felt themselves to be political refugees, volunteers for the army of President Chiang; many of them were in fact ex-members of the Chinese Nationalist Army who felt that they were simply at one stage of their liberation from communist duress and return to the CNA.

Why could they not be referred to as anti-communist heroes, the term they themselves used? There was only one possible answer, and anti-communist heroes they were from then on—really! There was, of course, some discussion as to whether or not "anti-communist patriots" might be preferable, but in the end "heroes" was democratically chosen, by vote.

The anti-communists were quite conscious of their role in history, and had developed quite a hero-martyr complex, not at all unjustified in their case.

"Because of our refusal to return to communism," one of the leaders declaimed, "the communists have suffered a serious setback on the world diplomatic front. Hence they regard us as their most bitter enemies."

The next question wasn't as easy to answer. Since the liberation of the 27,000 Koreans by Mr. Rhee and their ROKA guards in June, the Mosulp'o camp had been guarded by a regiment of U. S. Infantry. Why, since the heroes were our good and great friends, were they so heavily guarded?

That regiment was in garrison around them not to guard them, but to protect them, they were told. They would be protected as assiduously on their trip north by U. S. and U. N. naval units, and when they went into the DZ they would see on either side of the railroad an entire division of U. N. troops, there to protect them.

Mention of the trip north disturbed a number of the leaders. Could they not go by rail rather than LST (landing ship, tank)? On the trip from Koje to Cheju they had been horribly seasick and they had had no hot food. Furthermore, they had been overcrowded, with each LST packed to its capacity of 600, and when they were loaded and unloaded their compounds, companies and platoons had been all mixed up.

How the latter could happen was easy to see. No compound numbered more than 500 men. If a compound of 400 and 200 men of another were loaded on one LST, and the first 500 men off directed to a new compound, it could be made up of 200 men from one compound and 300 from another, with friends separated from friends and even brothers from brothers.

It was pointed out to them that a sea trip would be necessary anyway, to get to the mainland of Korea, and that the mainland rail lines would be crowded to capacity by the Korean anti-communist heroes. How much simpler it would be to sail all the way to Inchon, one compound to an LST and with room and facilities for heating their food! Furthermore, each man would be issued even before he boarded the LST, one pill for each day of the trip of a medicine invented by the Americans and called dramamine, a pill positively guaranteed to prevent seasickness.

Besides, if a man couldn't face a trip from Cheju to Inchon in an LST, how could he contemplate a trip from Inchon to Taiwan?

That did it. The Navy gave in on not over-crowding the

133

LSTs, and the hot food, but the Army medics balked on a pre-issue of dramamine. With the confidence of the Chinese in pills, they maintained, no one would be awake to cook the hot food. The aid men on each LST, however, would be provided with a plentiful supply of the pills.

The next series of questions was cheering. What would happen when they moved, they wanted to know, to the rehabilitation project. Could their American and Chinese instructors go to the demilitarized zone with them? What would happen to their study classes? The vocational shops? Their fields and gardens?

The answers were as varied as the questions. Their American and Chinese instructors could and would accompany them on the trip, right up to the edge of the demilitarized zone. Farther than that they could not go because of the armistice agreement. But they would remain nearby, at Munsan-ni—Munsan-ni was pointed out to them on the map—and they would see them every day of the explanations, for they would serve during that period as United Nations Command representatives, observers or interpreters. They would be on hand to greet them, too, on Freedom Day, and many of their Chinese instructors, whose jobs would be at an end on that day, would accompany them to Taiwan.

Many of them did, too, for no matter where they had been recruited, the example of the anti-communist heroes had so inspired them that they too decided to cast their lot with that of the Nationalist Chinese on Formosa. Too much cannot be said for the heroism of the fifty Chinese who served as UNC observers and interpreters during the explanations in the demilitarized zone. Almost to a man they had families, relatives or friends within Red China, vulnerable to pressure and reprisals.

They could not escape identification. Many of them encountered schoolmates among the communist officers, explainers and interpreters, with whom they had attended mainland universities. Although the Indians barred cameras within the explanation area, they were constantly being surreptitiously photographed. During the explanations they were subjected to a constant stream of abuse and threats from the communist explainers, as "Chiang agents," and on one occasion one of them was physically attacked.

They discharged their difficult and dangerous assignment with honor and distinction, and the free world owes them a debt of gratitude for their magnificent performance.

As to the study classes, the POWs were told that it would be up to them to continue them themselves. They could take their current books and materials with them to the DZ on their persons, and the assistant instructors from among their own ranks would have to take over the teaching role in its entirety. The rehabilitation project instructors would give them lesson plans before they left, with daily assignments right up to Freedom Day, and the Indian Red Cross would be furnished the textbooks and other materials they would need to carry out the lesson plans.

If they thought the study classes were worthwhile, and wished to continue them until Freedom Day, it was up to them. The vocational shops were something else. The shop equipment, tools, raw material and so on were bulky and inconvenient to pack and ship. They would be in tents in the DZ, which as a purely temporary camp would have no buildings suitable for shops. Since they were to be there for only four months, it hardly seemed worthwhile to take anything beyond elementary barbering, tailoring and cobbling tools along, and those not for purposes of vocational education but to keep themselves military and presentable during the explanations. The rule on vocational tools would have to be that they would be limited to personal tools which a craftsman could carry on his person.

Every question and every answer set off a chain reaction. Permission to carry textbooks and light tools on their persons suggested, immediately, another line of questioning. Would they be permitted, it was asked from all sides, to carry their personal possessions with them to the DZ?

That was a stickler, and one on which the rehabilitation heads knew that they would collide head-on with the Prisoner of War Command. It's SOP—standard operating procedure— in any prisoner of war operation, no matter what the nation, to "shake down" POWs on the occasion of any move, to be sure that they move to their new location with only the possessions they are authorized by the Geneva Convention—personal toilet articles, a uniform change of clothing, etc.

In fact, in almost any prisoner of war operation it's a good idea to move the men occasionally, and on very short notice, so that they won't have an opportunity to dig up any escape equipment which they may have hidden. The capacity of any prisoners of war, not just Chinese and Koreans, for accumulating handy little items of that nature is simply amazing. A POW

136

society is one of the greatest proofs in the world that the communist dogma . . . "from each according to his ability and to each according to his need" . . . just won't work. Instead, it becomes "to each according to his ingenuity."

A compound of prisoners of war will start out on an absolutely equal footing, with toilet supplies and a change of clothing. (This, of course, applies only in the free world. A prisoner of war in the hands of the communists is lucky to keep a part of the clothing in which he was captured.) Cigarettes are issued, but some entrepreneurs who don't smoke or can control their smoking begin to save them. Those cigarettes are traded to a Korean guard for a pullet. The pullet, well-fed on scrapings of the rice pot and some choice greens pulled from the other side of the barbed wire, begins to lay an egg a day. With cigarettes and eggs now to trade, the possibilities are unlimited.

The Chinese anti-communist heroes had progressed to a point at which they were in possession of Korean currency, and conducted a brisk trade with the simple Cheju islanders—to whom, when they left, they sold their unharvested gardens. Had the Cheju islanders simply waited, they could have had the crops for nothing, and they advanced this idea. The Chinese pointed out that it would be catch-as-catch-can, with very little for anyone, while the purchaser, now, of one of the fine garden plots would have uncontested title. It really wasn't fair. The Cheju islanders, fisherfolk who are the product of one of the last matriarchies on earth, didn't have a chance.

The first purchase of an American POW, according to the movies, is a length of copper tubing so that he can build a still. In fairness to the Chinese and North Koreans, it must be said

137

that a 200 proof potable was not on their agenda. They were satisfied with a quickly brewed and only mildly exhilarating sort of rice beer, lightly fermented for immediate personal consumption only and not for sale. Had they contrived anything stronger on Cheju they would have definitely refused to leave for the DZ. They would have been too prosperous to leave.

There was another aspect to the matter of personal possessions. Some of these men had been behind barbed wire for nearly three years, and life behind a prisoner of war enclosure contributes to a "barbed wire fever" to which few men are immune. One of its manifestations is the loving care lavished on the few pitiful possessions which the POW may have been able to accumulate. A particularly good razor blade, for instance, becomes a sort of fetish, too precious to be used for shaving. It will be hidden from all eyes, in the safest place the POW can contrive. When he is alone, he will retrieve it, inspect it carefully for signs of rust, oil it by rubbing it gently with oil from his scalp, then re-wrap it in a bit of rag and hide it again.

He will give that razor blade the same tireless attention an American high school boy would give his "hot rod," for it, in effect, is his "hot rod," his most precious possession.

The matter of personal possessions, therefore, was postponed by the rehabilitation heads until higher authority in Tokyo could be consulted.

18

"Our Compound Has a Cow!"

In Tokyo, it developed that prisoners of war in transfer are authorized by the Geneva Convention to take up to 25 kilograms of personal effects with them. But while the judge advocates were finding the authorization, Major General Charles W. Christenberry, assistant Chief of Staff of the Far East Command for personnel and administration, within whose province the POWs came, decreed that the anti-communist heroes, both Chinese and Korean, could take all the personal possessions they could carry along with them to the DZ.

General Christenberry, now retired and the managing director in New York City of the American-Korea Foundation, at all times approached the problems of the prisoners of war with a depth of compassion and understanding which makes him an ideal choice for his new civilian assignment.

"Certainly they may take their personal possessions with them," he said. "A prisoner of war with everything he owns in the world on his back is a capitalist. He isn't going to make any trouble and risk losing all his earthly possessions."

Following Freedom Day, the Chinese anti-communist heroes sent handsomely embroidered banners to Generals Hull, Harrison and Christenberry and the head of the rehabilitation project, through the Overseas Chinese Association of Korea. General John E. Hull, succeeding General Clark as CINCUNC upon the latter's retirement, had won the undying gratitude of the anti-communist heroes by standing staunch in their defense, as General Harrison had in the truce talks. Gen. Harrison had already departed for his next command, in the Caribbean, and General Christenberry for the United States and retirement, and the rehabilitation head was arranging to send their banners to them, with translations. "Harrison" could be transliterated in Chinese by ignoring the r's, but the interpreter blushed when he attempted to render the transliteration of "Christenberry."

"What the hell," he finally admitted, "how can you transliterate Christenberry? It says 'Distinguished American General'!"

General Christenberry's decision was as important as any other one thing in persuading the anti-communist heroes to go back to the dreaded battle line, to be again a battle line for them. But it, too, led to further questions, at a subsequent meeting with the enclosure and compound leaders.

"May we take our pets?"

What sort of pets did they have?

"Well, we have chickens, and dogs and cats, and rabbits."

"Of course, you may take your pets. Anything you can carry."

Off on one flank a hand goes up, and when the anti-communist hero is recognized, he stands up, salutes smartly, states his name, his enclosure number and compound letter, and announces:

"Our compound has a cow."

If the cow had been ruled out because you can't carry a cow, they would have volunteered to carry the cow. The avenue of escape here was a discussion of the Hindu religion, the sacredness of cows in the sight of the Indians, and the difficulty of finding forage in the DZ in a newly bulldozed clay compound with winter coming on. They decided to carry her aboard the LST in quarters and eat her on the way to Inchon, and that's what they did.

Most of the pets were dogs. One compound favorite with a hint of Alsatian background produced puppies en route to Inchon. Her master passed the check point into the new compound in the DZ dutifully carrying her and followed by six of his fellows, each with a puppy.

This might have gone relatively unnoticed, with chickens in baskets and rabbits peering out of field packs on every hand. But the five hundred men of this compound, as a means of irritating the communist observers and newsmen at the take-over, wore, to a man, dark glasses. The glasses, resembling spectacles for 3-dimensional movies, were made of cardboard and ising-glass. Where they got the cardboard and ising-glass is not known, but an American corporal named Finnegan is suspect. For the glue, they probably boiled a horse!

"American agents, wearing dark glasses and leading fierce police dogs," Radio Peiping blared the next day, "led the terrorized prisoners of war between lines of sympathetic Indian soldiers, who averted their eyes from the shameful spectacle."

The idea had been to wear the dark glasses in the explanations, but they went over so big the first time they tried them on that they wore them continuously thereafter, and wore them out long before the explanations started.

With pets permitted, an element of competition entered into preparations for the trip to the DZ. Compounds and individuals without pets simply had to have them, and a brisk trade developed.

The following story is related with absolutely no intention of branding any of the Chinese anti-communist heroes as dishonest. But in justice to them it should be prefaced by a short dissertation on moral standards in a Chinese-Korean matrix.

From 1905 to 1945, Korea was occupied by the Japanese, first loosely and then tightly. During that period, if a Korean stole anything from a Japanese, it was patriotic rather than dishonest. When the Soviets replaced the Japanese in North Korea in 1945, it was similarly patriotic to steal from the Russians. When the Chinese "volunteer" forces entered North Korea in 1950, it became patriotic to steal from them.

The Chinese communist forces requisitioned supplies from the North Korean army and people, and the Koreans stole them back. But this time the Koreans were not dealing with astigmatic Japanese or mentally myopic Russians. They were dealing with clever Chinese, who realized that the simplest means to repossess the property of which they had been robbed was to steal it back. In time, in such a contest, property lines blurred and the whole thing was reduced to a sport with nationalistic overtones.

In short, the Chinese anti-communist heroes would rather

142

steal something from a vigilant Korean farmer than buy it from him, even if they had the money—and they had the money. It was more sporting, and morality simply didn't enter into it.

Colonel Robert J. Philpott, who built the two camps on Cheju-do and now builds homes on the Florida Keys, writes in "The New Age" of his experience in having Korean laborers unload the LSTs which brought in supplies for the Chinese prisoners of war. The attrition rate on supplies was extraordinary. The Cheju islanders would dig holes in the sand, and a big percentage of the supplies went into these holes on the "plant you now, dig you later" principle.

When the Cheju islanders were fired, and the Chinese prisoners of war themselves put to unloading the LSTs, not a single item was lost. The Chinese even located and dug up some of the Korean caches.

When the Chinese anti-communist heroes started acquiring more pets, one work detail of some twenty men returning from their potato field to their compound for supper stopped to negotiate the purchase of a pair of rabbits from a Korean farmer who had lots of rabbits. They bargained with him in rapidly alternating teams of six, five, four, three and two, until agreement was reached, the confusion was allowed to abate, money paid, one male rabbit placed in the arms of one of the final pair of purchasers, and a female in the arms of the other. Their fellows were well along on their way home.

Within minutes the Korean farmer was ashamedly calling on the camp adjutant. Twenty Chinese prisoners, he said, he didn't know which compound they were from, had just bought two rabbits from him at quite a good price. In the process, they had stolen eighteen more.

The questions most frequently asked by the POWs, once they could bring themselves to agree to moving to the DZ, had to do with the explanation procedure. These were difficult to answer, for the armistice agreement was most sketchy on this subject and the anti-communist heroes were as well informed on the armistice agreement as the rehabilitation heads.

Would they receive explanations individually or in groups? Seeking safety in numbers, they much preferred the idea of being interviewed in groups. That, they were told, would be up to the Neutral Nations Repatriation Commission, but they would have to be prepared for individual explanations. There would be a maximum of fifty NNRC teams, or "subordinate bodies" as the armistice agreement referred to them, to supervise the explanations, and there were 23,000 anti-communist heroes. There were 90 days for explanations, of which 14 were Sundays, the POWs' day of rest guaranteed by the Geneva Convention. If the NNRC could summon a full 50 teams a day for 76 days—and this was unlikely in view of the attrition which would be caused by illnesses that would develop in delegates unaccustomed to Korean winter weather—300 anti-communist heroes would have to be processed each day, or six per team in an eight-hour period.

So individual interviews were not only possible but probable, at the beginning, with group interviews at the end if the teams fell behind. The United Nations Command considered it important, they were told, that all of the anti-communist heroes receive explanations, to establish the fact firmly of their anti-communism before the Indians, the Swedes, the Swiss and the free world press.

The anti-communist heroes received this solemnly. The Chinese had already banded themselves in groups of five, sworn blood-brothers who were determined to resist brainwashing, no matter how intensive, in groups. Now they set about devising a means of resisting it as individuals.

What they came up with was nothing short of brilliant. It seemed an exaggerated precaution to the rehabilitation heads, who had never faced brainwashing and didn't know how diabolical it was. But these men knew what it was, and they were determined not to succumb to it, however paralyzing it could be.

Their solution was a series of plays, presented with variations in every Korean and Chinese compound. Compounds with particularly exhilarating versions—or exceptionally effective actors—toured other compounds, presenting their production to wild cheers and applause.

The setting was always the same—a table presided over by a turbanned actor who, so there could be no mistake, wore on his chest a sign proclaiming him the "Indian Chairman." At his left, always carefully at his left, also placarded and obviously in the role of minor villains, were a Czech and a Pole. At his right, upright and noble, were a Swede, a Swiss, a U. N. representative, a U. N. observer, and a U. N. interpreter. Sometimes the U. N. personnel were not seated at the curtain, but entered to resounding applause. Then the communist representative, observer and interpreter entered, to the accompaniment of stamping, hisses and whistles. Finally, the villain, the communist "explainer," entered and took his seat.

Then, to an accolade which was invariably deafening, the HERO strode on stage. Guess who!

The explanation scripts concocted by the average compound were considerably more intelligent than the text of the actual "explanation" later used by the communists in the DZ. The POWs considered every possible angle which might be employed to persuade them to return—and the hero had an answer to every avenue of approach. The answers, moreover, always confounded the "explainer" and convulsed the audience. They were so convincing and so eloquent that in some of the plays the explainer would wrench himself from the restraining hands of the communist representative and observer and exit arm in arm with the anti-communist hero, both of them shouting "Hui Taiwan"—"To Taiwan!" In others, even the representative and observer headed for Taiwan, with the Czech and Pole making abortive efforts to restrain them. And in one version, even the Czech and Pole sought asylum.

When the "explainer" remained unmoved, and resorted to threats or other violations of the armistice agreement, the United Nations representative would leap to his feet and protest to the NNRC representatives. The latter would solemnly debate the violation, and find in favor of the anti-communist hero and the U. N. representative by an invariable vote of 3 to 2. Sternly admonishing the explainer, the "Indian Chairman" would order the proceedings resumed.

It didn't always work that smoothly in the actual explanations, but it worked.

146

Some of the compounds staged other opuses, to further illuminate the problems faced by the anti-communist heroes. Two productions by the Korean POWs showed both sides of the spinning coin—"The Dawn of Freedom" and "Aftermath of Return to the Iron Curtain."

19

The Indians Take Over

With the completion of "Big Switch," the exchange of re-patriated prisoners of war during the first week in September, the anti-communist heroes began the move north. Flags waving and bands playing, both the Chinese and Koreans moved to their ships and trains in high spirits. They debarked at Camp Freedom in the same high spirits, and impressed observers with their snap, precision and military discipline as they marched to their new compounds.

Since the CFI—Custodian Forces, India—had no experience in a takeover of this sort and were not sure how quickly the rosters for a compound of 500 men could be checked and the men processed into their new compound in the DZ, it was agreed to turn over on the first day only two compounds, one in the morning and one in the afternoon. To assist in the processing, the NNRC asked the United Nations Command to supply a number of interpreters, and let it be known that they were asking the communist side for an equal number.

Major General William S. Lawton, commanding the Korean Communications Zone, which was delivering the prisoners of war, demurred at the presence of the communist interpreters and objected even more strenuously when he discovered that communist officers and newsmen would also be present. According to the armistice agreement, the turnover of non-repatriate prisoners of war to the CFI was purely a matter concerning each detaining side and the CFI, and there was no justification for the presence of communist observers, newsmen, or interpreters.

The NNRC decided otherwise, however, and his protest was to no avail. So before the transfer began the first morning he called on Major General S. P. P. Thorat, commanding the CFI, to point out the military aspects of the situation.

At this juncture it should be noted that the Indian delegation to the NNRC and the CFI were two quite separate entities. The armistice agreement provided for a senior representative of each of the five neutral nations to the NNRC, with the Indian delegate, Lieutenant General K. S. Thimayya, as chairman. Each senior delegate was to have not more than fifty assistants.

The CFI under General Thorat, on the other hand, had purely a custodial function. When NNRC staff members noted that the armistice agreement did not specifically bar personnel of the other side from witnessing the takeover by the CFI, it was to General Thorat that General Lawton addressed himself, in the hope of accomplishing the turnover without incident.

"If you have communist observers and interpreters present," he told General Thorat, "you will have a riot. These men are already nervous enough over the prospect of the explanations.

If you have communist interpreters at the processing tables, they will believe their names are being taken down in advance by the communists so that increased pressure may be brought upon them in the explanations."

"We will have no trouble," General Thorat assured him. "We are not without experience in this sort of thing, you know."

Both were right. There was a riot, but the Indians demonstrated pure genius in handling it. So did the prisoners, in dealing with the matter of communist observers.

The first compound to be turned over was Korean, from Koje. This was the compound made up of men who had represented themselves as communists for up to three years, but had decided to resist repatriation when they had their opportunity during "Big Switch." Now they were militantly anti-communist—the most determinedly anti-communist compound of the whole 47, perhaps, since they felt themselves obliged to prove their anti-communism to the United Nations Command as well as the NNRC, CFI and the communists.

The enclosures and compounds in the DZ had been built according to what is probably a universal plan. First a single fence of barbed wire, enclosing ten compounds. Then the compounds themselves, with a triple fence enclosing two alleys or runways, each some thirty feet wide, and then the inner compound.

In processing the prisoners of war, the CFI had them march to the compound in platoons of 25, matching the registers of 25 names each which the U. N. personnel turned over. Entering the outer gate of the compound, they proceeded around the inner runway in a clockwise direction, were checked off against the registers, and entered the inner gate of the compound. Both the U. N. and the communist observers were in the outer runway, but there were two communist interpreters at the check-off table in the inner runway. As the interpreters called off the names of the men in Korean, the observers ostentatiously wrote them down in their notebooks, until the anti-communist heroes created a diversion which kept the interpreters busy with something else.

The check-off table was the bottleneck, and platoons were soon at ease at intervals all around the runway, awaiting their turn. From their fellows inside the compound they learned of the presence of the communist interpreters at the check-off table, and the communist observers writing names just on the other side of the barbed wire.

Each anti-communist hero, accordingly, equipped himself with a rock, and when he came abreast of the communist interpreters, let fly. The Indian troops good-naturedly began inspecting their fists for rocks, and leading them past the check-off table, two soldiers to each prisoner of war.

Each prisoner of war also had a Republic of Korea flag flying on a short staff from his field pack. Prevented from throwing rocks, they resorted to what must have been a judo or ju jitsu device. The hand was quicker than the eye, but the result was that the Indian trooper holding the POW's right arm crashed into the soldier hanging on the left, while the anti-communist hero took his flagstaff from his pack and took a cut at a communist interpreter with it.

Still good-natured, four Indian soldiers began leading each

prisoner of war past the check-off table while a fifth carried his ROK flag for him. So the anti-communist heroes spat at the communists as they passed them, with a high degree of accuracy.

Some were more imaginative. One, a trumpet player in the compound band, was burdened down by an enormous duffle bag as well as his instrument case. Permitting one Indian soldier to carry his duffle bag, a second his ROK flag and a third his instrument case, he walked along tractably enough in the loose grip of the fourth. When he was opposite the table he beckoned to the Indian with the instrument case, flipped the snaps, took out his trumpet and smashed it over the head of the communist interpreter.

At this point, with about half of the men processed into the compound, a large NNRC delegation arrived to observe the takeover, and proceeded into the compound itself, where efficient Indian officers were assigning the men to tents. The POWs were polite and cooperative with the Indians, and smiling and affable with the Swedish and Swiss observers. They ignored the Czechs and Poles. But to experienced hands, trouble was brewing. At intervals of about one-half hour, during the morning, an anti-communist hero would prove to be a communist hero, one of the infiltrating agent-agitators, and just before entering the inner compound gate would cut and run, throw himself on the breast of the nearest Indian officer, and ask for repatriation.

When this would happen, the score of communist observers still in the alley and the Czechs and Poles inside the compound itself would applaud happily. The U. N. observers and U. S.

officers felt like applauding too, for they recognized the desirability of squeezing every last communist agent out of the compounds before they entered on their four-month ordeal. For obvious reasons, they refrained. But tension was building up.

General Lawton's warning of an incipient riot was repeated to approachable Indian officers, and pooh-poohed. The senior Swedish and Swiss officers were warned, and they suggested to the top Indian, Czech and Polish personnel that the interior of the compound was perhaps not the safest place to be in the event of trouble. They in turn were pooh-poohed.

A forthright representation was made to the senior Swedish and Swiss officers by a U. S. officer with long experience with the prisoners of war. The targets of any action by the anticommunist prisoners, he told them, would be the communist Chinese and North Korean observers and the Czechs and Poles. The men bore no ill-will toward the Indians, Swedes or Swiss, but with the difficulty of distinguishing between Swedish and Czech uniforms—they were very nearly the same color —it was not improbable that someone might be hurt quite accidentally. A rock flying through the air is not equipped with radar.

The U. S. officer didn't want the communists to be presented with so obvious a propaganda opportunity. He felt that if the Swedes and Swiss left the compound, the Czechs and Poles would probably not be so brave, and would also leave.

The Swedes and Swiss passed the word to their officers and began to saunter out. The Czechs and Poles scuttled out on their heels. The Indians from the NNRC made a dignified exit, leaving the Indian officers and men from the CFI who had legitimate business getting the prisoners of war settled.

The last NNRC member had hardly stepped through the inner gate when the 500 anti-communist heroes—now 491 in number but clearly more completely anti-communist—charged the barbed wire in four directions. Three directions were a feint, but the fourth—toward the communist Chinese and North Korean observers—was in deadly earnest. In that direction came the rocks, even a pickaxe which some U. S. engineer had carelessly left behind in the haste with which the compound had been constructed.

General Lawton had been right. But so had General Thorat. Into the compound at a dog-trot came a battalion of unarmed Indian troops, a ratio of roughly one Indian to one North Korean. Each Indian put his arms around the nearest Korean—plucking them from the top of the barbed wire toward the last—and, grinning amicably all the while, hung on for dear life. The riot subsided as quickly as it had flared. Not a single Indian struck a single Korean, or vice versa. The only casualty was a Bengali sergeant who had been standing next to one of the communist interpreters, and caught a rock on the top of his head. He rubbed his head and insisted that it had been nothing, really—a good, game guy.

There were mental casualties, however. The communist observers had fled to the far side of the wide outer road. One Red Chinese colonel, braver than his comrades and in the middle of the road, clung to that vantage point until out of

154

the very center of the compound a rock as big as a grapefruit arched out and up and down to crash on the road between his feet. It had traveled between seventy-five and one hundred yards, and for the rest of the takeover the communist observers preserved that distance. When on occasion they insisted on a more intimate position—the ground was rugged and one hundred yards from some compounds would have had them poised on a steep hillside—the Indians hung canvas on the exterior fence, to protect them from aimed rocks.

Korea is understood to be the only country in the world in which the young men, after an evening of sipping sake in the Korean equivalent of a gin-mill, go outside and throw rocks at each other for fun. Not even a Korean, of course, can pitch a rock the size of a grapefruit seventy-five yards or more. They did it with a sling, made from the laces of two combat boots and the tongue of one.

That was the only disturbance during the takeover, and it marred the relations of the Indians and the anti-communist heroes not at all. In fact, they developed a mutual respect which was extraordinary. They developed some fast friendships, and even renewed old acquaintances.

The deputy commander of the CFI was Brigadier Gurbaksh-Singh, a magnificent Sikh well over six feet tall and built in proportion. Conspicuous wherever he went because of his imposing appearance, he was not at all surprised when two North Koreans beckoned to him one day. He was surprised when he heard what they had to say.

"Were you not, sir," they asked him in easily understandable

English, "a prisoner of the Japanese in Malaya, from 1942 to 1945?"

"I was!" he replied. "But how did you know?"

"We were in the Japanese Army," they giggled. "We were your guards."

20

The Communists Stall

The terms of reference of the armistice agreement with respect to the prisoners of war were signed on the 8th of June, the agreement itself and the supplementary agreement providing for the move to the DZ on the 27th of July.

The communists remained coy on the question of whether or not any U. N. personnel would resist repatriation. Basing their belief on the curious communist mirror mentality, many on the U. N. side believed that, at the last moment, they would produce prisoners of war "not for direct repatriation."

The limitations of empirical communist psychology have already been outlined. The dogmatic communist, severely conditioned in his thinking by the distorted picture of free world methods and motives which has been tirelessly drawn for him, cannot project himself into the non-communist mind. In determining possible enemy courses of action, he considers enemy intentions rather than enemy capabilities. In the end, he convinces himself that the enemy has done, is doing, or will do what he himself would do in similar circumstances. Then, possibly in order to tempt his enemy into a denial, his propaganda accuses the enemy of having adopted a typical communist course of action.

The more vehement the enemy denial, the more the communist is convinced that he is right. Enemy silence is baffling, and even more convincing than a denial, for it shows that the enemy is unworried by the communist charges.

This communist trait is most useful for free world intelligence purposes. The Reds accuse the United Nations Command of using germ warfare in Korea. It is likely that they are trying very hard on their own part to introduce bacteriological agents into South Korea. If they succeed, they have a ready-made scapegoat. "Aha," they cry, "this vile plot of the Americans has backfired!"

Thus, throughout the long period in which negotiations in Korea were centered or stalled on the question of non-forcible repatriation of prisoners of war, there was never a mention of the fact that the communists held UNC prisoners who would allegedly resist repatriation. The Reds piously plumped for immediate repatriation of all prisoners, never presenting repatriation as a problem which they might also face, and assiduously propagandizing all the while their theory of American terrorization of their men in our hands.

This gave rise to a considerable body of opinion, on the UNC side, that the communists themselves were busy brainwashing and terrorizing a token batch of prisoners of war, to offset the exclusive attention centered on the anti-communist heroes. And we were right.

The original terms of reference with respect to prisoners refusing repatriation were so drawn as to be equally applicable to either side. Explainers would go to the locations where the prisoners were. But the supplementary agreement, since it constituted a modification of the armistice agreement re the demilitarized zone, called for designating special areas.

"If there are prisoners of war under their custody who request not to be directly repatriated," the supplementary agreement said, "the Korean People's Army and the Chinese People's Volunteers have the right to designate the area in the vicinity of Panmunjom between the Military Demarcation Line and the western and northern boundaries of the Demilitarized Zone (the DZ there made a right-angled turn to the east) as the area within which such prisoners of war will be turned over to the Neutral Nations Repatriation Commission and the armed forces of India for custody. After knowing that there are prisoners of war under their custody who request not to be directly repatriated, the Korean People's Army and the Chinese People's Volunteers shall inform the United Nations Command side of the approximate figures by nationality of such prisoners of war."

And so they did, in the last few days of the sixty allotted for prisoner of war movement, while there was a lull in world press attention after the turnover of the 22,604 anti-communist heroes. Three hundred and thirty-five Koreans, twenty-three Americans and one Briton. It was a puny riposte to the 88,000 Koreans and Chinese who had chosen freedom, and, as later unmasked, a phony counter-propaganda effort as well. But however excited the U. S. press became about the 23 Americans who professed to prefer communist slavery to freedom, it still could not obscure the drama of the thousands of anti-communist heroes awaiting the "explanations."

Four days had elapsed in July since the effective date of the armistice, 31 in August, and 25 in September—60 days, and the explanations were scheduled to begin on the 26th of September. An explanation compound, built to Indian specifications, stood ready, and the anti-communist heroes had checked off days 180-121 inclusive on their time-turned-backwards calendars.

In the small special compound housing the 85 suspected Chinese communist agents, the sixty days had been checked off too, and bright and early on the morning of the 26th of September the ostensible leader of this group requested a visitation by an NNRC sub-committee. The sub-committee came, was informed that this group had been coerced into refusing repatriation, that it really wanted very badly to be repatriated, and that it even hoped to lead a parade of all 23,000 prisoners of war back to communism.

As they came out to proceed to the special compound for prisoners who did indeed wish repatriation, however, a schism developed even in this group. Twenty hung back, and when they were safe from reprisals from the sixty-five who pressed forward, it developed that they still wanted no part of repatriation. Nor was there any simultaneous move toward Red China and Red Korea in any of the other forty-six compounds. And no word came from the communist side to the NNRC or the NNRC to the United Nations Command about the scheduling of explanations to the anti-communist heroes.

The truth of the matter was that at this point the communist side wanted no explanations whatever if they could possibly avoid them. They had been getting a thin trickle of intelligence from the anti-communist compounds, as an agent or two every few days gave up his assignment as a bad job and put in for repatriation to the Indian guards.

These agent-agitators, forced in their extremity to tell the communist intelligence network the truth whether it was palatable or not, informed their superiors that the anti-communist heroes were militantly, determinedly anti-communist in fact; that if explanations were attempted, they would screen out only a few remaining agents, and would get such a propaganda black eye that they would never live it down. They told them, too, that their story that the men were being terrorized by "American," Chiang" and "Rhee" agents would not hold water in the final test, that in groups or singly the men were ready, willing and able to affirm their anti-communism.

These facts came to light in February, 1954, when Captain Lee Chun Bong, a North Korean who had served in the Chinese Communist Army for nine years, slipped across the demilitarized zone and asked the United Nations Command for asylum. Captain Lee had been serving as the interpreter, between the Chinese and the Koreans, for the communist brainwashing braintrust, and his story confirmed in every particular the deductions of the UNC explanations staff as to what was going on on the communist side.

What needed no confirmation at the time was the distaste of the communist side for the explanation compound which had been provided to Indian specifications by the UNC. They voiced it loudly to the NNRC, although in their propaganda they simply ignored its existence completely, just as they failed

161

to mention the fact that they had entirely failed to build explanations facilities themselves on the other side of the DZ. In demanding "more suitable" explanation facilities, they ignored the fact that they could have started explanations in the existing compound on the 26th of September, right on schedule.

Assaying their intelligence, the communists concluded that anything was preferable to conducting explanations as a result of which they could only take a propaganda drubbing. The most desirable "out," from their standpoint, would be the creation of so much unrest among the prisoners of war that they would actually attempt a breakout. In the confusion following such an eventuality, with the POWs misdirected by the agents still remaining among them, they might recover enough of the men to bolster a claim that they had fled back to kind communist care from "terrorization."

Even if the entire 23,000 fled in the other direction, back to the UNC, the communists could still claim that they had been "kidnapped"—as they were already claiming with reference to the 27,000 released by President Rhee and as they actually claimed when Freedom Day came and the men were liberated in keeping with the terms of the armistice agreement. But in any event, they wouldn't have to face the loss of face they knew they would incur through putting the POWs' anti-communism to the test.

The first step in the campaign actually to terrorize the prisoners and provoke them to an escape attempt consisted of a heavy campaign on the part of the senior Czech and Polish delegates in which they insisted that the anti-communist heroes had never been informed of their rights under the armistice agreement, including their "full freedom to return home to lead a peaceful life." This was not, under the armistice agreement, a duty of the NNRC. It was the duty, immediately upon the signing of the armistice, of each detaining side, and the privilege of the "explainers." The UNC had discharged that duty, but although it considered similar action on the part of the NNRC unnecessary and redundant, interposed no objection to having the men again informed.

A sub-committee of the NNRC, therefore, went to work on a statement which explained the role of the commission to the prisoners, and reiterated the provisions of the armistice agreement pertaining to them, which they already knew so well. The statement as drafted by the committee was unobjectionable in every respect, and mimeographed copies in Chinese and Korean were scheduled for distribution to the compounds.

Here again the peculiar difference of attitude on the part of the communists toward the Chinese and Koreans came to light; Captain Lee in his story was unable to explain it. Just as the 65,000 Koreans already freed had been considered expendable by the communists, now the 8,000 remaining were spared the propaganda coup. The legitimate version of the NNRC message was distributed to the Koreans, who were merely politely bored by it.

On the Chinese message, however, the Czechs and Poles pulled a switch. Apparently another version had been prepared, on the communist side, paralleling the legitimate message, mimeographed at approximately the same time, and made ready for substitution at the critical moment.

In any event, the message from the NNRC to the Chinese

completely misrepresented the function of the commission. It assured them that it was the duty of the NNRC to see that they were repatriated, that "many" of their fellows had already asked for and received repatriation, and, in short, that any further resistance to repatriation was well-nigh useless.

The message was mimeographed on Red Chinese Army issue rice paper, and written in the ideological dialecticism of the "New China." The anti-communist heroes recognized it immediately for what it was, and were shocked and frightened by this physical evidence of communist penetration of the NNRC. But with their racial stoicism they accepted it as just one more cross to bear, and gathered up all the copies and burned them. They did not panic, although they spotted a few more communist agents within their ranks who were agitating for a break-out.

Had the communists employed this device on the more volatile Koreans, it might have been successful. Their tactics may have been more carefully thought out than they appeared to be. The Chinese unquestionably had their wind up to a greater extent than the Koreans. They were in a foreign land in the hands of foreign devils, and they might be expected to panic and bolt more readily than the Koreans. If the Chinese bolted, the Koreans would surely be right on their heels, all the more alarmed because they would not know why the Chinese were breaking out.

The attempt was cleverly timed, too, for it came after the takeover was complete but before all the CFI had arrived in the DZ. The turnover of the anti-communist heroes had gone so smoothly, after that first day, that it had been completed earlier than had been anticipated. Not one-half of the final number of Indian troops were on hand to cope with a break-out attempt.

Two more attempts by the communists, to provoke the anti-communist heroes to break out, also failed. Czech and Polish delegates insisted upon an inspection of the hospital, which was a CFI and not an NNRC responsibility, and instigated a shocking disturbance on the 1st of October in a ward containing 35 bed-ridden Chinese patients, as they had known they would. And a communist agent in a Chinese compound carefully staged a situation the following day which would make it appear that he was being "kidnapped" by Indian troops, in the expectation that it would bring his fellows over the fences to his rescue.

Prompt, firm action by the Indian troops, and wise counsel from their leaders which was heeded by all but a few of the anti-communist heroes, prevented both of these disturbances from spreading beyond their original compounds. The only untoward result was the cancellation of the celebration of Mahatma Gandhi's birthday, which the anti-communist heroes had planned for October 2d.

21

Tea and Cigarettes

"Additional provisions governing the explanation work shall be prescribed by the Neutral Nations Repatriation Commission. . . ."

The armistice agreement was extremely sketchy in the matter of the actual mechanics of "explanations," and as one of the first items on its agenda the NNRC turned its attention to its "Rules of Procedure Governing Interviews and Explanations" (Appendix C).

This document, published the last week of September, had several provisions which were disquieting to the anti-communist heroes, particularly the Chinese. The latter were already upset as a result of the forged NNRC message and the defection of trusted assistant compound leader who proved to have been a communist agent. The rules of procedure, in several particulars, did nothing to reassure them, and their mounting unease very probably contributed greatly to the disturbances of October 1 and 2.

The Chinese had been seriously shaken by the case of the assistant compound leader who had turned out to be a Red agent. This man, Wang Hsu by name, had been wholly un-suspected, and as one of the most vocal anti-communists had worked his way up to the next to the top position in his com-pound.

Following the failure of the forged NNRC message to panic the prisoners of war, Wang Hsu became as despairing of ac-complishing his mission as was the brainwashing braintrust on the other side of the demarcation line. He decided that the time had come for Wang Hsu, too, to bug out. "Bugout," a noun, was the POW Command slang term for a prisoner of war who changed his ideological allegiance in either direction. "To bug out" was the verb describing the action of bugging out. The defection of the 65 suspected communist agents on September 26 had been a "big bugout."

However, Wang Hsu (pronounced Wong Shu) had a plan which would get him out of the compound while still retain-ing the perfect trust and confidence of his fellows. Each anti-communist hero had come to Camp Freedom with one blanket. The nights were getting a little cool up near the 38th parallel, and the CFI had been so busy getting itself settled that it had not yet gotten around to issuing the three additional blankets to which each man was entitled, and which had been supplied for them by the United Nations Command.

There were six other communist agents in this compound, Number 31, in addition to Wang Hsu, and he got one of them to propose that the assistant compound leader go as a commit-tee of one to ask General Thorat to issue the rest of the blank-ets. It was agreed. He hailed an Indian guard and asked to be taken to General Thorat, and off he went. He even waved good-by. But he never came back.

The compound, already restive and nervous as a result of the needling and all-around agitation Wang Hsu and his six accomplices had been able to conduct, decided that he had been kidnapped—quite probably at the instigation of one or more of the other accomplices. So they kidnapped an Indian sergeant who entered the compound the next day with a rations detail, and they sent word to General Thorat that they would exchange the sergeant for Wang Hsu.

Wang Hsu had already appeared before an NNRC sub-committee, to validate his desire for repatriation, and was at that moment being interviewed by a group of admiring communist newsmen and spinning a wondrous tale about the nefarious Americans. But General Thorat was not the sort of soldier to submit to blackmail. He roared up to the compound in his jeep, strode through the gates and demanded to see the compound leader.

It was a tense and ugly situation, but General Thorat's courage was equalled by the finesse of his diplomacy. "What sort of Chinese are you," he asked when the compound leader presented himself. "You have offered me neither tea nor cigarettes!"

Tea and cigarettes were produced, and in a straightforward manner General Thorat convinced the men that, unbelievable as it seemed to them, Wang Hsu had asked for repatriation. They took up the matter of the blankets with him, and he promised to have them issued immediately. After more tea and cigarettes, and an exchange of salutes, he left with the sergeant in tow.

Tea and cigarettes had been up until that time a bond between the Indian troops and the anti-communist heroes. The Indians liked their tea in the English fashion, with milk and very sweet, and the Chinese took theirs straight, so interchange on that score was limited to exploratory courtesy. But most of the Koreans preferred the water in which they boiled their rice, as a hot drink, to tea, so they had extra tea to trade to the Indians for Indian cigarettes—straight Virginia tobacco, also on the English order—which they liked as a change from their American cigarettes. The Indians liked the American cigarettes about as much as the Chinese and Koreans liked Indian tea.

But tea and cigarettes could not assuage the disquiet produced by the rules of procedure. Explanations to individuals or groups had been authorized, as anticipated. But what had not been anticipated was the authorization of repeated explanations to individuals or groups. The anti-communist heroes, familiar as they were wtih the cumulative effect of repeated brainwashings, had particularly dreaded such an eventuality—and here it was.

"The Polish and Czech delegates assisted the communist leadership by giving advice at meetings with the communists or over the telephone," Captain Lee Chun Bong said in his broadcast testimony. "When the NNRC approved the 'rules of procedure,' the Polish and Czech delegates were given a banquet at which they made speeches saying that this was the beginning of the communist victory."

Happily, these "neutrals" were a little over-optimistic.

Another provision of the rules of procedure disturbed the anti-communist heroes not at all, but had hidden implications for the United Nations Command. Written explanations might be distributed to the prisoners of war. Had the communists taken advantage of this, and insisted on daily distribution of communist literature to each individual POW, they would have built up such pressures that trouble would have been inevitable. The material would have received the same fate as the forged NNRC Chinese message, but the mere fact of its distribution by the Indian troops would have irrevocably allied the latter, in the prisoners' judgment, with the communists.

The censorship obligation it would have put on the NNRC, too, would have been so immense that the possibilities of further fraud and deceit would have been multiplied.

Fortunately the communists did not take advantage of this opportunity. Their reason will have to await the arrival in the free world of some future seeker of asylum and sanctuary who is informed on this aspect of their operations.

But it was in provision fourteen that the Czechs and Poles in the NNRC brought off their big coup. "The representative of the detaining side," it ran, "shall not participate in the work of explanation or interfere with it in any way. He may, however, bring to the notice of the Chairman of the NNRC or its subordinate body at the end of each explanatory session, any matter which may be construed as violating the Terms of Reference."

The longest brainwashing of the explanations lasted well

over four hours, and interviews of three hours or more were commonplace. During that time the explainer would threaten the prisoner of war with death and his family with torture, time after time after time and with variations. At the end of the interview, the U. N. representative was permitted to cite these violations. The Indian chairman would admonish the explainer, who would proceed to commit the same violations in the very next interview.

Some Indian chairmen, too, interpreted "the end of each explanatory session" to mean the end of the morning session, or the end of the day, and not the end of a single interview. By the end of the morning or the end of the day they were often in no mood to put off lunch or dinner in favor of hearing protests by the UNC representatives.

The rules which provided for repeated explanations and the muzzling of the UNC representatives were properly and promptly protested by General Mark W. Clark. When the NNRC would not budge, he informed them that the UNC representatives would be instructed to act in the best interests of the anti-communist heroes, despite this manifestly unfair ruling.

The flagrant disregard by the communist explainers of the prohibition of threats of force of both the armistice agreement and the rules of procedure fully justified the UNC representatives in the plan of action they adopted under General Clark's direction. Adopt it they had to, to justify the faith and trust the anti-communist heroes had in them as their "legal counsel" in the explanations.

As a rule, the anti-communist hero himself would fling the

explainer's threats back in his teeth, and, if it were the turn of the U. N. interpreter to furnish the running translation for the NNRC committee, they got an accurate version and could immediately admonish the explainer.

If the communist interpreter were functioning, he would generally slide over the threat—but the U. N. interpreter would immediately call the attention of the committee to the violations, and the same admonishment would result.

But if the anti-communist hero, worn down by the ordeal, looked mutely to the U. N. representative for help, the latter leaped to his feet and protested despite the fourteenth rule. With the communists breaking every rule in the book, his conscience would not permit him to obey that one prohibition. He was there to represent the United Nations, and to a man the representatives did a good job.

Still one more provision of the rules of procedure was disturbing to the anti-communist heroes. This was number twenty, which read as follows:

"Prisoners who have applied for repatriation, those who have been given explanation . . . but have not submitted their applications for repatriation and those who have neither been given explanation nor applied for repatriation shall be kept separated in custody."

The anti-communist heroes interpreted this to mean that they would not be returned to their compounds, after they had received explanations, until they applied for repatriation. Under those conditions, they decided, they would not even leave their compounds in the first place. Let the explainers come to them and talk to them in their compounds, they said. After all, the armistice agreement said that the other side ". . . shall have freedom and facilities to send representatives to the locations where such prisoners of war are in custody to explain to all the prisoners of war . . . their rights and to inform them of any matters relating to their return to their homelands, particularly of their full freedom to return home to lead a peaceful life. . . ."

Some of the more accomplished "guardhouse lawyers" among the anti-communist heroes also pointed out that the segregation provision, except for those who actually wished repatriation, was in direct contravention of the Geneva Convention, while the armistice agreement specified that all arrangements with respect to the prisoners of war would be in accord with both the letter and the spirit of the Geneva Convention.

They were right, too. The Geneva Convention prohibits any segregation of prisoners of war except for disciplinary and health reasons.

The United Nations Command had rushed to completion the new explanation sites demanded by the communists and requested by the NNRC, despite delaying changes in the specifications. They were ready for use by midnight, October 13.

The Communists could put off the test of their propaganda claims no longer. On the morning of the 14th they requested that the NNRC deliver 1,000 Chinese prisoners of war for explanations the following day.

The NNRC agreed and the UNC concurred. Only the anti-communist heroes balked. They refused to come out of their compounds until General Thimayya promised that they would not be segregated after the explanations.

So the anti-communist heroes wrote the first amendment to the rules of procedure. Proper credit should be given to General Thimayya, however, for the magnificent leadership he displayed. The prisoners of war had other doubts and fears, but he allayed them. He even loaded a man from each "platoon" of the first compound in a truck, and brought them to the explanation site so they could get an idea of the lay of the land and tell their fellows what to expect. The thing that really sold them, though, was his sporting approach.

"You say you are anti-communist, and will resist repatriation to the death. Very well—come on and prove it!"

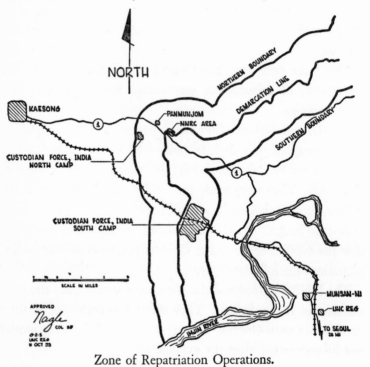

Zone of Repatriation Operations.

22

The Stage Is Set

To have been present at the explanations to the anti-communist heroes was, for the UNC personnel involved, at the same time one of the most humbling and most inspiring experiences of a lifetime. For the prisoners of war, it was a life and death struggle, replete with drama and pathos, and yet even to them not without flashes of their irrepressible humor. To participate in their ordeal was to become emotionally involved with them, without exception.

Among the UNC personnel, there were fifty Chinese and Chinese-Americans, under Mr. Chen Yih, journalism master and former tennis coach at the University of Missouri. There were fifty Republic of Korea Army officers, all English-speaking, under young, efficient Brigadier General Park Yong Zoon. There were seventy-five U. S. officers—Army, Navy, Air Force and Marines—under Colonels Willard B. Carlock and Howard L. Bresee, U. S. Army.

The Chinese and Korean personnel were admittedly chosen for their proficiency in English, but they proved themselves equally efficient in all other respects. The Americans were

chosen from among former lawyers, teachers, ministers, sales-
men and, of course, soldiers—men able to think and talk on
their feet. Language ability—Hindi, Urdu, Mandarin, Cantonese, Korean, Swedish, French, German, Italian, Czech, Polish, Russian—was sought but not stressed, although one U. N.
representative, Lieutenant Colonel Vaughn F. Meisling, U. S.
Army, spoke Chinese, Swedish, French and German (of the
languages useful in the operation!).

Awaiting announcement by the communists of the identity
of the renegades in the token refusal of repatriation on the
other side of the demarcation line were Australian, Belgian,
British, Canadian, Colombian, Ethiopian, Filipino, French and
Greek officers. Most of these left when it was discovered that
none of their nationals had been brainwashed, but some who
stayed and distinguished themselves by their efforts in behalf
of the anti-communist heroes included Lieutenant Colonel
Gordon McNabb and Major Desmond B. Ryan (brevetted
from captain for the occasion) of the British Army, Captain
Tefesse Lemma of the Ethiopian Army and Captain Vesto
Pablo Taylor y Robinson of the Colombian Army.

These men tumbled out of their sleeping bags at the provisional camp which had been set up for them at Munsan-ni,
the morning of Thursday, the 15th of October, long before
dawn. It was cold, damp and dismal. They shaved, dressed,
breakfasted and collected their passes—one to get into the demilitarized zone and one to get past the CFI checkpoint—
before the convoy departure time of 0630. The convoy
consisted of six jeeps, a communications truck and four busses,

each flying a U. N. flag and another blue and white flag for identification purposes in the DZ.

Despite their heavy wool olive green Army field clothes and field jackets, and in some cases parkas, they were cold and uncomfortable as they jolted along the bumpy dirt road past hills and fields which until recently had been bitterly fought over. There were twisted barbed wire entanglements, pockmarks of machine gun bullets on concrete retaining walls and abutments, and mangled railway cars along the track which paralleled the road. As they crossed the Imjin River over Freedom Bridge, the original railway bridge which now had a one-way plank roadway as well, the contorted frame of the original highway bridge lay in the current to the right, where it had toppled.

At the bridge approaches, half a dozen tanks manned by U. S. Marines were posed, covered with camouflage nets. When the anti-communist heroes had crossed this bridge, moving to the DZ, the guns of the tanks had pointed west by north, toward the enemy, to assure the prisoners of quick support in the event of any move against them in the DZ.

Now the guns pointed east by south, toward the Republic of Korea, to bring comfort to the CFI. The disturbances of October 1 and 2 had brought rumblings from Seoul that any further clashes between the CFI and the anti-communist heroes would bring Republic of Korea Marines on a rescue mission.

From the river the UNC convoy climbed over a hill, their cold jeeps still sputtering in the quiet morning air. (The name Chosen—Korea—means "morning calm.") Then they descended into a comparative plain which stretched unimpeded, except for a few prominences, all the way to the tall and forbidding Korean mountains north of Kaesong and the 38th parallel. North Korean anti-communist heroes from Kaesong, in compounds on those intervening prominences, could look right down on the smoke of the morning fires in their home town.

On their left, as the UNC convoy proceeded, they passed the warehouse which had supplied the prisoners of war repatriated in "Big Switch," the return of the 75,000 communist prisoners, and which now supplied Camp Freedom. Past the tents of the personnel who manned the warehouse was the gate into the DZ, with a military police checkpoint at which they stopped only long enough for the convoy commander to sing out the number of persons in the line of vehicles.

Then they traversed an embankment spanning a wide marsh, with covered pipes on their right carrying water into Camp Freedom. Over the marsh, thousands of ducks and geese circled, disturbed by the convoy but careful not to cross the line marking the demilitarized zone. The 1st U. S. Marine Division, on the other side of that line, had a few shotguns as well as a few tanks.

On the far side of the marsh was the CFI checkpoint, manned by a military police sergeant of the Rajputana Rifles, formerly the Napiers from the fame they gained in a battle under a British brigadier, and before that the Bombay Light Infantry. He was resplendent in a red turban topped by a pleated green cock's comb, and the convoy halted for several minutes while he checked passes and inquired politely in each vehicle for weapons and cameras, the first barred by the Military Armistice Commission and the second by the CFI.

178

Opposite the checkpoint was the first Korean compound, on a fair hill not more than a hundred and fifty yards away. The anti-communist heroes were drawn up with military precision in four ranks, each overlooking the one below because of the slope of the hill. In the center of this array was their band.

Each man had a small Republic of Korea flag in his hand, and standing on elevated platforms holding larger flags were their cheerleaders. Executing a precision drill with their flags which would have done credit to a line of Tiller Girls, they repeatedly shouted in unison "Mansei!" ("May Korea Live 10,000 Years!"). Then they launched into martial Korean songs, each sung with intricate and involved flag movements. On a flagpole thirty feet high, over the whole spectacle, an enormous ROK flag stood out in the breeze.

The effect was electric. It made every man in the convoy want to go over and tell these men who had so much trust and faith in the United Nations Command, "We will merit your trust; we will fight for you at the explanations and whenever you need us!"

But all they could do was wave in acknowledgment as the convoy proceeded. Even this show of appreciation distressed the Rajputana sergeant dreadfully. He shook his upraised finger in admonishment at each vehicle as it passed him, commanding sharply, "No signalling! No signalling!"

As a result of communist nagging, the entire Indian element was susceptible to suggestion that signals were being exchanged between UNC personnel and the anti-communist heroes. What could have been passed by "signals" other than "Keep a

179

stiff upper lip!" would have been difficult to determine, but suspicion lingered—of which more later.

The convoy proceeded through the camp, past the hospital with the patients lined up and cheering, past another Korean compound with the same precision demonstration, to the demarcation line. Each compound had a flagpole at least thirty feet in the air, and some went up to seventy-five feet. They were made with eight-foot flooring boards from the tents, two placed one way and the next two turned ninety degrees. They were guyed at frequent intervals, since they were most insubstantial, with barbed wire from the fences, or former loudspeaker wire. Flying from each was the biggest possible ROK or Nationalist Chinese flag; many Korean compounds had smaller poles flying a Chinese flag, and vice versa.

Doubling up in their living tents, each compound had set aside one tent as a chapel, and these were surmounted by white crosses. A second tent in each compound was utilized as a theater stage, facing open ground where the men could congregate for the presentations. The long sides of these tents facing the audiences were thrown upward and outward on long poles, with the canvas draped in graceful scallops, pagoda style.

At the demarcation line the convoy turned left to the explanation area, one half dropping off at the first compound, the other half continuing around a hill to the second. The narrow road, newly built, was very muddy from the heavy rain of the night before, but fortunately had a firm base. Although the entire road distance from Munsan-ni to the first compound was only a little more than 12 miles, the trip with the two halts had taken an hour. The communists were late; the communists were always late. They seemed to be the victims of a psychological block about the whole thing.

The two explanation compounds were built on exactly the same plan, and similarly located, out of sight of each other and out of sight of the main camp. Each faced a low hill, and each had a hill behind it.

Picture a rectangular area about 400 by 100 feet surrounded by barbed wire, enclosing sixteen U. S. Army squad tents, each about 30 by 15 feet. Facing the long side of the compound from the hill in front of it, these tents are ranged along the back side of the enclosure; behind the tents is an alley enclosed in barbed wire, on which the back entrances of the tents give. You are facing east, so that this back or east entrance to the explanation tent is the one by which the anti-communist hero will enter, and, if he is not successfully brainwashed, also leave the tent. The west entrance, giving on the compound proper, is to be used by the NNRC committee, the UNC representatives, the communist representatives and explainers, and any POW choosing repatriation.

The foreground of the compound is relatively clear, except for three tents strung along for the use, one each, of the one neutral and two enemy groups in the exercise, in the event of rain. All of the tents are floored and "winterized," that is, walled with wood to window level and from that point to the slope of the roof with translucent plastic. Entering the tents from the western entrance, each has plank furniture: a table and bench on the immediate right for the NNRC committee, a table and bench farther along to the right and facing across

181

the tent for the communist representatives and explainers. In the middle of the left side of the tent and facing the communists' table, a bench for the anti-communist heroes. In the far left corner, a bench for the UNC representatives. It suited the whim of some Indian chairmen to seat the communist representative on this bench, too, reserving the center bench and table for the explaining staff.

On this first day of explanations, the Swedish and Swiss NNRC personnel arrived on the dot of eight in U. S.-supplied busses, the Swedes in green-brown uniforms, tall and serious, the Swiss in smart peaked "overseas" caps and light-blue uniforms. In no time at all the Swiss were demonstrating their caps to the waiting UNC personnel; the Swiss caps unfold into an ingenious skiing headpiece covering the entire head and neck, with just a small face opening.

Fifteen minutes later, the communists arrived, in a long line of fully fifty dark green Russian-made jeeps, each flying a red flag in addition to its blue and white DZ flag. The Chinese wore soft, round, formless "Lenin" caps and drab gray-green uniforms suggestive of prison garb, buttoned at the throat and with no insignia of rank. Each man had a tape sewn above his left breast pocket, with his name and job assignment.

The North Koreans, on the other hand, were very elaborately turned out, in dark blue, belted and booted, with kepi-style caps, gold rank insignia on shoulder boards, Russian-style blouses and red stripes on their baggy pants.

The Poles and Czechs arrived in greatcoats with fancy gold shoulder insignia and brass buttons. In the European military tradition, many carried shiny dispatch cases swinging on long straps.

In contrast to the Indian officers in the varied uniforms of their several services—there were Indian Air Force and Navy personnel, as well as Army, on their NNRC delegation—and the Swedes, Swiss and UNC personnel, who were now smiling and getting acquainted, the communists were stone-faced, even among themselves. No one smiled, no one laughed. Too dangerous in a communist society. What is he smiling about? Who is he laughing at?

Now the weather cleared, the sun began to shine brightly, and the short pine trees and scrub oaks on the hillsides took on their full fall colors, the yellow, brown and russet of the oaks contrasting with the green of the pines. The lacy fronds of tall pampas grass on the flats waved in the fresh breeze.

Everything was ready; everyone was there except the anti-communist heroes.

23

The Anti-Communist Heroes Prove It

The UNC representatives were worried. If the prisoners of war did not present themselves for the explanations, the communists could make their claims of terrorization and fraud until doomsday and many would believe them. Any attempt to explain to an entire compound at once would have been drowned out by demonstrations such as that in the first Korean compound the UNC party had passed that morning. Any attempt to explain to individuals or small groups in the compounds would inevitably lead to disturbances.

Proof of the militant anti-communism of these men, of their oft-repeated affirmation that they would resist repatriation to the death, could be established only by their attendance at explanations.

Nine o'clock came, and the UNC personnel silently prayed for General Thimayya's success in his mission. At intervals a staff car with an Indian officer would pull up, and a fresh rumor would sweep the area.

At nine-thirty a truck load of prisoners could be discerned on the road leading to the holding compound, before it disap-

184

peared back of the hill behind the explanation compound. NNRC, UNC and communist personnel began a slow movement into the explanation compound. But at ten the truck reappeared, still loaded and heading back to the main camp. These were the platoon leaders on the reconnaissance conducted by General Thimayya.

At ten-thirty male voices massed in a stirring chorus could be heard, more than a mile away. Then a long convoy of trucks lumbered around the hillside into sight, loaded with singing, shouting, flag-waving anti-communist heroes. General Thimayya had proven himself capable of leading Chinese troops as brilliantly as he had led Indian troops.

The POW-eye view of the explanation set-up took the form of a succession of shocks. First, a holding compound which could accommodate 250 men. Then a roughly bull-dozed path skirting the slope of the hill between the holding compound and the explanation compound, with Indian troopers in green uniform and sloppy-brimmed fatigue hats at intervals of 50 feet. The troopers were "unarmed"; they carried lathis.

When one reads of police in an Indian city controlling a crowd by means of lathis, the word "lathi" somehow carries the connotation of lath, and conjures up a mental picture of gentle, non-violent control of crowds almost as if with wands.

A lathi is a round pole of teak or some similar hard, heavy wood, one and one-quarter to one and one-half inches in diameter, about four feet long, and sharply pointed at one end. Of pick-handle potential, it could be a lethal weapon. To the credit of the Indian troops it must be said immediately that no instance was known of an Indian trooper employing a lathi

185

in conjunction with the explanations, despite not infrequent emergencies when an anti-communist prisoner, in pure terror at facing the brainwashers, would turn on the Indians just as a dog hit by an automobile will bite a beloved master in an extreme of fear and pain.

They did not need their lathis. They had leadership too.

On the right-hand slope of the hill before them, the anti-communist heroes could see a small compound with one small tent. There the prisoners of war who still refused repatriation after the explanations, General Thimayya had told them, would wait until a truckload had accumulated, when they would be taken back to their original compound. They would be separated, not segregated, but only until they all got back to their compound, and only because, their escorts explained to them, to Indians all Chinese look alike. How could they tell which ones had received explanations and refused repatriation, and which had not heard the explanations?

All but a few of the anti-communist heroes thought this very funny, because, to Chinese, all Indians look alike. The few who did not laugh were disappointed. They were irrepressible hams who had played the hero to such applause in the Cheju Chautauqua that they had in mind volunteering for explanations as often during the day as they could get away with it.

So they volunteered to be first, and away went sixteen of them to each explanation area, each man escorted by an Indian trooper.

As they came over the hill, the next shock. There were fifty communist jeeps drawn up in line, each with its red flag and

186

its driver. The few jeeps and several busses of the UNC group did not loom nearly so large, and their drivers were badly outnumbered.

The next shock, however, was to the communist explainers. As the anti-communist heroes entered the alley back of the explanation tents, they peeled off, one to a tent, and the curtain raised on the drama.

To the "general observers" pacing the compound in front of the tents, the effect was somewhat that of one of those musical arrangements in which one section of the orchestra takes up a theme, another comes in, one more is added, and so on until the whole orchestra is going full blast. But in this instance the crescendo reached its climax in the time a man could walk four hundred feet—about a minute and a half.

Two general observers per compound were permitted each side, although the communists blandly disregarded this as they disregarded all rules while vehemently insisting that the other side obey them to the letter. The communists maintained their stony stares—they had been warned by the "bugouts" to expect this, although they could not possibly have anticipated the violence of it.

The UNC observers, try as they would, could not conceal their jubilance. The tables were being turned on the communist explainers with a vengeance.

The NNRC observers were perplexed. They had not been warned to expect it, and they began peering into one tent after another, puzzled. If this din, this bedlam, constituted the communists' "explanations," the Geneva Convention, the armistice agreement, the terms of reference and the rules of pro-

187

cedure were all clearly being violated to the grossest degree.

The poor explainers were wholly innocent. Innocent for possibly the first time in their lives and certainly for the last time during the explanations, they were nevertheless guiltless in this instance.

The anti-communist heroes were explaining to the explainers.

The Indian chairmen of the sub-committees in each tent were prepared with a reassuring statement as to the role of the NNRC in safeguarding the interests of the prisoner of war, and advising him that he need not answer questions if he felt that the answer might be used to threaten or coerce him directly or indirectly. But unless an individual chairman had a commanding voice and a compelling personality, he rarely had a chance to finish it. Since it was in English and only a handful of the anti-communist heroes could understand it anyway, the chairmen soon gave up and delegated the reading of the statement to an interpreter.

The average anti-communist hero, entering the tent from the bright sunlight outside, could see no one except the U. N. representative, at his right hand as he entered. He would salute the U. N. representative, who would stand and return the salute.

Next he saw, diagonally across the middle of the tent, the communist explainers. This gave him a momentary setback. He had been led to expect, in his rehearsals for his role, an explainer, a communist representative, a communist observer and an interpreter.

The rules of procedure had not clarified this to any extent,

188

for they stated in one paragraph: "The explaining representative shall have the right to distribute to the prisoners of war . . ." and in another "The explaining representatives may ask the prisoners of war . . ."

The communists interpreted these conflicting provisions to permit them no less than five explaining representatives per anti-communist hero, and dwelt on their own sweet reasonableness in insisting upon only three explainers per POW in the average tent. When the word spread that an anti-communist hero was weakening in any tent, however, they quickly shot in two more expert explainers as reinforcements. Then, since the explanations on this first day were to Chinese, the communist representative was Chinese and the communist observer was North Korean. In addition to the interpreter for the NNRC, the North Korean required two interpreters, Chinese-English and English-Korean, because, as they blandly explained, they had so few Chinese-Korean interpreters.

Thus in the average tent there were at least eight communists, and sometimes as many as ten, not counting the Czech and the Pole. Add to that the flagrant disregard by the communists of the limitations on the number of general observers outside the tents, and the fifty communist jeep-drivers outside the compound, and the communists had a substantial—and intentional—preponderance of strength.

But the anti-communist hero was never taken aback more than momentarily. His surprise at this stacking of the deck against him generally turned to anger, and he would launch himself into his well-prepared diatribe.

To cover his chagrin at the failure of the anti-communist

hero to be properly frightened, the communist explainer who had drawn the first shift would begin reading *his* prepared statement. The result was a situation in which the Indian chairman was vainly shouting and pounding on the table for order, his interpreter was attempting to complete the opening statement to the POW, the anti-communist hero was shouting at the explainers and an explainer was trying to drown out all the others.

It was a Donnybrook for fair.

When the chairman succeeded in restoring some semblance of order, the explainer would go back to the beginning of his prepared statement. This, surprisingly, was simply an adaptation of the amnesty statement of April, 1952.

"Captured comrades—" the explainer would begin, only to be interrupted immediately.

"Don't call me comrade, you aren't my comrade!" the anti-communist hero would shout. "Nor was I captured! I surrendered to escape your filthy exploitation of the Chinese people!" This would go on until he stopped for breath.

"Captured comrades of the Korean People's Army and the Chinese People's Volunteers—"

"Volunteers! Ha! I didn't 'volunteer.' No one asked me if I wished to fight in your murderous war in Korea." Again, a tirade until he ran out of breath.

"Captured comrades of the Korean People's Army and the Chinese People's Volunteers: The Korean People's Army and the Chinese People's Volunteers, during negotiations with the opposing party, have in accordance with the provisions of the Geneva Convention with regard to the treatment of prisoners of war, firmly demanded that following the armistice you have the right to return to your respective fatherlands—" By this time the anti-communist hero had his breath back.

"Yes, I have the right to return to my fatherland! But not while it is in the blood-stained hands of you running dogs of the Russians! I will return to my fatherland in a liberating army led by President Chiang Kai-shek!"

". . . you have the right to return to your respective fatherlands to lead a peaceful life—" the explainer would plow on doggedly.

"A peaceful life? I was leading a peaceful life until you came to my village and impressed me into your so-called people's volunteers and forced me to fight in Korea!"

". . . to lead a peaceful life, and have, on April 6, 1952, issued a statement wholeheartedly welcoming you back—"

"On April 6, 1952, I said what I would rather do than go back! I would rather die than go back to your blankety-blankety-blankety-blank oppression!"

There was, it is to be feared, a strong admixture of profanity in the replies of the anti-communist heroes. There was nothing in the armistice agreement, the terms of reference, or the rules of procedure specifically barring profanity under these circumstances. There were, of course, the provisions of the Geneva Convention enjoining soldierly conduct upon prisoners of war, particularly with respect to officers—and the explainers were plainly officers. But the obscenity most often employed was not, to the Indian chairman, either obscene or profane.

". . . wholeheartedly welcoming you back to the embraces of your fatherlands—"

"Ha! The embraces of my fatherland as it is ruled by you sons of turtles, you sons of turtles for a thousand generations, are the garrote and the hangman's noose. I do not want the embraces of my turtle-headed fatherland!"

This was deadly, and the explainer could only complain to the chairman.

"So he called you the son of a turtle," the Indian chairman would sympathize. "What's so bad about that? Please get on with the explanation."

This forced the explainer to explain that a female turtle, because of her carapace, could copulate only—so far as Chinese and Koreans are concerned—with a snake. This made her an adultress, her mate a cuckold, and her offspring bastards. If one were a thousand times the son of a turtle, this illegitimacy had been compounded a thousand times. It was an insult no man could bear. Even if you smiled, you couldn't say that.

Yes, he could see how that could be, the chairman would agree. And the anti-communist hero would be duly admonished.

"Now the Korean armistice has been realized, the time for you to return to your fatherlands has arrived—"

"It has not yet arrived, but it will arrive! We will return to our fatherland in an army of liberation under President Chiang Kai-shek!"

"According to the provisions of the 'Terms of Reference for Neutral Nations Repatriation Commission,' nobody is allowed to threaten you and prevent you from realizing your desire to return to the fatherland. We deeply understand your longing

192

for your fatherland and the misfortunes that have fallen upon you following your capture—"

"I have told you that I was not captured—I surrendered. And my surrender was the greatest good fortune which has ever befallen me! Now I am free from your grasp, free to go to Taiwan to join the forces of President Chiang!"

"Some of you have, during the detention period, been forced to tattoo your arms—"

"Forced to tattoo our arms? I have willingly tattooed my entire body! Would you like to see what I have tattooed over my heart? Here—" ripping his shirt open with a histrionic flourish worthy of a Drew or a Barrymore, "look at this one! 'Resist Russia, Oppose Communism!' And this one, 'Hui Tai-wan' (To Formosa)! And this one! (Generally an obscenity directed at Mao Tse-tung.)"

". . . tattoo your arms, write certain documents, join certain organizations, work in POW camps, or otherwise engage in similar activities. We consider that you have done all these not out of your own free wish and should not be responsible for them—"

"But we are responsible for them! We were forced to do nothing by the United Nations Command! We were treated by the United Nations Command always in accord with the Geneva Convention, better than we were treated when you captured some of us from the army of President Chiang, better than we were treated when we were miserable cannon-fodder in your so-called People's Volunteers, your army which is neither the people's nor volunteers! Yes, we wrote certain documents opposing communism—I learned to read and write as a prisoner of war of the United Nations Command! Yes, we worked in the POW camps, learning trades and how to be better farmers! And we will do all of the same in freedom and liberty on Taiwan—and on the mainland when we take it back from you puppets and lapdogs of the Russians!"

This was hard for the explainers to take, and the first one would be perspiring and literally green in the face at this stage. What was worse, the delight of the UNC personnel at this anti-communist testimonial on the part of the POW, the respect being engendered in the Indian, the Swede and the Swiss. . . . The Czech and Pole looked worried; the North Korean was still stony-faced. Another explainer would take over.

"We therefore seriously announced and with responsibility: our captured personnel (if he was lucky he got by with the word 'captured'; if not, he got the same harangue as his predecessor), no matter what kind of the above-mentioned activities he has engaged in in the POW camps of the opposing party, will not be questioned about his past deeds after returning to this fatherland; all returning personnel will be reunited with their families—"

"My family? I have no family! You killed my mother and father, you murderers!"

". . . with their families, join the construction work of the fatherland and lead a peaceful life. We have sent our representatives to give comfort to you, notify you of matters relating to your return to your fatherlands, and welcome you back to the fatherland. We, together with the peoples of Korea and

194

China, are concerned about you and anxiously await your return."

And the explainer would repeat the names and titles of Kim Il Sung and Peng Teh-huai. He would repeat them, that is, if he were quick enough to get them in before the peroration of the prisoner of war.

With a performance like that on the part of the prisoner, the explainers had no appetite for further "explanation," and the chairman would sum up, carefully using the language of the terms of reference.

"You have had explained to you your right of repatriation," he would state in clipped English, "and you have been informed of matters relating to your return to your homeland, particularly of your full freedom to return home to lead a peaceful life. If you wish to be repatriated, leave the tent by this (pointing to his left) door; if you do not wish to be repatriated, leave the tent by that (pointing to the door by which the POW had entered) door."

This, even if it were translated by the UNC interpreter and therefore honest and accurate, could still be confusing to the anti-communist hero. By the terms of the armistice agreement, "the act of delivery of a prisoner of war by one side to the other shall . . . be called 'repatriation' in English, 'song hwan' in Korean, and 'ch'ien fan' in Chinese. . . ." The latter two mean, literally, "go home." A fast choice between "if you wish to go home, leave by this door; if you do not wish to go home, leave the tent by that door," often completely defeated him.

There was not a man in the lot who did not wish to go

home. But they wished to go home via Formosa, to go home to a liberated, free, once more happy China at whatever date in the future that might become possible. They were willing, eager, to fight to make it possible. The choice they were making was not whether to go home or not go home, it was between returning to Red China or going to Formosa, between returning to communism or going free.

If the interpretation were the turn of the communist interpreter, he would point only to the door to Red China, and it would be difficult indeed for the anti-communist hero to hear the "not" in the last sentence. It was not surprising that even some of the most militant of the men, tired by their tour de force, became confused at the very last.

When this would happen, and a man would hesitate between the two exits, the door to Red China would swiftly fill with six to twelve of the surplus communist general observers, representatives, observers, interpreters and hangers-on in the explanation compound, twittering and clucking and making enticing beckoning motions to the prisoner of war as if he were a Thanksgiving turkey whom they were trying to coax to the chopping block. In this group there were always two or three women.

If the Indian guard dispersed this further show of strength, they would scatter for the seconds it took him to proceed on his rounds, then reassemble and redouble their efforts. It would have been easy for the UNC general observers to call the attention of the guard to the disregard of his orders behind his back, but they never did. That covey of decoys told the hesitant hero quite plainly which was the door to Red China.

The communists made many errors of judgment in their explanation efforts, but one of their worst was the standard of appearance they set for their feminine colleagues. One of the fears of both the Chinese and North Korean anti-communist heroes had been that they would employ pretty girls as explainers; worse, that they might tour the compounds with strip-tease shows as a prelude to using the same girls as explainers, or that they might frankly be solicited by prostitute-explainers.

They had been behind barbed wire for a long time, and they could stand it for six more months—but not with pretty girls being flaunted before them.

Were they such fair-weather anti-communists that a pretty girl could lure them back to communism?

No, but pretty girls in combination with brainwashing would increase their problems. The rehabilitation heads who were trying to reassure them realized neither how powerful brainwashing could be nor how beautiful a pretty Chinese or Korean girl could be after up to three years behind barbed wire.

Chinese and Korean girls can be pretty, too, even to a man who has not been behind barbed wire for three years. But the anti-communist heroes need not have worried. The only requirement the communists laid down for their feminine personnel was that one be able to tell them, at a glance, from a mud fence.

"To weaken me in my determination," the average anti-communist hero would say when he encountered one of them as an interpreter or otherwise, "you will have to find a prettier girl than that crow! Are there no pretty girls dedicated to communism? Or must a woman be so homely that she can get a man only among you ugly cadres to become a communist?"

If the perplexed POW turned to the chairman for repeated instructions, to be sure of the door to Taiwan, he got only the set speech, together with more flagrant cheating if the communist interpreter thought there was a chance of further confusing him. The word "Taiwan" was absolutely forbidden to the UNC interpreter, and pointing to the door leading to Taiwan by the UNC representative or observer was "signalling," and grounds for disqualification.

An extra UNC team had always to be held in readiness, immediately to replace those disqualified.

24

"Hui Taiwan!"

The explanations, that first day, had not started until eleven
o'clock. By one o'clock, when the tents emptied and the participants in the unfolding drama headed in some six directions
for lunch, about one hundred and seventy-five anti-communist
heroes had received explanations—and not a single one had
opted for repatriation.

When the explanations resumed shortly after two o'clock—
the communists were only a little late this time—it quickly
became obvious that their team had spent most of the inter-
mission in skull practice. They had asked, "What do we do
now, Coach?" and Coach had told them what to do.

The anti-communist heroes' first team, the stars of the compound plays, had dominated the first half. There was still an
occasionally eloquent prisoner of war who could give the explainers a thoroughly bad time, but the majority of the men
that afternoon were just simple, scared soldiers, with only one
or two good denunciations apiece at their command. For the
greater part of the time they simply chanted, giving each other

strength as the chant spread from tent to tent, "Hui Taiwan!
. . . Hui Taiwan!"

The change in communist tactics became obvious immediately. When a prisoner of war was obviously anti-communist and wholly lost to them, they wasted no time on him and waved him on to freedom.

But if a man was not articulate, not so quick to dispute their statements, listening to them more or less quietly with only an occasional "Hui Taiwan," they passed the word for reinforcements and two boss explainers would join those already in the tent. Then the real brainwashing started. If they could get the prisoner of war tired, then quiet, they read to him, over and over and over, the Kim-Peng statement, interspersed with a few soft-voiced, persuasive arguments. When the arguments were to no avail, the statement again, and again, and again.

The statement, when read without the interruptions with which the majority of the anti-communist heroes punctuated it, seems innocuous. It could be read, if not interrupted, in about three minutes. But when it was read, re-read, repeated, with varying emphasis but always the same round of words, for one hour, two hours, three hours—it was hypnotic in effect.

The reaction of the anti-communist heroes who were subjected to this followed a definite pattern, and one which had undesirable results.

Talked out, then shouting "Hui Taiwan" until he was hoarse or even dumb, the prisoner of war would subside on his bench while the brainwashing droned on. Feeling himself endangered by its hypnotic effect, he would appeal to the chairman to make them let him go. There was nothing in any of the agreements, terms or rules limiting the time of an interview. The chairman could only ask the explainers if they had finished with the man. No, they would reply politely, and go on and on and on.

In despair, worn out by his vocal action, the anti-communist hero then took physical action. Some blindly charged and attacked the explainers with their heads, fists, elbows, shoulders and feet. Others used more guile, moving their benches closer and closer as if to hear better, then picking up the bench when near enough and swinging it. Several, seeming interested in what the explainer had to say, moved closer to accept a cigarette from him, then smashed the pack or the lighted match into the explainer's face.

This placed almost everyone connected with the explanations in a most difficult position—particularly the explainers. Already so discomfited by their failure to persuade even a single man of his full freedom to return home to lead a peaceful life that even their North Korean colleagues seemed to be enjoying their loss of face, they were now in physical danger. This increased the strain they were under and tempted them to more outrageous lengths—which in turn increased their physical danger.

The CFI were placed in a difficult position. They were responsible for maintaining order—and the conduct of the anti-communist heroes, however much they were provoked, was definitely becoming disorderly. One Indian trooper had been standing beside each prisoner of war in the tent. Now they had to station a trooper on each side, with instructions to grab him if he made a move toward the explainers. Soon, in every tent in which the explanations were protracted, the anti-communist hero had an Indian trooper hanging on each of his arms.

The anti-communist heroes coming around the hill had, up until this point, been escorted by a single trooper. Now, as they passed along the alley back of the tents on the way to a tent which was ready for a new explainee, they could see their fellow POWs being held down on a bench or even struggling with two Indian troopers. This to them was definitely "use of force," and several of them made a break into a "busy" tent to help their comrades-at-arms. It became necessary for each to have two escorts, and as the tension mounted, they began struggling with their escorts. With some of the physically more powerful POWs in the tents it took four Indians, one to each arm and one to each leg, to restrain them.

The UNC representatives could not protest at the right of the CFI to maintain order, but could and did protest the unnecessary lengthening of the explanations and the forcing of the prisoners of war to sit and listen beyond a reasonable length of time. The anti-communist heroes were quick to follow up on this by putting their fingers in their ears and daring the Indian troopers to make them listen.

When the Indian troopers took the dare, as they often did, the UNC representatives and the Swedish and Swiss NNRC members protested.

It was a mess, and it steadily got worse, as the communist explainers and representatives doggedly insisted on their right to explain for as long as they wished. Increased force employed by the CFI to keep the explainees on their benches resulted only in increased effort by the anti-communist heroes to attack the explainers. When they could get loose, their violence was more extreme; tables were upset in the communists' faces and then used as battering rams to pin them against the wall of the tent. Here and there the general observers outside the tents would hear a shout and a scuffling of feet, then see a plastic tent wall back of the communist bench crash outwards.

The communist general observers gloated. As Coach had counselled, they had provoked so much disorder that it looked as though they just might have broken up the explanations, and saved themselves any further embarrassment such as they had undergone that morning, and thus far in the afternoon.

Then the communists gloated still more. Almost simultaneously in each of the two explanation areas, a prisoner of war stopped struggling with his escorts as he entered a tent, either ignored the UNC representative or spat at him, strode to the communist table, saluted, shook hands with each person sitting at it, and asked for repatriation. Without even waiting for the chairman's charge, he strode to the correct door for Red China and out into the compound, there to be greeted with a round of handclapping from the communist claque. Excitedly surrounding him after shaking hands all around again, they scuttled out the front gate with him and his Indian escort, up over the hill to where another NNRC subcommittee had waited vainly all day, up until that moment, to validate any requests for repatriation.

Communist agents both, over the hill but not yet out of the woods, for in giving themselves up during the first explanation session they had not accomplished the missions assigned to them.

In one compound, late in October, the anti-communist heroes discovered a communist agent before he had a chance to "bug out" or give himself up during explanations. His name was Wong Tsun-fei, alias Wong Wei-tsu, 23 years old, a native of Kiangsu, who had worked as an accountant in the finance bureau of the local government before he "volunteered" for service in Korea. (These details are included so that the faculty of the communist espionage school which he attended for three months may finally know what became of him.)

In April, 1953, he was assigned to secret team Code #424 for special investigation, assassination and counter-espionage duty. On June 25, 1953, he surrendered to the United Nations Command, swore that he was anti-communist, and was sent to join the anti-communist heroes on Cheju-do.

His mission was to collect data on all the leading anti-communists in his compound and enclosure, their true names, backgrounds, original units, etc. He was, further, to attempt to break up the anti-communist organization, create friction among the leaders and cultivate any wavering elements.

He was further instructed that when he presented himself for explanations he was to whisper his code number, 424. The communist explanation team would check his name and pass him a weapon for carrying out secret assassination.

According to Wong Wei, he was just one of three agents who surrendered at the same time to infiltrate and agitate in the anti-communist camp. The second was Chu Kuo-chang, 21, the other Sung Yu-kung, 24, both natives of Kiangsu.

In the explanations another day, one anti-communist hero amused newsmen no end by accepting one cigarette protruding from a freshly opened pack handed him by an explainer, then blandly putting the remainder of the pack in his pocket, denouncing the explainers, and going out the door to Formosa.

Now that the cigarette-pack pistol of Captain Kholkhov has been revealed as a standard Soviet assassination weapon, one cannot help but wonder if he were Chu or Sung. No word has ever come, at any rate, that it was a pistol and not an innocent pack of cigarettes.

As for Wong Wei, in the two months remaining for explanations his compound successfully converted him. He cried "Hui Taiwan!" when his compound underwent explanations, one of the last three days of the 90-day period, instead of "424!", and Taiwan is where he is today.

The net gain to the communists on this first day of explanations was only nine, however. This was Wang Hsu's compound 31. Wang Hsu had alibied his early bugout by telling Coach that Compound 31 was ready for repatriation en masse as a result of his fine work, and Coach had asked the NNRC for that particular compound by number, so that his boys could make a good showing in the first game of the series. Don't you agree that Wang Hsu was probably shot, and that night?

Explanations ended, in one tent at a time, around six o'clock. The UNC party at Compound A, that nearest the camp, waited some fifteen minutes for the convoy from Compound B, and it was not until they arrived that the total of six men lost to the communists from A and four from B was known to the UNC personnel, when the two groups added their scores for the day. The convoys joined, and ten minutes later came abreast of the first compound in the main camp. The compound, Korean, was out in force with its band, the men demonstrating as they had that morning. Barely discernible in the fading light were banners in Korean and English: "Congratulations, Chinese Compound 31!" they exulted. "Only ten traitors!" The POW communications system had scored another scoop. Each succeeding compound had similar banners, some thanking the UNC representatives, but all with the total of ten!

Notes could be tied to the always handy Korean rocks, for sling propulsion, and each compound had a high tower, as well, for flag, hand and arm signals.

The UNC representatives got back to Munsan-ni at seven-thirty, a fourteen-hour day and a fifteen-hour day by the time they had showered and suppered. They had never worked as hard in their lives, they had never gotten as emotionally wound up in their lives, they had never been as tired in their lives, and they had rarely been as happy. Each man could derive deep personal satisfaction from having shared in saving 481 fellow humans from death or a slave labor camp.

The post-mortems at the UNC headquarters went on until dawn. The consensus was that the Chinese anti-communist prisoners of war were the real heroes of the occasion.

Compound 31 held a post-mortem too, all night long. At noon the next day, when the men in the other compounds were taking the sunshine, playing volley ball or basketball, or thinking up new devices to baffle the explainers, Compound 31 was soundly wrapped in slumber. They had it made.

25

The Brainwashing Braintrust

In July, 1944, World War II was going badly for the Japanese, and Korea was being squeezed to the utmost for men and munitions as well as foodstuffs. Lee Chun Bong, a twenty-five-year-old primary school teacher in the South of Korea, with a wife and two children, found it impossible to reconcile his small wage with the rocketing price of food. He had been lucky, however, to avoid conscription at his age, even with a family.

Leaving his wife, son and daughter at home to work on the farm of a landlord, he beat his way to Manchuria to see if he couldn't find a better job. He found a job, but it didn't pay anything. The Japanese Kwantung Army authorities picked him up in Mukden and put him to work at forced labor in the Fushun coal mine—the same mine, formerly British-owned, which was shown so proudly to the visiting British Labor Party delegation by the Chinese communists ten years later—still being worked by forced labor in contrast to the silly British system of paying wages.

In the confusion attending the end of the war Lee escaped

from the coal mine, but, unable to find other work or make his way to South Korea, was finally reduced to joining the Chinese communist army. Although a Korean, he spoke acceptable Chinese by this time, and because of his educational background—twelve years of schooling, the equivalent of a U. S. high school education—he made rapid progress. In three years he was permitted to join the Communist Party, and in May, 1950, when 45,000 North Koreans in the Chinese Communist Forces were sent to Korea in preparation for the June invasion of the Republic of Korea, he was kept with the CCF. By this time he was a captain.

When the CCF entered the Korean conflict in October, 1950, Capt. Lee came along. Because of his proficiency in Chinese, Korean and Japanese he was often given political, liaison and interpreting assignments. With the signing of the armistice in Korea and the assembling of the brainwashing braintrust on the communist side, he was assigned as chief interpreter to North Korean Lieutenant General Lee Sang Cho, chief communist delegate then to the Military Armistice Commission.

As far as the UNC knew, during the explanations, General Lee Sang Cho was also the head of the communist brainwashing braintrust. It was he who signed all letters and made all representations from the "Northern Command" (the NNRC euphemism for the CCF and NKA commands) to the NNRC.

But behind Lee Sang Cho, who was only a three-star general and a Korean, there was an even more powerful, completely anonymous Chinese who was accorded four-star rank and honors, although he was a civilian. His name, according to Captain Lee, was Chiao Kuan-hua, alias Chiao Mu. In February,

208

1956, one Chiao Hisao-kuang, according to Radio Peiping, relieved Pan Tzu-li as Red Chinese ambassador to North Korea —another alias? By November, 1956, Chiao Kuan-hua had been promoted to assistant foreign minister of Red China, and left Peiping with Chou En-lai for a six week Asian tour.

A former newspaperman, Chiao has always been close to Chou En-lai, and was with him in Chungking during World War II. It was Chiao Mu who accompanied communist General Wu Hsiu-chuan to the U. N. General Assembly at Lake Success in 1950, assisting him in the diatribes against the U. S. and the U. N. which resulted in U. N. condemnation of communist China as an aggressor in Korea.

Now a major functionary in the Chinese Communist government, Chiao's career has not suffered too greatly because of his defeat in the Korean prisoner of war explanations, for he accompanied Chou En-lai to Geneva during the summer of 1954 for the conference there on Vietnam, as an advisor to the Red Chinese delegation. Another reason he may have survived the debacle in Korea, in addition to his friendship for Chou, may be the influence of his wife, Keng Peng, a long-time communist who was also included in the delegation to Geneva, as deputy to Huang Hua, delegation spokesman. Huang Hua will be remembered for his rage, during the abortive conversations attempting to arrange a political conference in Korea, at U. S. Ambassador Dean's uncomplimentary references to the lack of sanitary facilities and other amenities at Panmunjom, which the communists were urging as the site of the political conference.

General Lee Sang Cho did not even rank immediately under

Chiao, Captain Lee said, but was third man on the totem pole, under Tu Ping, chief of the CCF Political Department, and CCF delegate to the Military Armistice Commission. But he had two North Korean underlings, Major General Kim Il, chief of the North Korean explanation team, and Chu Yon, secretary of the North Korean delegation to the MAC.

As the interpreter between Chiao and Tu Ping, who spoke no Korean, and Lee Sang Cho and Kim Il, who spoke no Chinese, Captain Lee was present at every conference of the brainwashing braintrust. He also attended all of the explanation sessions, both Chinese and Korean, to interpret between General Kim, the Korean team chief, and Colonel Lee, the Chinese team chief.

"On the first day of explanations," Captain Lee broadcast for the Voice of the United Nations Command after he sought political asylum in South Korea in February, 1954, "only four Chinese communists requested repatriation. (He confirmed the fact that the other six had been communist agents.) This figure was far below expectations, so they reported this fact to Peking by message and asked for instructions. Peking wired back that the explanations should be stopped if they could not do any better. However, Lee Sang Cho and Chu Yon argued that it was too early to assess the chances of the explanations by the results of one day only, and insisted that they continue the explanations. This recommendation was transmitted to Peking. Peking wired back approval."

The brainwash braintrust stalled for one day, October 16, to permit this interchange of messages, by asking to explain on that day to 1,000 North Korean prisoners of war. General

Thimayya had as yet been unable to persuade the Koreans to leave their compounds, even with a guarantee that they would not be segregated. With Peiping's okay, they asked for 1,000 Chinese for the following day, October 17th, and two compounds of Chinese anti-communist heroes came out with a bounce, hoping to beat Compound 31's record.

The preceding day had been spent, on the communist side, in debriefing the explainers, a skull session on the part of the brainwash braintrust in which the (neutral!) Czech and Polish delegates to the NNRC participated, and extensive briefing of the explainers for the following day's work.

"When the anti-communist prisoners were reported to have said that they wanted to go to Taiwan," Captain Lee continued in his broadcast, "Chiao instructed the explainers to say that Taiwan would be 'liberated' soon. Even the Polish and Czech delegates objected that this violated the NNRC Rules of Procedure and the terms of reference of the armistice agreement, for it constituted a threat to the prisoners. Chiao over-ruled this objection, saying that this was the only way to win back the prisoners. As a last resort, Chiao ordered the explainers to stretch out their explanations for 4 to 5 hours to exasperate the U. N. observers and the Indians. Some explainers who refused to do this were later on told to 'criticize themselves,' and those who had been thus punished were so mad that they could not eat their suppers that night."

The anti-communist heroes were not idle that day, either. When the first Chinese prisoners appeared for the explanations the following morning, it was apparent that they had used their excellent communications network thoroughly to debrief Compound 31, and to be briefed by Compound 31.

The men came over the two hills to the explanation compounds laughing and joking with their Indian escorts, completely tractable and doing everything within their power to prevent development of a situation of physical conflict such as that of two days before. Realizing that the individual explanation sessions were going to be protracted, they were saving their strength for the communist explainers, not the Indians.

The first men into the explanation tents sat quietly and listened to the Kim-Peng statement. Then, ignoring the explainers, they turned to the NNRC chairman and politely expressed their choice—Taiwan.

With this the explainers embarked on their new routine.

"You want to go to Taiwan?" they asked. "Taiwan is a small island. Traitor Chiang had eight million troops, and we defeated them and him. Now he has only eight million defeated troops and civilians together. Sooner or later Taiwan will be liberated. Why, then, do you want to go to Taiwan? How can you go to Taiwan?

"It is unlawful for you to go to Taiwan. The armistice agreement carries no provision which permits you to go to Taiwan.

"To go to Taiwan is death!"

That was the approved text. Depending upon the enthusiasm of the explainer and the supposed susceptibility of the explainee, there were embellishments and additions, the purport of which was always: "If you go to Taiwan, we will take Taiwan and we will kill YOU!"

The resolve of the anti-communist heroes not to come into

conflict with their Indian guards, this day, was to no avail. All hell broke loose.

At the words "Traitor Chiang" the anti-communist heroes were galvanized. They ripped off their shoes and threw them at the explainers. When their guards again restrained them, they swung their guards themselves about so that they crashed into the explainers' tables.

The UNC representatives did not have to protest. The Swedish and Swiss NNRC members were on their feet, shouting. This was so flagrant a violation of the terms of reference, so direct a threat of force and violence, that it could not be permitted to continue.

In virtually every tent the Poles and Czechs were silent— which was unusual. Even they seemed to be ashamed of this excess on the part of their enforced allies.

In every tent, the Indian chairman immediately ruled against such tactics.

In every tent, the communist explainers completely ignored the ruling. They were out to break up the explanations. By fair means or foul does not apply; they knew no fair means. Some of them even went so far as to asseverate that Chiang Kai-shek was dead, that Taiwan was already ruled by Peiping.

The day degenerated into an even more shameful exhibition than the afternoon of the preceding explanation session. The communist explainers insisted on holding explainees with whom they thought they might stand a chance, for two hours, three hours and more. It was necessary to force the anti-communist heroes to sit and listen. The Swiss representatives threatened to go on strike and bring the explanations to a complete halt if this use of force did not stop. The Swedish representatives sent a senior officer to bring General Thimayya to the scene.

Nerves were wearing raw, all around. When the Swedish representative in Tent 16 of Area A protested at the protracted explanation there, the chief explainer leaped to his feet and roared, "The Swedish delegate is full of ——!"

This was a mistake. The Swedish subcommittee member in Tent 16 was the chief of staff of the Swedish component of the NNRC. A substitute explainer became necessary in Tent 16.

When the NNRC committee in another tent stumbled out for a break after another excessively prolonged session, the Swedish representative politely stood aside for an elbowing explainer. Then, following the explainer, the swagger stick under his arm barely touched the Chinese communist between his shoulder blades.

The Red yelled bloody murder. Someone had tried to stab him!

By dusk, six o'clock, only 429 anti-communist heroes—one compound—out of 1,000 who had volunteered for explanations had been interviewed. The usual six agents had been winnowed out, and three others had chosen repatriation. Explanations had concluded in Area B. Only one explanation was still in process, the one in Tent 16 of Area A. It had just passed three and one-half hours.

Indian guards had cordoned off Tent 16. Around them milled twenty-odd newsmen, ten from the U. N. side and a supposed ten but actually several more from the communist side. There were two-score UNC personnel, but two hundred communists. Tempers were thin, the air tense and the situation explosive.

The senior U. N. general representative, arriving from Area B, ordered all UNC personnel except those working in Tent 16 out of the compound and to their busses.

General Thimayya arrived and strode into Tent 16. The Indian troops had lighted gasoline lanterns inside the tent. All eyes turned to the general. The prisoner of war, now completely terrified, seized that opportunity to bolt out of the back of the tent, the door to Taiwan. In the alley he halted, in an agony of confusion as to whether or not he had made the right choice. No one else knew his choice; he had been mute for the entire three hours of expert, assiduous brainwashing.

As he hesitated in the alley, some thirty communists surged to the gap between Tents 15 and 16 and, egged on by communist propagandist Wilfred Burchett and a Czech officer, launched a noisy demonstration intended to turn him their way.

The two UNC representatives remaining in the compound had overlooked one U. S. Department of the Army civilian of Chinese birth, Charles Chao.

Chao was in the middle of the thirty-odd communists, their number now swelling as General Thimayya talked to the prisoner of war. He was not only in their midst, he was making almost as much noise as they, yelling "Hui Taiwan! Hui Taiwan!"

The communists started kicking Chao from all sides with their heavy boots, coldly, silently and efficiently, first in the knees and then, as he crumpled, in the groin, stomach and kidneys. One of the two UNC representatives saw him going down and dove in to the rescue, inadvertently bowling over the Czech in the process.

The UNC representative might also have been kicked to death in the dusk along with Chao had he not thought to yell, at the top of his voice, "I want Indian troops! I want Indian troops to protect this man who is being murdered by these communists!"

The Indian common soldiers, posted to keep the crowd away from Tent 16 and understanding only Hindi or Urdu, didn't budge. But a Sikh, Major H. S. Sandhu, six feet two, two hundred pounds, and every inch and every ounce an officer, plunged into the melee, together with most of the ten free world newsmen. The communists and their pseudo-newsman mentor faded away in the gathering darkness.

In his story on the fracas, one American correspondent said that a U. S. officer called a Polish officer a son-of-a-bitch. An investigation was ordered immediately. UNC personnel were enjoined to be on their best diplomatic behavior.

This gave rise to the usual wisecracks on the working level at the Munsan-ni camp in the post-mortems that night and the next day, Sunday. The first one to become current was "It wasn't a Pole, it was a Czech." The next one was a paraphrase of the old story about the piccolo player: "It isn't a question of who called the Pole a son-of-a-bitch; the question is, who called the son-of-a-bitch a Pole?"

There was pretty solid ground for this last question. In two days of explanations, it had already been noted by the language-skilled U. S. personnel that it was not unusual to hear two supposed Czechs conversing with each other in German, and two Polish officers who found it necessary, if they were to understand each other, to speak R-u-s-s-i-a-n.

General Thimayya had taken the brainwashed prisoner of war to the Indian field hospital, where, the next day, he was still so thoroughly terrified that he opted for repatriation. The score was now UNC 900, communists 20. If one excepted the obvious agents, as the communists did in their reckoning, it was 900 to 8.

The investigation established that no U. S. officer had called either a Pole or a Czech a son-of-a-bitch.

26

"To the Republic of Korea!"

For explanations on Monday, October 19, and each day that followed, the Northern Command again asked the NNRC for 1,000 Korean prisoners of war, fairly secure in their estimate that the Korean anti-communist heroes, obstinate as only Koreans can be, would persist in their refusal to leave their compounds.

When they did so persist, the Northern Command, backed by the Czechs and Poles on the NNRC, insisted that the CFI use force to make them leave their compounds and attend explanations. The Swedes and Swiss quite rightly opposed illegal use of force for such a purpose, the Swiss going so far as to threaten to withdraw from the NNRC if force were used. The Indians sided with the Swedes and Swiss. President Rhee also voiced his relentless opposition. So another plot of the Northern Command to provoke wide-scale disorder and a possible breakout attempt was defeated.

Each day, the Northern Command requested 1,000 Korean prisoners for the following day, and each day General Thorat informed General Thimayya and General Thimayya informed the Northern Command that they refused to leave their compounds. One thousand Chinese, however, would be happy to present themselves for explanations. No, the Northern Command wanted Koreans.

On the 30th of October, the brainwash braintrust got a shock. General Thimayya informed them that the North Korean prisoners of war would be pleased to present themselves for explanations at 0800 the next morning.

The communists had underestimated the leadership abilities of Generals Thimayya and Thorat and their principal subordinates, who now demonstrated that they were capable of commanding Korean troops as well as Indians and Chinese. Again, the argument which carried the day had a sporting flavor. In their daily visits to the Korean compounds the Indian generals and their brigadiers dwelt on the remarkable anti-communist showing made by the two Chinese compounds to undergo explanations, and the fact that other Chinese compounds were clamoring to better their records.

"We could beat them," the Koreans began to remark.

"Perhaps you could, but the Northern Command doesn't think so," the Indian officers would observe. "They ask only for Koreans, and will not accept any of the Chinese compounds which are volunteering to take your place, each day."

"We can beat the Chinese!" the Koreans affirmed.

"Right-ho," General Thimayya agreed. "What day shall we choose for the test?"

With leaders like that, the CFI didn't need to use force.

The first explanations to Korean anti-communist heroes came off on October 31. While they didn't do quite as well as the Chinese, with 21 repatriates out of 459 explainees that day, it cannot be said to have been entirely their fault. They had simply been infiltrated by more agents than had the Chinese, and they had not screened their ranks as thoroughly as had the Chinese at their last opportunity, at the time of "Big Switch."

The explainers were even more insulting with respect to President Rhee than they had been to the Chinese with respect to President Chiang. As a result the same violence developed as the day wore on, until it was taking up to five Indian troopers to hold one anti-communist hero quiescent. In addition, the UNC observers were now officers of the Army of the Republic of Korea, and when the explainers got out of line they did not hesitate to protest to the NNRC chairman, politely but firmly. In not one single instance did a ROKA officer depart from perfect diplomatic protocol—but they made their presence felt. But it was still, after all, a violation of the NNRC rules of procedure to make these objections before the interview had concluded.

Here was drama of a high order. Here was a direct contrast. Here were officers of the same blood, same language, same background, sitting in the same tent after an armistice in what had been for them a civil war. The communist Korean officers lied, cajoled, cheated, threatened, breaking every rule in the book in an attempt to get men who had served in their commands to come back to them.

The Republic of Korea officers were proud, upright, legitimate in their every protest, and unswerving in their defense of the right to freedom of these soldiers who had fought against them and whom they had captured or whose surrender they had accepted.

Comparing Koreans after eight years of communism and eight years of true democracy, it was easy to understand why these soldiers chose the Republic of Korea, even sight unseen. What was difficult to understand was why even 21 of them chose the so-called "People's Democratic Republic of Korea." The latter is a semantic travesty.

At six-thirty on this first day of Korean explanations, it is quite dark and all of the tents have emptied except, again, troublesome Tent 16, into which a crowd of communists are peering. The last explainee has already gone out the back door, headed for freedom in the Republic of Korea, and the Indian chairman was adjourning for the night.

"Just a moment, Mr. Chairman," the UNC representative said, politely but firmly. He was Captain Alfred Phillips, U. S. Army. He had not lost a single anti-communist hero to the explainers the whole of the day, but he had a protest nevertheless.

"Mr. Chairman," he continued, "in the very first interview this morning the explaining representative of the other side repeatedly violated the Geneva Convention, the terms of reference and the rules of procedure. He insisted on continuing to talk when the prisoner of war represented to you that he did not wish to hear any further explanations, and that he wished to go to the Republic of Korea, that he did not wish to be repatriated to North Korea.

"He directed abusive language toward the observer of the United Nations Command, an officer of the Army of the Republic of Korea. He insisted on continuing his explanations while the delegate of Switzerland had been excused to go to the latrine and the session should have been suspended. He threatened the prisoner of war with allegations of future communist military victories, by gesture and bombast, and by promising reprisals against the family of the prisoner of war. He demanded from the prisoner of war answers to improper questions.

"When the prisoner of war chose not to be repatriated and, in complete compliance with the rules of procedure I had waited until the interview was finished to call your attention to these violations, you said, 'Later, later, at the end of the morning session.'

"When, at the end of the morning session, I again attempted to call your attention to these violations, you said, 'Later, later, at the end of the day.'

"The explaining representatives, encouraged by your laxity and exacerbated by their failure to persuade a single prisoner of war in this tent to choose repatriation, simply increased the number and variety of their flagrant violations. Had these violations influenced a single prisoner of war, I should have made this representation to you at that time; since they did not, I make it now in behalf of the prisoners of war who may receive explanations in this tent tomorrow.

"I now ask you to admonish these explaining representatives respecting these violations, and to warn them that such violations will not be tolerated in the future. If you do not so admonish and warn them, I shall repeat what I have just said to

222

the representatives of the world press, whom I now see congregating outside the door of this tent."

The chairman had caught a Tartar. But he apologized handsomely, and he duly and fully admonished and warned the explainers.

"I have been tense and over-wrought as a result of the highly emotional situation in these explanations," he told Captain Phillips. "You are quite right. I should have heard you, and warned the explaining representatives, at the end of the first interview."

He shook hands contritely with Captain Phillips. The Swedish and Swiss delegates congratulated him on his fine stand and pumped his arm effusively.

The Czech and the Pole hung back until the tent emptied and the crowd of newsmen and communists had left the door. They too, then, shook hands with Captain Phillips, bowed correctly, straightened, saluted, and left the tent.

There was never any more trouble in Tent 16. Captain Phillips was roundly berated by Radio Peiping for his "insolent and outrageous conduct"—but that, in a way, was a sort of citation.

Radio Peiping was thumping hard on another drum at the same time. Early in October, two communist agents had "bugged out" of Chinese Compound 28, with a wondrous tale cooked up between them. One Chang Tzu-lung, they said, had refused to participate in a demonstration following the disturbance on October 2, Ghandi's birthday, and had therefore been beaten to death by "Kuomintang agents," shouting to the last, "Long live Chairman Mao! Long live the Communist Party!"

These "Kuomintang agents" were then supposed to have eaten—so help me—his heart, liver and kidneys. Then the body was alleged to have been buried, deep under one of the tents in the compound.

In the subsequent explanations, one of the rehabilitation chiefs was not only accused of having ordered Chang's murder, but of having helped eat his heart and liver, in an effort to alienate any dependence the anti-communist heroes might have placed upon him. "Heart and liver," incidentally, is a single Chinese word with a connotation much the same as the Southern American "liver and lights."

After hearing this tale of grisly cannibalism half a dozen times in one morning a Swedish sub-committee member braced the rehabilitation chief, now serving as a general UNC observer, in the enclosure.

"How did you have this liver?" he inquired. "Well done?"

Too much liver was a constant gripe among the UNC explanation staff, who followed up liver for lunch, while they looked enviously at the Swedish contingent's steak, with liver for dinner. The explanations staff camp was expertly organized in every respect save one, the mess. Major Ryan of the British component audibly wondered how a steer could be driven that far north in Korea with no legs, marching only on his liver.

Not only Radio Peiping but General Lee Sang Cho pounded away at the NNRC and CFI on this alleged murder, for the remainder of the month of October. While the CFI during the last two weeks of October, backed by a majority of the NNRC, rightly refused to use force to make the North Korean anti-communist prisoners of war come out of their compounds for explanations, murder was something else. The CFI had every right under the Geneva Convention to insist that the prisoners of war live up to the disciplinary standards of the Indian Army. And the code of military justice of the Indian Army, as of every other army, is very sticky on the subject of murder.

On November 1, therefore, while the second day's explanations to the Korean anti-communist heroes were under way, CFI troops surrounded Compound 28 and ordered the Chinese occupants into the inner alley of the compound. Then the two communist agents, Chien Sung-kuei and Yu Hseuh-ho—the NNRC neutrals and the CFI, of course, had no way of establishing that they were communist agents—led a digging party to the very tent where the body was supposed to be buried.

As with virtually every other compound in the camp, the site of Number 28 had been bulldozed bare and level, and beyond the first foot or so it was immediately obvious that no shovel had ever turned the soil under this particular tent. But sweating Indian soldiers with engineer tools dug an enormous hole through the virgin Korean clay, stopping only to pry aside a particularly obstreperous rock, until at a depth of four feet they came to something just about the size of a man's body.

It was an enormous root, flooring with its appendages the entire excavation. It was obvious that it, too, had never been disturbed. Both the communist and free world press had been invited to witness the exhumation, and the free world press gave their Red confreres quite a working over at this development.

Despite the farce of the exhumation, General Lee Sang Cho renewed his pressure. There had been a murder, he insisted, and he had two eyewitnesses. If the CFI would shake the compound down properly, the murderers could be identified and more witnesses produced.

On the 2d of November, the CFI did just that. The men in Compound 28 were paraded one at a time past Chien and Yu. They put the finger on seven "murderers"—the most militant anti-communists in the compound—and ten "witnesses"—the fellow communist agents they had left behind. The NNRC took all seventeen into custody. The "witnesses" had a ready story to explain the disappearance of the body. The alleged murderers, they said, had been tipped off to the investigation, four days ahead of time, and had dug it up and burned it. This was quite a trick, since there had never been a Chang Tzu-lung in the compound, and the earth of his "grave" could NEVER have been turned *five* times—out, in, out, in, out!

On the 1st, the explainers had regained only 19 out of 483 Korean explainees. The North Command asked for neither Koreans nor Chinese for explanations the 2d or 3d, but on the 3d they suddenly asked for Chinese for explanations the 4th. Compound 28 would be just dandy, they said.

This was the test. If the Chinese anti-communist heroes were actually terrorized, as Communist propaganda clamored, by "Kuomintang agents," and so prevented from requesting repatriation, then, with the seven supposed Kuomintang agents in Compound 28 neatly removed and their organization disrupted, Compound 28 should unanimously opt for repatriation.

226

Compound 28 received explanations on November 4. Two men requested repatriation.

With the score now at some 2,300 for the anti-communists and 62 for the communists, Coach heard from the alumni association.

"Peking angrily accused Chiao of having continued explanations despite their instructions not to do so," Captain Lee Chun Bong's story continued, "and told him to assume the full responsibility for the failure. Chiao was therefore upset and decided to take revenge. He asked the Indians to produce 500 prisoners out of which he only gave explanations to 250. (Actually, he gave explanations to only 136 in an entire day.) He then returned the entire 500 back to their compound, being fully aware that it would be practically impossible to segregate the 250 who had been explained to from the 250 who had not been explained to. He then demanded that the other 250 be produced for explanations, but the Indians were unable to segregate these two groups. Chiao then declared that it was impossible to go on with the explanations and so the explanations came to an end."

The handwriting was on the plastic walls of the explanation tents. Of the 136 Chinese anti-communist heroes who received explanations on November 5, only two were persuaded to request repatriation despite the extended brainwashing they received. In thirty-two tents, in eight hours, only 136 received explanations—an average of between four and five men per tent for the whole day, and two hours for each explanation. Actually, the explainers alternately droned and shouted at some of the prisoners for as long as five hours.

In Tent Number 3, Area A, an obviously ill POW withstood this hammering from about 9:15 a.m. until noon. The explainers demanded that he be presented again after the lunch recess. The chief UNC general observer insisted that he be examined by an Indian Red Cross doctor to determine his physical condition. In a cursory examination, without a thermometer, stethoscope or any means of determining his blood pressure, the doctor reported that his pulse and temperature seemed normal, and that his *physical* condition did not rule out his ability to withstand prolongation of his ordeal.

The chief UNC observer accepted this, since the Indian Red Cross personnel were all Indian Army medical, sanitation and welfare officers, seconded to the Red Cross for the occasion, and their solicitude for the prisoners of war was unvarying. But the UNC representative in Tent 3 (Colonel Meisling, Chinese-speaking and fully cognizant of the growing terror in the mind of the man) told newsmen during the lunch break that it was "like watching mankind die before your very eyes and not being able to do anything about it."

The inquisition was resumed after lunch and the prisoner requested repatriation. However, at the validation tent the Swiss member protested that the man seemed out of his mind, and the chairman ordered him sent to the Indian field hospital. After a thorough physical examination which still found him physically okay, and after twenty-four hours' rest, he recovered from the near-coma to which the brainwashing had reduced him. He came to feebly whispering "Hui Taiwan." He had no recollection of having requested repatriation.

Close attention by the free world press to the explanations

was the greatest guarantee the anti-communist heroes had against injustices such as the foregoing, and some distinguished correspondents blazoned their valiant stand far and wide. Outstanding among the correspondents covering the explanations were Bob Alden of *The New York Times,* Jack Casserly and Bob Elegant of International News Service, Frank Jordan and James Morrissey of United Press, Dwight Martin and Jim Greenfield of *Time,* John Osborne of *Life,* Bob Pierpoint of the Columbia Broadcasting System, John Randolph of the Associated Press, Walter Simmons of the *Chicago Tribune,* Alfred Smoular of *"Paris Match"*, Earl H. Voss of the *Washington Star* and Jimmy Wei of *China News.* There were many others, and omission from this list by no means dismisses their efforts.

A vote among the others would probably have awarded the palm to Jimmy Wei, publisher as well as chief foreign correspondent of *China News,* Taipei's leading English language daily, and managing director now as well of the China Broadcasting Corporation, the Nationalist Government's radio network on Taiwan. During explanations to the Chinese anti-communist heroes, Jimmy could translate for his fellow newsmen, honestly and ably, and to him his compatriots owe a deep debt of gratitude.

27

The Achilles Heel of Communism

By the device of asking daily for the remainder of the Chinese compound interviewed on November 5, Chiao was able to bring the embarrassing explanations to a halt for another ten days. In the meantime, Peiping clamored noisily on the one hand that "Chiang agents" were guilty of halting the explanations, and Lee Sang Cho was strongly pushing the position that the Northern Command could have 90 days of explanations, not 90 days within which to conduct explanations, as provided in the armistice agreement. Since the communists had actually conducted explanations on only 6 days, and knew that they could put them off indefinitely, to accede to such a preposterous position would have permitted them to prolong the period indefinitely, for months and even years.

Attrition, as malcontents "bugged out" not because they had relaxed in their anti-communism but because of a flare-up in their barbed wire fever, and death, as the men grew older, would liquidate the troublesome problem of the prisoners for the communists.

The United Nations Command steadfastly insisted that the other side abide by the terms of the armistice.

At this stage of the explanations the free world press was also giving the communists a hard time. On November 10 the distinguished military commentator of *The New York Times,* Hanson W. Baldwin, wrote as follows under the heading "Red Faces in Korea."

"The prisoner of war 'explanations' at Panmunjom have resulted, so far, in a major loss of face for the communists.

"The interviews and explanations have been grotesque and fantastic. . . . Yet the whole process, difficult though it has been for the individual prisoner, has resulted in a triumph of individualism. Men have dared to pit their desires and beliefs against the conformist doctrine of communism. And so far, the men have won.

"The stout opposition of most of the 22,000 Chinese and Korean prisoners to a return to communism is undoubtedly one of the most severe ideological defeats communism has suffered since the desertion of thousands of Red Army men in the first months of the German invasion of Russia in World War II.

"Slightly more than 200 of these 22,000 prisoners have elected to return to their communist-dominated motherlands, and only sixty-five of these 200 as a result of the enforced 'explanations.' No amount of double-talk on the part of the communists can explain away such statistics.

"This victory in the war of ideas is of major importance in Asia, where anti-communist fortunes have long been at low ebb. 'Face,' or a sort of indefinable pride, is an important element in Oriental politics. There is no doubt that Peiping and

Pyongyang and their communist overlords have lost great face during the Panmunjom 'explanations.' . . . Panmunjom has again revealed the Achilles heel of any communist or any dictatorial government. Moscow can never be sure of its armies. Least of all, after Panmunjom, can Moscow be sure of the armies of its satellites and friends. . . .

"These events, in addition to a new understanding of the malevolent nature of the communist evil gained by the Indian troops at Panmunjom by first-hand contact, may have a lasting importance in Asia. The more adult understanding of communism which experience has given to the Indians may even have some effect in New Delhi. Certainly the immediate impact of all recent Korean events is to put the communists on the psychological defensive . . . the unwilling puppets at Panmunjom by their exposure of Communist weakness may yet influence the course of history."

John Randolph of Associated Press had this to say at the same time:

"The United Nations and the United States have won their greatest moral victory in Korea since they took up the communist armed challenge forty months ago.

"The victory was the smashing defeat of the communists last week in the prisoner of war explanations and in the eyes of the three truly neutral nations serving in Korea, Sweden, Switzerland and India.

"Long delayed in coming, costly in blood and treasure, it will remain one of the brightest achievements of the free world. For it is the establishment and living proof of a principle of free choice that could some day topple the communist empire into ruins.

"There were many heroes in the battle.

"Part of them were the disillusioned, vengeful and enormously resolute little Chinese and Korean soldiers who marched into the interview tents after three years of captivity and voted—ninety-seven percent—to spurn home if it meant communism.

"The others were the GIs, the ROKs, and the other United Nations fighters who suffered and died during an extra year of war to buy them the right to reject their Red masters.

"Powerful allies in the struggle were the Swiss, the Swedish and the Indian neutrals, who stood firm for right last week and showed up the communist drive for what it was—a ruthless, cynical and utterly heartless power play for the possession of the prisoners' bodies and souls.

"As the week drew to a close yesterday the communists were routed. They knew it. Every move they made was a desperate groping for escape from a defeat and rejection so overwhelming that for once these grim world politicians were made to look ridiculous on the world stage.

"And just as it was a defeat for the communists, so it was an overwhelming vindication for the United Nations leaders, most of them American. For two long years these men had been working in Washington, in the United Nations and here at Panmunjom to give these prisoners, victims of communist wars, the right to choose their future. They were often misunderstood and criticized and so was their country.

"As far as is known, none of these men have been here to

233

watch the actual explanations. This is a pity. For this sight, one of the most unusual in the history of nations, would have been an unforgettable reward. . . .

"By Friday, when the talks were cancelled as the result of the Reds' slowdown tactics and 'inhumanly long' interviews, a total of 2,204 prisoners had appeared before the desperate Red explainers. Sixty-four returned, 2.9 per cent. . . .

"How can such overwhelming figures stand up? How could such figures still be valid 18 months after the original screening?

"There are three reasons:

"1. These men are anti-communists. They didn't need to be wooed or persuaded. All they needed was an opportunity to revolt against the machine that had oppressed them, used them for cannon fodder and even in many cases murdered their families.

"2. They had decent treatment in captivity. Once the UN got its communist dominated compounds under control, these men got better food, clothing and shelter than the ROK Army itself. They were treated, perhaps for the first time in their lives, as human beings. All they lacked was freedom, and they were amazingly patient in waiting for it. As one North Korean told an explainer this week, 'I lived better the last three years in the compounds than I did the five years before in North Korea.'

"3. They were not overpersuaded. Contrary to what the communists and many neutrals thought, the United Nations never solicited these men. In fact, at the time they were screened, everything possible was done to persuade them to return home so as to speed the Armistice. To enter an anti-communist camp, a prisoner had to be a real anti-communist.

"And here the United States owes a great debt to some unknown officer or State Department advisor for one of the most brilliant strokes in the history of psychological warfare. That was the extraordinarily important wording of the first key question in the prisoners' screening last year.

"That question was 'Would you resist repatriation?'

"There were other questions, too, but if the answer to this was 'no' or even hesitation, the prisoner was sent to a communist camp. Only those whose minds were so firmly made up that they were willing to fight, even to die to be free of the Reds, were admitted to the anti-communist camps.

"The wording of that question and its first place on the list has had its end result—the triumphant vindication of the United Nations' long fight against neutral doubts and communist slanders. It was well done. If it had not been, the United States today might be suffering a moral disaster as great as the communists are actually suffering.

"For it is a disaster and they realize it.

"It has seemed to everyone on the scene that from the end of their first shocking rejection on October 15 the Reds have done only two things: Try to convince themselves it just isn't so, and to get out of it when they realized it was.

"In doing so they have exposed themselves as cynical manipulators to the upright and idealistic Indian command. They have disgusted the stoutly neutral and stubbornly honest Swiss and Swedes . . .

"The reaction of the communist high commands to this

brutal disillusionment must be extremely serious. Not only have they miscalculated an extremely important principle and propaganda move, but they have an even more serious reason for alarm, one that must chill even the Kremlin.

"This is the exposure before the whole world that even a Red Army is only three fifths Red at most. This is a terrible admission. What would America think if its Army and its people were found to be two fifths communist? For the United States and for the rest of the free world, this week just past is a bright week, the reward for months and years of shaping morality and idealism into workable principles—a difficult and unappreciated task . . .

"This, for the communists, is a staggering defeat. For its effects will spread and penetrate sooner or later into all parts of the world, inside and outside the communist empire.

"That empire today is reckoned at about 800 million people, almost half the world population.

"But this week Panmunjom revalued those figures. They are no longer what they seem. For by vindicating the fact that two fifths of the Red Armies in Korea were bitter anti-communists this week's development has greatly shrunk that empire.

"For these figures overwhelmingly suggest that inside the communist lands there are not millions, but hundreds of millions of hate filled anti-communists. Silent allies, waiting only for the chance to fight, even to die, for their freedom."

The Kremlin read what Messrs. Baldwin and Randolph wrote, and what many others wrote. In his belligerent foreign policy speech in February, 1955, on the occasion of the abject resignation of Premier Malenkov, Soviet Foreign Minister

236

Molotov drew particular attention to the fact that 77% of the members of the Red Army are either Communist Party or Young Communist League members.

That won't help. In a survey of the Chinese anti-communist heroes on Taiwan after they were liberated, the Ford Foundation found that more than 4,000 of these men, too, had been members of the Communist Party.

28

"Resist Russia—Oppose Communism!"

But despite the resounding defeat of the communists, at this point an unfortunate rivalry—unfortunate from their standpoint as it turned out—sprang up between the Chinese and Korean brainwashers.

From the first day of the explanations, one could not escape the observation that the Korean observers enjoyed the discomfiture of the Chinese explainers, and vice versa. When the Chinese were on the receiving end of the anti-communist heroes' counter-explanations, the Korean observers were impassive so long as they were with the Chinese in the explanation tents. But at the noon recesses and when they knocked off for the evening and gathered among themselves, they exhibited the only indications of amusement to come from the communist side during the explanations—except the parallel indications from the Chinese when the POWs were dishing it out to the Koreans and the Koreans were taking it.

On a percentage basis, the Korean explainers had done a better job than the Chinese explainers, for probable reasons which have already been advanced. And it was Chiao, a Chinese, who was masterminding the operation, and Chiao who was under fire from Peiping.

Under such circumstances, a little needling was inevitable, and on November 15th, General Lee Sang Cho—a North Korean—requested a Korean compound for interviews the next day. There may have been a little needling from the NNRC, too, for with each request for the remainder of the Chinese compound which had already undergone partial explanations, the NNRC was enabled to suggest interviewing one of the ready and willing Korean compounds.

The senior Swiss member of the NNRC, veteran diplomat Armand Daeniker, pointed out to Robert Alden of *The New York Times* that the communists still had plenty of time, at the rate of 500 prisoners of war a day, to complete explanations to all of the anti-communist heroes within the remaining days of the allotted ninety.

"But they (the communists) just do not seem to want to go on with the explanations because they have been going against them," Mr. Daeniker said. "We have had to overcome one obstacle after another that they have set in our path."

Two hundred and twenty-seven Korean anti-communist heroes received explanations on November 16, and only six requested repatriation. If the usual ratio prevailed, the six included four communist agents and two victims. General Lee Sang Cho demanded the remainder of this compound for interviews the following day, and thus brought the explanations to a complete halt for thirty-four of the remaining thirty-seven days of the 90-day period.

It was the only out for the communist side. The United Nations Command would have vastly preferred daily explanations, and a daily propaganda beating for the enemy—but Chiao and Peiping had had enough. There had been sufficient explanations to both Chinese and Korean anti-communist heroes, chosen not at random but in a pattern which the communists' own intelligence told them best stacked the cards against the POWs, to prove that they were far from terrorized, that they were not controlled by "Chiang and Rhee agents," and that they genuinely, wholeheartedly rejected repatriation to communism.

The POWs were frankly disappointed at the end of the explanations, for by this time there were wagers galore between compounds and between nationalities on who could make the better anti-communist showing.

The anti-communist heroes had learned to spare their strength, and in the later explanations each compound turned up with a different set of tactics.

Every man of the 483 Koreans on November 1, for instance, had worn a mask. These depicted goats, pigs, horses, Marshal Kim Il Sung of North Korea, etc. Those who wore Kim Il Sung masks—and fat, pudgy Kim was a subject who lent himself beautifully to caricature—took them off and stamped on them once they were in the explanation tents. Others insisted on wearing their animal masks until the explainers had run through their routine, then took them off to point out politely that even a pig would be smarter than to fall for such guff, and so on. The masks were really works of art, and Brigadier Gurbaksh-Singh, the Sikh with the Korean friends, proudly carried one off at the end of the day as a souvenir.

240

The men of another Korean compound happily ran foot races with their Indian escorts, all day long. This may have been a CFI tactic to restore good feelings all around, but no matter who thought of it, it was a big success and everyone enjoyed it, even, a little surreptitiously, North Korean Major General Kim Il. The Koreans are notable track stars and fans, and the Korean anti-communist heroes invariably won their sprints.

Coming over the hill for the explanations, the POW would race against his Indian escort until the latter, exhausted, dropped out of the unequal contest. Then another trooper would take him on, until the anti-communist hero arrived at the explanation compound completely out of breath.

Then he would listen attentively to one run-through of the explanation patter, and quietly, reasonably, still seated on his bench, take command. One Korean listened to everything the explainers had to say, then calmly and in English for the benefit of the NNRC committee, chided the explainers.

"That was not a very convincing explanation," he told them. "You know, I used to be a company political officer. If I had your job, I would say—" and he launched into a persuasive harangue which was, really, far more devastating than the material with which the explainers had been provided.

Here the explainers protested to the chairman at the fact that he was speaking in English, and insisted that he be made to speak in Korean. The chairman consulted the remainder of the NNRC subcommittee, and they, vastly bored at the deadly repetitiousness of the usual round of explanation and highly intrigued by this novelty, agreed that there was nothing in

241

any of the regulations compelling him to speak in Korean. In fact, there was nothing in any of the regulations compelling him to speak at all. The Czech and the Pole voted right along with the other three, perhaps the only instance of unanimity in the entire NNRC proceedings.

"Then *I* would say," continued the anti-communist hero—and he proceeded to blast his own argument to bits.

The explainers got rid of him as quickly as possible, all of them pointing to the door leading to the Republic of Korea.

A Chinese, one of many to employ the same tactics, spoke to the explainers quite calmly and reasonably. "I was one of your recruiters in Hopeh Province," he said. "I visited the villages and persuaded the young men to join the so-called People's Liberation Army, promising them everything. Those who still refused to join, I noted for the press-gangs who followed me. Then, along with my victims, I suddenly found myself a 'volunteer' in Korea, with Koreans who had no wish to be 'liberated' fleeing before us. Is it any wonder that neither I nor the young men to whom I lied in your behalf wish no return to such a vicious system?"

The standard ending for each such gambit was an invitation for the explainers to accompany the POW to Formosa or the Republic of Korea. The fifty communist drivers just outside the compounds were a potent reason none ever accepted the invitation. Despite the prohibition on weapons in the area for which the CFI was responsible, there was an occasional glimpse of a sub-machine gun butt or muzzle under the seats of their jeeps. One day General Kim Il himself waddled into the explanation compound with his pistol still strapped to his waist, and gave it up to an Indian custodian most ungraciously when it was noted. The shoulder holster market in Kaesong must have boomed during this period.

Other POWs were less eloquent than the ex-recruiter but no less resourceful. From the moment of the first attempted violence against the explainers, each anti-communist hero was greeted as he entered the explanation compound alley by a giant Sikh officer who had gone to the trouble of learning how to say "Don't be afraid!" in both Korean and Chinese. As he said it, he patted their pockets to be sure they were smuggling in no weapons.

Despite these precautions a number of Koreans produced baseball-sized rocks on occasion, and one whipped out a knife with which he came within an ace of slitting an explainer's throat. But these were elementary compared to the ruse of one Korean.

His right forearm was in a neat, clean sling. It had obviously been broken—you could see the splints protruding from the bandage at his wrist. Pretending full acceptance of what the explainer was saying, he kept pulling his bench nearer with his one good hand, and finally accepted a cigarette. As he rose and manipulated the cigarette awkwardly with his left hand in letting the explainer give him a light, he slipped his right arm out of the sling and started beating the hapless communist about the head and ears with his cast. Surprise is an important element in any military maneuver; he got a number of good licks in before he was recaptured, and several more on top of those before he could be said to have really re-surrendered.

Not only were the nerves of the prisoners of war and the

explainers strained; had the explanations continued on a daily basis it is not at all improbable that incidents such as the attack on UNC Observer Chao might have multiplied. As the explanations which were scheduled proceeded, everyone got a little short-tempered. The communist violations were so flagrant and the brainwashing so vile that even the Czechs and Poles again seemed ashamed of these allies of theirs.

That there were no incidents involving others than the anti-communist heroes and the communist explainers, aside from the attack on Chao, was due in large measure to the vigilance and unfailing good humor of Generals Thimayya and Thorat, and their senior staff officers.

The junior officers of the Indian NNRC delegation were also outstanding. This is no reflection on the efficient junior officers of the CFI, who were, of course, the regularly assigned officers of the crack troops making up the brigade. But the junior officers of the NNRC delegation were put through extensive psychological and personality tests before they were assigned, to be sure that they had the cool-headedness, judgment and other necessary qualities for their most difficult assignment.

It was just as well that they had been chosen so carefully, for the whole of the Indian NNRC delegation were under constant pressure from the communists. The few instances in which their nerves too became raw were wholly excusable. One of the subjects on which communist pressure was unremitting was the subject of "signalling."

As a result of the CFI's prohibition on cameras in their area, a ban with which the United Nations Command was most happy to cooperate since most of the prisoners were terrified

of being photographed and most of the Chinese UNC observers not pleased at the idea, photographs of the area were at a
premium. One Sunday a number of UNC personnel disregarded the danger of mines and climbed to the top of the
highest hill outside the DZ and overlooking the camp. With
telephoto lenses—standard equipment for anyone who had
inexpensively indulged his camera hobby in Japan—they photographed the entire panorama.

Not a day elapsed before the communists officially complained of "signalling" from this height. The NNRC was
forced to pass the complaint to the United Nations Command,
and it became necessary to put the hill off-limits.

The day the Chinese POW was made mentally ill by the protracted brainwashing, and called back for more of the same
after the lunch recess, the chief UNC observer with an assistant was on a hillside overlooking the compound. Directly in
line with, but fully seventy-five yards from Tent 3, in which
the recessed explanation had now resumed, he was sitting on a
shooting stick with arms crossed, thumbs back of his biceps,
four fingers of each hand in front. In the bright autumn sunlight, he could see nothing inside the dark tent; the groggy
prisoner of war could not possibly see him.

Nevertheless, the communist explainers protested that he was
"signalling" to the POW, and the Indian Air Force chairman
was forced to come out of the tent and shout a request that
he move . . . "and stop signalling, please!"

Laughing, the observer and his assistant withdrew some
twenty-five yards to the north, where General Thimayya and

his chief of staff, Brigadier B. M. Kaul, were also watching Tent 3 with interest.

"So help me, General Thimayya," he said, still laughing, "I wasn't signalling!"

"Oh, come now," said Brigadier Kaul. "I've heard about this 'four finger' signal of yours. Just what does it convey?"

After a warning that the information was most un-neutral, they were told.

Four fingers upraised—not horizontal with crossed arms—is the "V" sign of the anti-communist opposition in Red China. Along with the figure four, in both Chinese and Arabic configuration, it is found everywhere, drawn in the dust, scratched or painted on walls and scrawled on communist posters.

The anti-communist heroes brought it with them to the prisoner of war camps, passed it on to the Koreans and then to the UNC personnel. It has many meanings, of which the simplest and most direct is "Death to the Communists!" It also means "Resist Russia—Oppose Communism!" and "Freedom will come from the four corners of the earth, across the four seas, on the four winds."

The word *four*—*ssu* in Mandarin and *shi* in Japanese—is a direct homonym for the word *death* in all of the languages connected with Chinese or borrowing from it. The ROK Army did not dare have a Fourth Division, so they made it the "Capitol" Division instead.

When the UNC representatives waved back to the demonstrating compounds in Freedom Camp, they tucked in their thumbs and spread their fingers. When an anti-communist hero in the explanation tents who was being brainwashed almost beyond human endurance threw a despairing glance at any of the UNC personnel, they would do their best to flash him the four fingers. All it meant was "Keep a stiff upper lip" or "Stay in there—fight!" And who could wish him less?

The communist explainers, however, who knew very well the other meanings, were always prompt to protest when they detected it, and it began to assume in the minds of the Indian personnel some vast significance of great import. Well, it does have great import.

One UNC representative who won the hearts of the POWs —he had traveled to the DZ with them on an LST and then the Korean train from Inchon—was Captain David E. Pihl, U. S. Air Force. Captain Pihl had been selected for DZ duty because he spoke fluent Swedish. The invariable salute to the UNC representative and observer with which the anti-communist heroes had started the explanations had become a little difficult to render when the prisoner of war entered the tent with an Indian trooper on each arm. But when the men entered Captain Pihl's tent, they never failed to pivot with their escorts and salute, with the Indian if he could not be shaken off. The Indian troopers, however, magnificently disciplined and respecting military courtesy, usually cooperated.

This began to get on the nerves of the communist explainers, and they protested to the chairman. The chairman inquired if Captain Pihl could not dispense with these exchanges of courtesies. Captain Pihl expostulated that it was the men who initiated them, that they were not prisoners but prisoners of war, soldiers, and that when a soldier of any army saluted him—and that included members of the CCF and NKA, if *they* ever got around to military courtesy, he, by golly, was going to stand up at attention and return the salute.

The chairman bought that, and the men went right on saluting Captain Pihl come hell or high water.

The UNC representatives and observers wore, in common with all U. S. and many United Nations troops in Korea, U. S. Army fatigue caps with cardboard inserts so that they stood straight, stiff and military, somewhat on the order of a French Army kepi. Captain Pihl had two of these caps. Pasted on the inside of the top of one of them, where a Chinese anti-communist hero could not fail to see it as the captain held it in his lap by the visor, was a 3 by 5 inch Chinese Nationalist flag. The other cap, for days when there were Korean explanations, had a ROK flag.

The Indian troopers got the biggest boot of all out of it, and never gave him away.

All of the UNC representatives had been carefully grilled in diplomatic protocol, and were most punctilious in addressing the NNRC subcommittee members and in referring to the explainers. The latter, in keeping with the language of the armistice agreement, were always referred to as the representatives of the Korean People's Army or the Chinese People's Volunteers, although it was admittedly difficult to do so without an access of nausea.

In a heated exchange one day, therefore, it was understandable that Colonel William R. Robinette, USA, in speaking to the Indian chairman, referred to the KPA representative as the "communist" explainer. The explainer was on his feet in a flash, insisting upon being referred to correctly as a member of the Korean People's Army. Colonel Robinette duly apologized for having called him a communist, and went on to say that if the KPA explainer were not in fact a communist, he, Colonel Robinette, stood ready to offer any further amends and apologies the KPA explainer thought were due him for having been the target of so opprobrious an insult.

But he *was* a communist, the explainer made haste to say.

"Then what in the hell are you kicking about?" roared Robinette.

29

"This Is No God Damned Good!"

Much credit should go to Brigadier Kaul, General Thimay-ya's chief of staff, and to Lieutenant Colonel J. K. Khanna, MC, his operations officer, for their intelligent handling of such minor flare-ups as were beyond solution by the subcommittee chairmen in the explanations.

More often than not these incidents had their funny aspect. One Korean morning just before noon, still cold despite the bright sunshine, UNC representative Major George V. Lane, USAF, reported to the chief UNC observer that the chairman in his explanation tent had ejected the UNC observer—Lane's Chinese assistant—and would neither permit him to re-enter the tent or recess the explanation until a replacement could be secured. The explanation, therefore, was proceeding illegally.

The UNC general observer duly reported this to Brigadier Kaul, who summoned the chairman from the tent, automatically suspending the explanation. The chairman, a distinguished and decorated British combat veteran of the Indian Army in World War II who had been retired as a lieutenant colonel as a result of his wounds and had decided to remain in

India as a citizen of the new Republic, had been recalled to active duty for the NNRC assignment. Now, his face pink with anger and his moustaches bristling with indignation, he did not wait to be questioned but pointed an accusing finger at the UNC observer.

"That man," he roared at a stentorian parade ground level which brought every unoccupied neutral, anti-communist and communist in the compound hurrying to see what the excitement was, "called me a son-of-a-bitch!" The chairman's committee joined the crowd, too.

"I did not!" the observer retorted as angrily. "I called myself a son-of-a-bitch!"

"Wh-a-a-t?" Brigadier Kaul interjected unbelievingly, "you called *yourself* a son-of-a-bitch? How can a man call *himself* a son-of-a-bitch?"

Here the UNC general observer took a quick hand. He knew this particular observer, Chung En-huang, quite well. Chung had learned his English in college in China when it was Free China, not Red China. But he had served as an interpreter with the U. S. Army in China during World War II, and again in Korea, and he now spoke amazingly American GI English. He had never been nearer the United States than Pusan, Korea, but it would have done no good in this small emergency to have attempted to explain all the foregoing to Brigadier Kaul and his irate chairman. Instead, it seemed better to proceed with them on the unspoken assumption that Chung was as American as he sounded.

"In America," the UNC general observer interjected quickly, "it's possible. It's like this. When an American feels put-upon beyond endurance, he says to himself or to the person or persons who are doing this to him, 'I'll be a son-of-a-bitch if I let you get away with this!' He is not insulting his own mother; he is saying that if he accepts this injustice he will be unworthy of his own mother. This locution is normally shortened to 'I'll be a son-of-a-bitch!', or in cases of extreme provocation, simply 'Son-of-a-bitch!'

"I'll warrant," the UNC general observer continued quickly to the lieutenant colonel, "that what Chung said in your hearing was simply *'Son-of-a-bitch!'* Right?"

That was right, the colonel affirmed. But what, Brigadier Kaul inquired cautiously, was the unbearable situation which provoked such a protest?

Major Lane took up the story.

"We have been on one explanation all morning," he said mildly, "with no recess. The NNRC delegate from Czechoslovakia is, er . . . not feeling too well, and every fifteen minutes he asks the chairman's permission to go to the latrine, and says to continue the explanation without him."

The Czech hung his head sheepishly.

"The chairman always gives his permission, but when *I* asked for permission for Chung to go to the latrine about half an hour ago, he refused, and when I asked again ten minutes later he refused again. So when Chung just *had* to go, ten minutes after that, and he refused again, Chung just said *'Son-of-a-bitch!'* and went anyway."

There was laughter, in which the Czech and Pole participated.

"It was only a brief bit until lunch," the chairman said. "I

252

didn't realize he *had* to go. I was so annoyed with the Czech captain here trotting off all the time, and so anxious to bring the explanation to an end so that we could *all* go, that I was inconsiderate of Mr. Chung. I apologize!"

Mr. Chung also apologized. Everyone shook hands, all around. The committee re-convened briefly to ascertain the wishes of the prisoner of war still within the tent as to repatriation or non-repatriation. The POW went to Taiwan. Everyone else went to the latrine. Lane got there first, so the communists all had to wait until the "other side" and the non-communist neutrals had finished. It was forbidden to the communists even to be alone in a latrine with a non-communist.

"Children!" Brigadier Kaul snorted as he strode away to put out another fire.

Two of the most popular U. S. Army non-commissioned officers with the Chinese anti-communist heroes in the rehabilitation project were Master Sergeant Lindle M. Hancock and Corporal Lawrence M. Finnegan. Their efforts went quite a bit beyond the call of duty. They were interested and active in the POWs' behalf and they took the trouble to avail themselves of the wealth of available instructors and to learn to speak some Chinese.

Their charges placed so much dependence upon them that they not only petitioned that they accompany them to the DZ, but also that they act as UNC representatives in the explanations. This brought the plans for bolstering the morale of the anti-communist heroes in the DZ into a second clash with Army regulations.

One of the morale boosters, in so far as the Chinese POWs

253

were concerned, was the issuing of China-Burma-India patches to all U. S. military personnel in the explanation operation. So many of the Chinese were ex-CNA soldiers and familiar with the patch. Those who were not were quickly briefed on it by their fellows.

The CBI patch, a large, handsome shoulder insignia, combines the sun of China and the star of India with the red and white stripes of the U. S. flag, and there was some thought that it might also establish a small bond between the U. S. and the Indian personnel. To avoid embarrassment if Indian officers commented on it to anyone who had not really earned the right to wear it, those in this category were instructed to say that all of their service in that particular theater had been in China, where they had had no Indian troops.

But the service in World War II of virtually all of the Indian officers of the NNRC and CFI had been in Africa, Italy and Greece. They had not been as well briefed on U. S. insignia as the U. S. personnel and the anti-communist heroes had been on theirs, and the question never came up. They didn't recognize the patch at all.

Permission for general wear of the CBI patch, when it came through, laid down one inexplicable restriction. It was not to be worn when visiting Seoul. Since its shape, a shield, lent itself readily to attachment by three snaps instead of painstaking stitching, this presented no difficulty. But when the military police in Seoul began picking up Eighth Army personnel, wholly unconnected with the explanations but with a legitimate right to wear the CBI patch, some embarrassment developed.

254

No such embarrassment attended the brevetting of Hanock and Finnegan. While the British Army had made Captain Ryan a major for the explanation operation, in keeping with their system of long standing of giving officers the rank—and pay—appropriate to a particular assignment, the U. S. Army has no regulations whatever either for or against such an arrangement. But the requirement for UNC representatives was for officers, since a certain amount of rank was absolutely necessary in dealing with the officers of the NNRC delegations and the CFI, not to mention protecting the anti-communist heroes from the slashing tactics of the communist officer explainers.

Permission was therefore obtained verbally, from a high level, to pin captain's bars on Hancock and first lieutenant's on Finnegan, for the explanation period. Regrettably, they did not get the pay of their brevet ranks, for they certainly earned it, and more. They were carried, of course, on the repatriation group's administrative records in their proper ranks. Master sergeants do not normally figure in fatigue rosters, but the senior observer had to intercede when Corporal Finnegan drew head count duty at the mess one day. Lieutenant Finnegan, he explained, would be busy up in the DZ.

And busy he was. Hancock and Finnegan were recognized and saluted as punctiliously as was Captain Pihl, and what's more, congratulated on their recent promotions.

Finnegan starred in the abrupt termination of one brainwashing. The pitiable POW had been held in place on his bench by four Indian troopers for almost four hours. He had incautiously admitted, in charging the communists with dis-

255

possessing his small-holding landlord father from his ancestral acres, that his parents were still alive in Red China. Now the three explainers had sent for two reinforcements, and the five of them, like buzzards on a branch waiting for a man to die, were chanting at the prisoner of war, sometimes singly, sometimes all together, sometimes in duet, trio or quartet:

"Your father and mother await you."

Just that. Nothing more. The effect was wholly hypnotic even if you didn't understand it. After three hours, the nose of the anti-communist hero began to bleed. The Czech and the Pole were asleep.

To Finnegan, who could understand it, it was more than flesh and blood could stand. Throwing protocol to the winds, he leaped to his feet and shouted—in Chinese—"This is no God damned good!"

It threw the explainers into an uproar. This particular prisoner was the first of the day and had not recognized Finnegan; this set of brainwashers did not know that he spoke any Chinese and immediately assumed that he had understood everything they had said, up to that time. And in that time they had broken every rule in the several books which obtained.

The chairman pounded for order, and demanded an English translation of what Finnegan had said. This particular chairman hadn't suspected that Finnegan knew so well what was going on, either, and since it did no good to reprimand the explainers for their violations, had simply let them continue.

Finnegan told him in English what he had said.

"I quite agree with you," the chairman said crisply. "This *is,* as you put it, no God damned good. Ask the prisoner of war if he wishes to be repatriated, or if he does not wish to be repatriated."

The anti-communist hero numbly pointed to the door to Taiwan. By this time the POW grapevine had spread the word to leave the explanation tent by the door through which you had entered if your choice was Taiwan or the ROK.

Hancock and Finnegan conducted themselves throughout the explanations as officers and gentlemen, and have Bronze Stars to attest to their discharge of responsibilities above and beyond the call of duty. Hancock, a career soldier, continues to ornament the ranks of U. S. Army non-commissioned officers, and Finnegan, a draftee, is out of the service and back at school under the GI bill of rights. If any commanding officer in any future emergency needs a good captain and a good first lieutenant, or a good major and a good captain, their current addresses will be furnished on request.

The communists had no compunctions about asking non-commissioned officers to assume officer rank, or vice versa. When the anti-communist heroes pulled the wiring and loud-speakers out of their compounds to defeat electronic explanations, the Northern Command brought up psychological warfare ground loudspeaker and amplifier units, truck-mounted, and proposed explaining to them from outside the compounds.

They selected a North Korean compound for the first such broadcast. The compound was across a ravine from the Indian Red Cross encampment, and they proposed to set up their loudspeakers on the edge of the Red Cross area, well out of rock-range and given further immunity by the Red Cross flags

257

flying all about. Their broadcasters, with their truck and microphones, were set up in complete defilade on the far side of the Red Cross area—absolutely out of rock-range. If the Indians had been Burmese, the communists couldn't have been more frankly hiding behind their skirts.

The Korean anti-communist heroes could see what they were up to, and asked their guards if they might see a representative of General Thorat. Then they grouped at the posts on which the compound barbed wire was strung, on the side of the compound facing the loudspeakers. Singing rhythmically, they started pushing the posts back and forth, back and forth.

The compound posts were six by sixes, a good sixteen feet long, with six feet of their length in the earth. At their top, braced two by fours nailed on each side of the posts supported an additional three feet of wire, at an angle slanting into the compound. The fencing as a whole was not impossible to climb, but mighty difficult, and in the process a man made a spread-eagled target of himself.

But as they started swaying the posts, it became evident that this was an exercise in which they had indulged before, snickering quietly in the night. The tops of the posts described arcs of six feet. It was immediately obvious that it would be impossible to climb this particular fence. With the weight of only a few men on it, it would simply fall flat. The posts were so loose that with the number of men assigned to each one they could easily pull the entire fence out of the ground and throw it back over their shoulders, to advance on the next line of barbed wire.

258

One couldn't help wondering if the next two lines of fence hadn't also been worked on, during the starry nights.

When the emissary from General Thorat arrived, the few men not busy at the fence politely informed him that if the loudspeaker broadcast went on as scheduled, the whole compound was coming across the ravine to beat the communist broadcasters to death with their own loudspeakers. No Indian troops or Red Cross personnel would be harmed, if they would please stay out of the way, and once the broadcasters had been disposed of, the anti-communist heroes would march in disciplined ranks back to their compound and put the fences back up. The fences weren't keeping them in, but they did keep riff-raff like the communist broadcasters out.

The broadcast was delayed for some time. Indian Red Cross personnel tossed a coin and briefly served tea to the Korean communist broadcasters and the Chinese officers who were keeping an eye on them. Then they served tea to the UNC observers, and complimented them on the books and other materials being supplied by the UNC, through the Indian Red Cross, for the educational program which the prisoners of war themselves were conducting in their compounds. They liked the movies, too; would the UNC mind if they showed them to their own personnel and the CFI?

Finally another emissary arrived from General Thorat, with word that the broadcast was cancelled. He was terribly sorry; he didn't know why it had been cancelled.

That particular Korean compound was on the schedule for explanations the following day. The broadcasting team and Colonel Lee, the chief Red Chinese explainer, turned up at

0800 with a request to the NNRC that they be permitted to broadcast to the prisoners of war in the holding enclosures. The request was granted, and after some delay in getting the electrical generator to work in the freezing cold, a North Korean major who had been hanging in the background the day before went to work on the microphone. He gave them his name, rank and serial number in the North Korean People's Army, then the name and internment number by which they had known him until two days before, when, after more than two years of earnest agitation in their midst, he had bugged out "at the risk of his life" so that he could tell them all of the welcome awaiting them in Red Korea. He himself was being treated magnificently. Could they not see him in his uniform? He had been promoted to major, since he had been only a captain when he had been directed by the all-wise Nam Il to surrender and work among them as a mere private soldier. And he was going to get all of his back pay, and so would they if they chose to go home!

The anti-communist heroes never heard a word he said. The enclosure posts, without previous preparation, were too tightly rooted to permit the maneuver of the day before. But they sang, and waved their flags, and when they grew hoarse they accompanied the "A" detachment of their band by beating on tin cans—the butt cans for their cigarettes—with sticks and stones. The same thing happened in Area B, and the explanations got off to a late start that day.

Captain Lee Chun Bong knew of six North Korean and three Chinese communist agents who bugged out of the compounds and then turned up in officer uniform as explainers.

The anti-communist heroes, when Freedom Day came, said there had been many more than that. They particularly dreaded them as explainers. They knew that any intelligence the agents had on their families and home villages had gone to the other side with them, but they just didn't like to be specifically reminded of it in the explanations.

The sturdy Swedes and Swiss of the NNRC stuck to the principle that it was the man and not the rank, so long as he knew his job. One of the most able of the many able Swedes, a missionary of long experience in the East who could read, write and speak Chinese fluently, was a private first class, his reserve rank. And one of the Swiss, an extremely prosperous business man when he was not serving in his nation's citizen army, was a corporal.

30

Soviet Technical Progress

The explanations provided an arena in which Communist East met the Free West before an interested audience. One could only guess at the judgments formed by the Indians, Swedes and Swiss—and Czechs and Poles—but it became quite evident at times that the West was getting none the worst of it.

One of the most noticeable communist outrages upon Chinese culture is the business of shaking hands. This may be one of the seeds of eventual communist self-destruction in China. For untold centuries the Chinese have been accustomed to bow when meeting some one or when taking leave. The Free Chinese still bow, and physical contact between one man and another is actually abhorrent to them.

The Russians shake hands. The Chinese communists shake hands. It's a compulsion. If an Indian general encountered a group of twenty Red Chinese, the ranking communist would pump his fist, and then in order of descending importance he had to shake hands with the other nineteen. By the time he got down to the enlisted interpreter at the end of the line those hands were a little grubby, and you could see that he didn't particularly enjoy it. Each Red Chinese would bob a little instinctive bow with the handshake, but you could see that they hated it too.

The Indians are like Americans; they can shake hands or nod pleasantly, and before long they began to wonder at this communist compulsion. Besides, they were busy men, and hand-shaking took up a lot of time.

On the hillside which afforded a vantage point overlooking the whole of explanation compound A, the matter was taken up with Chen Yih, chief Chinese advisor to the UNC group, by an Indian general officer who shall be nameless lest he be accused of being un-neutral.

"Tell me," the general said, draping his arm familiarly about Chen Yih's shoulders, "isn't it true that the Chinese simply don't like physical contact of this sort, all of this hand-shaking and all that?"

Chen Yih could have said simply, "Yes!" and shrugged the general's arm away. But he knew that, despite his Missouri background, his career as a *New York Times* man and his long residence in the United States, as chief Chinese advisor of the UNC group he was also, to the communists, the CHIEF CHIANG KAI-SHEK AGENT! Every pair of communist eyes in the compound and out was focussed on this unprecedented display of camaraderie between an important Indian and the "chief Chiang agent." The wires to Peiping would certainly hum with it that night, and perhaps the wireless from Peiping to New Delhi. Well, it had been done now and couldn't be helped; the only thing left to do was do it up brown.

So for fifteen minutes, while the general's arm remained about his shoulders, he gave him the general background of handshaking in Red China, and wound up with the admission that handshaking, in fact any such personal physical contact with a man, was personally repugnant to him and all Chinese, free or Red.

A "bugout" came through one of the tent doors during that quarter of an hour and the communists were in such a state of shock that they neglected to applaud him.

Chen Yih also acted occasionally as an assistant to Captain Garnett D. Hargrave, the U. S. Army officer who was in charge of supplying the Indian Red Cross with the educational materials for the anti-communist heroes in the DZ. Since these materials were in Chinese and Korean, and Captain Hargrave had worked only on the Korean side of the rehabilitation project, he needed help when he had to clear Chinese materials with the Red Cross officials.

On one of these occasions a box of books turned up quite accidentally and, by strict NNRC standards, most improperly. Destined for the libraries in the anti-communist compounds on Cheju-do, it had arrived late. One of the clean-up men there forwarded it to the DZ without inspecting it too closely. Chen Yih recognized it immediately and quite frankly told the Red Cross official the title and author of the volumes.

"Ah, yes," said the Indian officer. "Seems familiar. '1984,' by George Orwell. What is it?"

"Science fiction," said Chen Yih. "English author—died recently."

264

"Yes, yes," said the Red Cross man. "Good reading for the lads, what? Take their minds off their troubles."

Captain Hargrave had succeeded a Lieutenant Reddick as chief of the rehabilitation project at Pusan Camp #9, for Korean anti-communists, early in 1953 while the weather was still bitterly cold. Reddick had one of the best programs in the entire POW Command, assisted by the fact that the field headquarters for the project was just up the road, ready, willing and able to back him up with anything he needed. Pusan #9 was also the easiest camp for visiting VIPs to inspect, and was therefore a model operation in every respect, including the rehabilitation work.

It would have seemed almost impossible to improve on Reddick's project. He had 100% POW participation; full cooperation from the camp command. Virtually the only aspect of his program that was seemingly susceptible of improvement had to do with the dirt-floored huts in which it was housed.

In just five months, up to the time President Rhee released all of the anti-communist patriots in Pusan #9, Captain Hargrave, a teacher in civilian life, had transformed Reddick's college into Hargrave's university. He trained POW instructors, tripled the number of classes. He moved the project from Reddick's scattered huts—no better and no worse than the other stone-faced buildings of the camp—to a Quonset campus of nine centrally located buildings. He accomplished, in short, a miracle, by tackling an operation which was already superb and making it sensational.

Many of the Indians had arrived at the DZ almost afraid that they would find evidence to support communist propaganda with respect to supposed racial discrimination by Americans. They encountered, instead, all kinds of evidence to refute it.

They found explanation teams of Americans, Chinese and Koreans living and eating and sleeping together because they were working together and the better they knew each other the better work they could do together.

The Indian Army lieutenant colonel on Red Cross duty whose task it was to pass on educational materials going into the compounds for the prisoners of war was taken aback at first to find that his opposite number in the UNC, entrusted with this most important liaison assignment, was a Negro U. S. Army captain, Hargrave. By the time Freedom Day came around, he was urging every U. S. officer with whom he came in contact to be sure that Captain Hargrave received a commendation for his tireless efforts in behalf of the prisoners of war.

Hargrave received not only a commendation but a decoration.

Without exception the Negro U. S. Army officers among the UNC representatives discharged their duties with distinction. A few of the Indian officers, however, gave up hard on their pre-conceived ideas of American racial discrimination. One of the last was one who remained on duty throughout the explanations in the tent to which Captain Wendell W. Long's UNC team was assigned.

Captain Long is an outstanding officer, dignified in speech and manner and distinguished in appearance. Soft-spoken and diplomatic, he had qualities of leadership which enabled him

266

to out-think and out-maneuver the communist explainers and the Czech and the Pole on the NNRC sub-committee to the extent that there were very few extended brainwashings in his tent, the only prisoners of war he lost to the Reds were obvious agents, and there were no clashes whatever in his tent between the several elements. His calm manner quieted frightened, panicky prisoners, so that his team experienced a minimum of assaults on the explainers.

By the end of the explanations, the chairman in Captain Long's tent had had full opportunity to observe the respect accorded Long by his seniors and juniors alike, and the confidence reposed in him by everyone from the senior UNC observer to the most pitiable prisoner. And this chairman, too, was campaigning for a commendation for Long.

Captain Tefesse Lemma of the Ethiopian Army served the United Nations Command as a general observer, and it irked the communists no end to observe him, almost daily, deep in conversation with Lt. Col. H. Reutersward, chief of staff of the Swedish NNRC delegation.

They were simply old friends from a tour in Ethiopia by Colonel Reutersward, the sixteenth generation in an unbroken line of Swedish Army officers, when Col. Reutersward was training the Ethiopian Army. The seventeenth Reutersward, in fact, was born in Addis Ababa.

The most striking contrasts to the eye between the free and slave worlds at the explanations were in matters of logistics—uniforms and transport.

From Captain Lee Chun Bong's report on the explanations over the Voice of the United Nations Command:

"Q: Were the explainers issued new clothes, gloves and shoes?"

"A: Yes, but they had to return them upon completion of the explanations. Many felt and complained bitterly about that."

Despite these steps on the part of the communist command, there were still glaring insufficiencies. While the UNC group from senior colonel to private first class interpreter all wore the same uniform—artic cap, parka or field jacket, warm winter wool olive green shirt and trousers, dry and comfortable combat boots—there were wide variations in uniform between the top-ranking and lowly communists, particularly among the Chinese.

While explanation days were almost invariably sunny, it had also almost invariably poured rain the night before. The Red Chinese enlisted men, interpreters, drivers, etc., wore low-cut rubber-soled tennis shoes, originally white but soon red with Korean clay. What was worse, when the men had to step in the sticky mud they would walk right out of their shoes, a matter of intense embarrassment to them if anyone from the UNC side was looking on—and someone always was.

On the day of the cancelled communist broadcast to the Korean compound, the group of Indian Red Cross officials and UNC representatives, while they were having their second cup of tea, were feeling sorry for a little Chinese communist interpreter who had lost his shoes in the mud more times than you could count, and consequently so much face that he felt thoroughly miserable even in the presence of his Chinese and Korean companions. To have been issued such miserable footgear, they decided, his rank must have been the lowest—as low as his morale.

"How on earth do the communist Chinese military themselves tell their officers from other ranks when they are too far apart to read the little squiggles on their name labels?" asked one of the Indian officers.

"It's very simple," Chen Yih replied. "If he is wearing boots, he is a general officer. Good-quality high shoes, a field grade officer. Low shoes, a company grade officer. Tennis shoes, a peon."

Whether it was because Colonel Lee may have overheard this, or because it was repeated in the Voice of the UNC commentary on the explanations that night, the next morning the little interpreter *almost* smiled when he encountered the UNC group, then looked quickly and shyly at the ground.

"He's trying to thank us," Chen Yih said. "Look at his feet."

He was wearing leather shoes.

But it was in the matter of motor transport that the contrast between the two worlds was most marked.

The communists arrived at the first few explanations in an interminable convoy of Soviet jeeps, fifty of them dropping off at Area A and the other fifty continuing to Area B. These jeeps looked like the product of a mésalliance between a U. S. jeep and a Model A Ford. Dark green, with a little more pretense to upholstery than a U. S. jeep, the hood, dash and transmission were virtually identical with those of a Model A—even the trademark on the radiators resembled the old Ford insigne.

269

But there the resemblance to either of their prototypes ended.

October is cold on the 38th parallel in Korea, and when the communists started to leave for lunch on the first day of explanations, the "Feep" which would respond to its starter was exceptional. The drivers leaped out and cranked vigorously— they had the old Ford in-place cranks, too. A few more started banging, coughing and spitting on two or at the most three cylinders. The majority still stood silent.

Then began the damnedest pushing and shoving and pulling and hauling in automotive history, in the slippery mud of the parking area. Because of the fixed cranks one feep couldn't straightforwardly push another to get it started. The feep that was mobile had to back into the immobile one, spare tire to spare tire, and push backing up. They looked like copulating turtles, and there were frequent collisions and near collisions between adjoining pairs.

When the U. S. jeeps and busses which carried the Swiss away—the Swedish contingent had lunch in the area—leaped to life at a touch on their starters, much face was lost by the Chinese and North Korean drivers. The Czechs and Poles simply couldn't stand it; they got out of the feeps and walked on up the road, to let their vehicles pick them up later if they ever got that far. As they passed the warm, heated busses in which the UNC representatives were enjoying their lunch, they simply couldn't help looking longingly at them.

When the communists returned from lunch, they parked all their feeps uphill, to see if they could start them that evening with a short run. Since no one coordinated the order in which the short runs would be attempted, fifty feeps came slipping and sliding and skidding downhill more or less at once, only one or two with any power and all reluctant to put on their brakes, into a bigger mess than they had had at noon.

That was the 15th of October. The 17th was even colder.

When the explanations resumed on the 31st, it was still colder. But the communists had had time to get down from Pyongyang to Kaesong two of the fifty Moscow busses promised and the ten actually delivered for the revitalization of the Pyongyang city transport system.

These were magnificent affairs, half a city block long and as close to a Fifth Avenue bus as Soviet inventive genius could come. They may have been great for Pyongyang's one paved street, but they were underpowered and not at all suited for the mud and narrow roads of the DZ. The U. S. busses, on the other hand, were short-coupled, built on Army 2½-ton truck chassis, and capable of going anywhere.

The communists may never have gotten their Moscow busses back to Pyongyang, or even to Kaesong, but they got them out of the DZ, very late that night, and suffered in silence and shame thereafter with their feeps. Their drivers started getting the motors idling each morning at eleven and each afternoon at four, so that they would be well warmed up when the time came to go.

Then, of course, they started running out of gas halfway out of the area.

31

Cultural Exchange

The long, empty spaces between excitement in the explanations afforded both the Indians and the Americans an amplitude of opportunities to get acquainted. There is no evidence to determine if the Americans advanced appreciably in Indian estimation, but there is no question but that the Indians made vast strides in American appreciation.

The Indian delegation was not completely military, by any means. There were also representatives of the Indian diplomatic corps, the superlative Civil Service, and the Indian press representatives organization.

Jeep-riding one day with an Indian Air Force officer, Wing Commander P. S. Gill, the chief U. N. observer pointed to the U. S. Army combat boots discarded along the way by the communist POWs returned in "Big Switch."

"Damned fools," he said. "They could use those boots, this winter."

"Of course," the Commander agreed amicably. "But you see, we Asians are proud. We resent the way you Americans press these evidences of your wealth and technological superiority upon us. And these communist prisoners of war simply had to discard your good boots and warm uniforms, or they would have been suspect when they were returned."

"Ah, ah," said the American. "Remember, you're neutral. Didn't the British give you good boots and warm uniforms when they ruled India? Did you resent that?"

"Yes, we did," he replied, calmly. "We want to provide our own good boots and warm uniforms. You realize," he added quickly, "that with us, cool uniforms are more of a problem!"

If one praised the British to an Indian, he was quick to counter with a disparagement. But if you criticized them, he was equally quick in their defense. The British may not have the Indians' love, but they have their respect.

Aside from General Thimayya, the chief U. N. observer perhaps grew closer to Lieutenant Colonel A. K. Khanna and Majors Sandhu, Nair and Klair than any of the other Indian officers, and among the Indian civilians, Messrs. W. S. Anand, N. V. Rao and I. J. Bahadur Singh.

Colonel Khanna, a Sandhurst graduate and a Military Cross winner in World War II, was an intellectual, ready with an argument on any subject.

"This is a difficult assignment," the UNC observer remarked one morning. Col. Khanna, Brigadier Kaul's operations officer, had just ruled once against the UNC on an appeal, and once for it.

"Not at all," Col. Khanna said modestly. "We and the Swedes and the Swiss are the only real neutrals here, because we lead from strength." (Colonel Khanna was also a fine bridge player.)

"It seems to me that you Asians have a different concept of the means of maintaining firm neutrality than the Swedes and Swiss," the UNC observer observed. "They can afford to be neutral because they have two of the toughest citizen armies in Europe, and no one can wittingly afford to take them on. But aside from you in Asia, there are only three big, tough armies, the Turks, the Pakistanis and the Thais. The Turks are in NATO, the Turks and Pakistanis are going into this new Middle East Treaty Organization, and the Pakistanis and Thais are talking up the similar Southeast Asia Treaty Organization. But you and the Burmese and the Indonesians seek safety in neutrality."

"I am just a simple soldier," Col. Khanna declaimed, "and know nothing of politics. But I can tell you why the Burmese and Indonesians seek safety in neutrality.

"When the Japanese took Indonesia," he continued, "they took Mr. Soekarno out of a Dutch jail and made him the head of as much government as the Indonesians were permitted to have. Two days after the Japanese surrender, he became the President of Indonesia. Then the Dutch returned and put him back in jail. This time it took the U. N. Security Council to get him out of jail and back at the head of the government. Mr. Soekarno is neutral simply because he doesn't want to be liberated again."

There was a bond between Major H. S. Sandhu and the UNC observer because both had served under Brigadier H. S. MacDonald in Greece, the former as a battalion commander in the Indian Army chasing the Nazis north, the latter as a military observer for the United Nations Special Commission on the Balkans, watching the communists retreat much more slowly. But both had enjoyed Danish bleu cheese, imported by the Germans, on the Yugoslav frontier, and ditto pickled herring, ditto, on the Bulgarian border. Brigadier MacDonald, a South African officer of the Indian Army, had been retired as a lieutenant colonel when India became independent, and then became Chief Observer for UNSCOB in Greece. Major Sandhu was crushed to hear that Mac was now an advisor to the Pakistani Army.

When General Thimayya was absent from the explanations, because of the press of other duties, Brigadier Kaul was present. When the brigadier was absent, Colonel Khanna was present. When Colonel Khanna was absent, Major Sandhu was present. Major Sandhu was always present, and the UNC observer fell into the habit of yelling for him in emergencies, which were frequent.

One day he sang out for Sandhu, and junior Indian officers clustered about delightedly. "Did you call for Major Sahib?" they questioned quickly, as they sent runners for Sandhu. Major Sahib was what they called him, and what the UNC observer called him thereafter. It brought him even more quickly.

Where Colonel Khanna, was argumentative, Major Nair was philosophical. He watched the Chinese and Korean anti-communist heroes closely, and the communist observers, representatives and explainers as well. A devout Hindu, he was puzzled at the apparent irreligion of the Chinese, and simply could not believe that a majority of the anti-communist Koreans were Christians. The UNC observer tried the story on him of the

275

Christian missionary in China who gave up, asking how you could persuade Northern Chinese to become Southern Baptists, and got nowhere with it.

"You know," the major observed out of the blue one sunny November afternoon, "the Koreans, I think, and the Chinese, yes, and the Japanese too"—he was just back from R & R (rest and recreation) in Tokyo—"are very cruel. They can watch an animal, a dog or a cat, die in the gutter, and feel no compassion whatever."

It fell to the UNC general observer to have to explain to an Asian that reincarnation did not figure as importantly in the principal religions of these other Asians as it did, perhaps, in his, and that one could not always tell by their facial expressions how they felt. When it counted, they were as kind, as compassionate, as Indians, or Americans, or anyone else.

Major Gurdial Singh Klair was a Sikh, a hard-working officer who drew a most difficult assignment, on a general observation team which toured the entire anti-communist complex. The Czechs and Poles put two of their toughest representatives on it, to start fires; the Swedish lieutenant colonel and the Swiss captain did their best to put them out. Major Klair was in the middle. The UNC general observer and his opposite number, Colonel Lee of the Red Chinese explainers, were at the far right and far left, respectively.

The first day the team functioned, the UNC observer found himself in profound disagreement with Major Klair. The major's accent was Oxonian and his conduct impeccable, but the UNC observer, a middle-aged, crusty character, just couldn't get his position across to Klair. The argument waxed, and both

276

lost their tempers. Protocol had been scrupulously observed, up until this point, particularly with respect to and by the Czech colonel and Polish lieutenant colonel involved, but the UNC observer, feeling affronted by a final ruling by Major Klair—who because of nationality rather than rank was the chairman of the team—demanded the name of the major's commanding officer. It was Brigadier Kaul, the major said stiffly, and the session adjourned.

Splitting up for the ride back to the explanation area, the Swedish colonel swung naturally into the right-hand front seat of the UNC observer's jeep, while the Swiss captain vaulted into the back seat.

"You didn't handle that well, colonel," the Swedish officer remarked. "The next time this question comes up, you leave it to me." Where the Indian officer's accent had been very, very British, the Swedish officer's was surprisingly American, and midwest American at that.

"How do I know you can handle it better?" the American asked, still testy.

"Well," said the Swedish colonel. "I was born, and lived until I was sixteen, in a Swedish city called Detroit, and I was selected for this assignment because it was cheaper to send me here from my temporary duty at a Swedish hospital called Walter Reed, than to send someone else all the way from Sweden."

This does not compromise the neutrality of the Swedish delegation to the Neutral Nations Repatriation Commission. The colonel was a Swedish reserve officer. At sixteen, his parents had moved from Detroit to Copenhagen. He had gone on to a university in Sweden. When World War II erupted, because his parents were in Denmark and because he was quite a guy, he had joined the Danish underground. For his exploits against the Nazis, Sweden made him a citizen. The U. S. really lost one there.

There was an easily discernible elite among the Swedish officers of the NNRC, surprising in representatives of so democratic a citizen army. Pressed for the explanation at a party, one of the top Swedish delegates broke down and confessed.

"To really get ahead in the Swedish Army," he said, "you must have either fought with the Finns against Russia, against the Nazis in the Danish underground, or both. Now we have a third category—Finland, Denmark and Korea!"

At the next meeting of the NNRC sub-committee, Major Klair drew the UNC observer aside. "You didn't report me to Brigadier Kaul," he said accusingly.

"No," said the observer. "I've seen the kind of an eating-out the brigadier puts on, and I'm a soldier too. Let's forget it."

"You know, colonel," Major Klair said as they shook hands on it, "I learned my English in India. I've been told my accent is excellent, but this is the first time I've had to depend exclusively on English, and I find my vocabulary is really not what it should be. You talk so fast, and use so many American words, that half the time, actually, I don't know what in the hell you are talking about."

The Messrs. Bahadur Singh, Rao and Anand were representatives of the Indian Foreign Service, and representatives of which any nation might well be proud. It was just that they looked like they represented three different nations.

Bahadur Singh was a tweedy, pipe-smoking type, and might

have been an Italian educated at Cambridge. He knew well that it was neither the U. S. nor the Republic of Korea which had been guilty of aggression on the 25th of June, 1950; he had been the Indian delegate on the United Nations Committee in Korea, and had seen the North Koreans pour across the 38th Parallel and had subscribed to the committee's cable to the Security Council.

There was no mistaking Mr. Rao and Mr. Anand for Italians. Mr. Rao, political advisor to General Thimayya, dressed in the manner made known all over the world by Mr. Nehru. He was fascinated by details of the rehabilitation project among both the communist and anti-communist prisoners of war, and particularly by the literacy project and the progress the POWs had made.

Mr. Anand is a Sikh, and made his appearances always in turban, hacking jacket and jodhpurs. One looked behind him, always, for his horse. It was the agricultural part of the rehabilitation project which he found most interesting.

General Thimayya, the winter of 1953-54, ranked seventh among thirteen lieutenant generals in the Indian Army, and it was known that the Chief of Staff of their army was about to retire. His American friends kept their fingers crossed when he returned to India, especially Major Roger Ranck.

As a captain, Major Ranck had been sent to the Indian NNRC camp at the start of the prisoner of war turnover, to act as liaison between General Thimayya and the UNC delegation, and to make himself generally useful. He did, and General Thimayya was most appreciative. Just at the close of the operation, an IBM machine in the Pentagon gave him a well-deserved promotion to major.

Passing through Tokyo on his way home, General Thimayya summoned Ranck to the Imperial Hotel for tea, and presented him with a really magnificent rug which had decorated his quarters in the demilitarized zone.

"I want to thank you very much indeed for your help," General Thimayya said. "I have written a letter of commendation about you to General Hull, and I am happy to see that your army has recognized your worth and ability by promoting you to major."

"Thank you, sir," said Ranck.

"Now that you have so successfully finished this assignment, Capt-,-er, Major, what will your next job be?" The General took a sip of tea.

"Oh, I've been on the same job all the time, sir," Ranck replied cheerfully. "I work for Colonel—"

"I suspected that," the General interrupted sympathetically, nodding his head and lowering his cup. "Psychological warfare."

Ranck, the chief of psychological warfare, and General Thimayya's many American friends—every American who met him in Korea—were disappointed when he was relegated to command of Poona, the Indian West Point, but reconciled by the assurance that some more crackerjack officers would be developed under his aegis. Late in 1956, they were made extremely happy by the announcement that he had been named Chief of Staff of the Indian Army.

They were momentarily hurt early in 1957, when, welcoming General Zhukov to Dehra Dun, he acclaimed him the greatest living general. But, they reflected, he's modest. Meant to say the greatest living general in Dehra Dun, no doubt. Psychological warfare.

32

Comrade Big Ear Wong

The only printed "explanations" the communists gave the anti-communist heroes were copies of the Peng-Kim statement, with which the POWs blew their noses or made even more graphic gestures of contempt.

The prisoners of war, however, did not let the explainers off so easily.

At the first recess in one tent on the first day of explanations, the UNC representative scooped a pamphlet up in some excitement from the empty explainers' table as he made his exit, thinking he had an example of communist printed material. His Chinese-speaking observer quickly disabused him. Part of the last POW's denunciation of the communists had been an indictment of their espousal of the opium trade in China, and as he had declaimed his choice of the door to Taiwan, the prisoner of war had flipped the pamphlet, a psychological warfare brief of a United Nations committee report on the same subject, to the explainers.

Somehow the prisoner of war, who seemed to feel quite keenly about the Red government's sponsorship of traffic in

282

opium in Asia, had brought the pamphlet with him from North Korea to Cheju and now back to North Korea.

This turned out to be only the first of many such incidents as the explanations proceeded.

One of the favorite psychological warfare leaflets thus preserved by the Chinese and Korean anti-communist heroes alike and finally delivered in various stages of decrepitude to the explainers was a caricature of a communist soldier clad only in a pair of pants held up by a piece of rope, leaning contemplatively on a big hammer-and-sickle symbol. The cartoon showed the soldier with big ears, a small head, a tiny waist, and big hands and feet. The legend in Chinese read as follows: "COMRADE BIG EAR WONG. RUSSIA WANTS EVERY CHINESE TO GROW LIKE THIS!

"With a small head, Wong doesn't have to think because Russia will think for him.

"With big ears, Wong can listen to each new change of the Russian party line from his political officers. He can also listen to his friends and report them as reactionaries.

"With a smiling face, Wong shows his happy feelings for Russia.

"With a small stomach, he doesn't need the food sent from China for Russia.

"With both big hands he can work nights and carry a Russian rifle to fight in Russia's aggressive wars.

"With both big feet, he can march and fight in Russia's aggressive wars.

"DOES WONG REALLY WANT TO BE A SLAVE FOR RUSSIA?"

Because the leaflet had been dropped in North Korea, the following message in the Korean language to Korean civilians appeared on both sides:

"This is a UN message to the Chinese Communist Forces. Post it for them to see."

North Koreans, disgusted with their communist government and with the presence of the Chinese communist forces in North Korea, could strike a blow for liberty by slipping out in the dead of night and tacking the leaflet to a tree or wall. The explainers, in their regular jobs as CCF unit political officers, were already familiar with Big Ear Wong to the point of apoplexy without this further ribbing from the anti-communist heroes.

The Korean version of the leaflet substituted only Big Ear Kim for Wong, and Red China for Russia. Whenever either Wong or Kim turned up the explainers knew immediately that their task was hopeless.

One Korean explainer made the mistake of insisting that it was not Red China but Soviet Russia whose influence was paramount in North Korea, and went into ecstasies about "our great liberator, Soviet Russia!" The anti-communist hero quickly replied that it seemed to him that Soviet Russia had been the enslaver of North Korea.

"Our Korean rivers, streets and mountains you have renamed after Russians," he shouted. "Our Taedong River in Pyongyang is now the Lenin River!"

It was not an enjoyable time for the communist observers and explainers. The former, standing in knots in the explanation area awaiting the occasional agent "bugging out," would

284

fall silent, but stand their ground, when the UNC observers walked by. If the group were Chinese—they mixed with the Koreans only when it was inescapable—Chen Yih would tell an anti-communist joke in Chinese to the chief UNC observer and Major Ryong C. Hahm, the Korean-born U. S. officer who had so distinguished himself in the pilot rehabilitation project. All three would laugh on cue—Major Hahm really spoke Chinese. When the communists were out of earshot, Chen Yih would repeat it in English.

If the group were Korean, Major Hahm would tell a joke in Korean or Japanese. To the Big Ear Kims, an anti-communist joke in Japanese was doubly infuriating. All Koreans, except those who entered school in the fall of 1945 or later, speak Japanese, but not unjustifiably feel that it is unpatriotic to do so.

Juvenile, but it passed the long stretches of time between "bugouts." It so enhanced the reputation of the chief UNC observer for being facile in both Chinese and Korean that he was frequently called upon to translate what the anti-communist heroes were shouting at the explainers in the tents, and vice versa, for NNRC members and newspapermen. When he disclaimed fluency, they would insist.

Between Chiao, their boss, and the anti-communist prisoners, the explainers were even unhappier than the observers.

"I was in a position to know about the communist leaders' attitude toward the repatriation of anti-communist prisoners," Captain Lee Chun Bong said in his VUNC broadcast and to the free world press after he too had asked for "non-repatriation."

"Although they knew that the prisoners had made a free choice in deciding to remain in the free world, they told the members of the explanation teams that the United Nations Command was forcibly detaining the prisoners. However, the actual explanation sessions proved that the anti-communist prisoners had rejected repatriation in a completely free decision."

Why, then, he was asked, did the Red leaders persist in continuing explanations?

"The communist leaders were afraid of losing face before the whole world in case they lost so many POWs; therefore, they felt that by telling the POWs about conditions back home at least a few might return."

Was that, he was asked, his personal conclusion?

"No. I heard it expressed time and time again at the Red leaders' meetings. No, it was not my personal conclusion. Chiao said, 'We must make every effort to persuade the POWs to return, because if we lose so many POWs we will lose face before the entire world.'"

"What did the communist leaders believe was the reason why the anti-communist prisoners rejected repatriation?" Lee was asked.

"They believed that the prisoners rejected repatriation because communism was bad, and that although the prisoners were members of the CCF and NKA, they were not communists at heart. Therefore they refused to go back."

Queried on the reactions of the leaders of the communist explanation teams, Lee continued:

"At the end of each explanation period, they said that it was

286

a failure. Chiao always said that it was a miserable failure, and that they had lost face once more before the world. When the explainers were briefed by Chiao, he said the POWs were forcibly detained by the UNC and they became convinced that the POWs sincerely refused to come home. In order not to offend Chiao, they did not report this fact, but among themselves they whispered and joked about it.

"Hurh Sang Ok, chief of the 1st Korean Explanation Team, and Kim Pyong Son, chief of the 2d Explanation Team, were among these. Other explainers also admitted that they had lost much face."

"What did the Red leaders do to the explainers who failed to win back prisoners?"

"They reported them as incapable to higher authority and consequently four North Korean and three Chinese explainers were relieved."

33

The Communist Heroes

When the communists, in keeping with their "anything you can do, we can do better" effort, decided that they too might hold prisoners who "did not wish to be directly repatriated," they hurriedly whitewashed an empty village right on their edge of the north half of the demilitarized zone, about a miie south of the Panmunjom-Kaesong road. The village had been larger than Panmunjom, but it was still too small to have its name on even the largest scale maps.

Barbed wire was thrown about the farmhouses, huts and shacks of the main part of the village, for the communist heroes. Another part of the village nestling in a valley over a small ridge was refurbished a little more elaborately for the detachment of the Rajputana Rifles which was detailed to guard these prisoners of war. And a new extension was built on a fair-sized farmhouse still further removed, and the place surrounded by barbed wire—no one quite knew why.

It was apparent that confusion and indecision beset the Northern Command right up to the moment they turned the communist heroes over to CFI custody. They had either planned to turn over fewer POWs, for which the farmhouse enclosure would have sufficed, or many more, which would have necessitated using both enclosures.

While the communists were complaining bitterly about the "inadequacy" of the explanation inclosure built for them in the South Camp, even before the explanations were scheduled to start, discreet inquiry disclosed that there were no explanation facilities whatever in the North Camp. But they would be built, oh, yes, and immediately.

Two days later they were reported as ready. Typical communist efficiency, speed and despatch. A UNC representative rode to the North Camp with Brigadier Kaul to inspect them.

Brigadier Kaul was embarrassed, and the UNC representative could only sympathize with him. After all, Kaul had been informed by the communist side that adequate facilities were all ready.

The "inadequate" facilities built by the UNC in the South Camp were stoutly made, floored and winterized, a large compound and sixteen explanation tents. In the North Camp, after a bulldozer—a U. S.-made Caterpillar—had levelled three or four hillside paddy fields, a crazy fence had been thrown up with posts leaning this way and that in two foot postholes dug with shovels in the sand. Inside the fence were five sleazy cotton tents, with no floors, no latrines—nothing.

The UNC representative pointed out to Brigadier Kaul for the benefit of the communist representative—who understood English very well indeed but carefully conversed in Chinese through an interpreter—that the terms of reference provided seven explainers per thousand prisoners of war, but in no event

289

fewer than five per nation. Three nations, the Republic of Korea, the U. S. and the U. K., were concerned. Eleven tents would be required, five each for the ROK and the U. S. and, since only one U. K. prisoner of war was involved, one for him. Brigadier Kaul repeated this to the communist representative.

Ten tents, the communist representative suggested. He pressed this point so painfully, almost in tears, that the UNC representative began to feel sorry for him too. It became apparent that the communists *had* only ten tents; more could not be procured without sending to Pyongyang, possibly even Peiping. With the roads in North Korea in the condition they were in, another tent might never arrive. . . .

They settled on ten tents, floored and winterized, with better tent poles than the present tents, which had hollow pipes of some base metal, bending dangerously already. And proper latrines.

Had the UNC representative been able to delay his trip from that afternoon until the following morning, he would have enjoyed himself still more. There was a violent windstorm that night, and, according to Major Kutky and Captain Chokra, the officers commanding the Rajputana detachment, the five tents already up were blown flat and their poles bent double or broken. When the communists erected the ten new tents, they built wooden cabins complete with roofs, and pitched the tents over them.

Even with facilities ready, the UNC shrugged off all questions as to when they proposed to start explanations. The chief UNC advisor in this situation was Dr. Joseph D. Lohman, celebrated sociologist, criminologist and penologist of the University of Chicago—elected Sheriff of Cook County, Illinois, in the fall of 1954.

After careful study of the records of the 23 U. S. renegades, Dr. Lohman recommended letting them stew in their own juice for a while. The British concurred with respect to their lone convert to communism, and the ROK Army with respect to theirs.

On the 20th of October Corporal Edward S. Dickenson requested repatriation, and then there were 22 Americans. This loss to the communists was offset almost immediately by the birth of a baby girl to the wife of one of the 335 Koreans, but that gain was more than offset on November 15th, when the father and mother requested repatriation along with their two children. Three other Koreans requested repatriation during the ninety-day period, but not a single communist hero recanted as a result of explanations.

The ROK explainers began brief, dignified and to-the-point explanations on December 2 and ran through 30 unflinchingly communist heroes the first day. The communist heroes had a definite set of tactics, too, but, typically, they were not their own. They borrowed them from an anti-communist hero who, when the long drawnout brainwashing started, cooperated completely with the communist explainers. He kept saying that he was interested in repatriation, but wanted more explanation. He asked them to explain Red Chinese and Soviet domination of North Korea, the June riots in East Germany, the execution of Beria. After four hours of this, the communists called quits.

It was quite obvious that having run through their hard-core communists and the POWs on whom they held hostages, the communists were not prepared to risk their 1.000 batting average.

The UNC asked to begin explanations to the 22 remaining Americans on the 14th of December, but they refused to present themselves unless the demands of the Korean non-repatriates for detailed disquisitions were met. So on each succeeding day the UNC put in a request for whomever the CFI might be able to produce, Korean, American or British.

Surprisingly, the communists asked on December 20, with only three days remaining of the explanation period, to interview Compound 3 on the 21st. Just as surprisingly, Compound 3, against all precedent, consented to be segregated if all of its members did not receive explanations in the one day.

The reason for Compound 3's consent became apparent in the next two days; it was loaded with communist agents. Fifty-six prisoners of war requested repatriation from that one compound, the communists' best score for the entire operation. One more compound had communist agents still to be wrung out, on the 23d, but it yielded only 11 repatriates, par for the course.

With the remaining Korean and American non-repatriates and the lone Briton persisting in their refusal to listen to UNC explanations unless they took the form of debates, right up until December 23, the final day, loudspeakers were used in the North Camp to inform them of their rights.

"After the UNC had made a final appeal to the UN prisoners through loudspeakers," Captain Lee said, "the communist leaders held a meeting at which Chiao asked the political officer whether he had carried out his instructions. The Chinese communist political officer said that he had, and that some UN prisoners of war had stayed inside their tents and wept.

"Chiao snorted and said that he was not interested in whether the POWs wept or laughed, and claimed that it was a victory for the communist side. 'This way,' he said, 'we have recovered the face lost to the UN side.'"

This small consolation to the communists was made even smaller on New Year's Day, when a second American, Corporal Claude J. Batchelor, asked for repatriation. It was smaller yet on the 20th of January when the NNRC, three days in advance of Freedom Day when by the terms of the armistice agreement the non-repatriates were to assume civilian status, turned the 22,000 anti-communist heroes over to the United Nations Command.

Chiao advanced a last, desperate plan to repossess these recalcitrants for the communists, a plan which, had the anti-communist heroes not proceeded out of the DZ in such disciplined, orderly fashion, might have renewed the Korean conflict. Here is the testimony of Chiao's own interpreter, Captain Lee:

"The communists heard from General Thimayya that the NNRC would turn over the POWs to the UNC. Chiao then called a meeting of the North Korean division in the Demilitarized Zone. Then, if a POW should make a break for the north, we must open fire to cover his escape. After that we must advance and head off the rest of the prisoners and kidnap them by force. If anyone were to criticize us later, we must

293

say that the U. N. forces had opened fire first to retrieve escapees.

"But when the final day came the communists merely tried to regain the POWs through loudspeaker broadcasts, but they failed to get back any. No prisoners broke away from the column and thus the communists lost face once more.

"I carried out my assignments faithfully for nine years in the Chinese Communist Army and as a member of the Communist Party for six years," Captain Lee Chun Bong concluded. "But when I came to Kaesong and sat in on the countless meetings between the North Korean and Chinese communist leaders, I was horrified to witness many political intrigues and dishonesties, and I discovered what communism really was. Then and there I decided to escape to the free world to tell the whole truth about it."

34

The Final Screening

The Custodian Force, India, massed at each compound in turn on the morning of January 20, and as the anti-communist heroes marched out on their way to freedom each single individual of the more than 22,000 was given one more final chance for repatriation if he wished it. This was, actually, the seventh choice the prisoners of war had had to return to Red control had they so wished.

They had had their first choice during the original screenings on Koje. They had a second choice when they were removed from Koje to the mainland of Korea and to Cheju. They had a third choice when they arrived at Cheju and on the mainland. They had a fourth choice when the repatriates were assembled for Big Switch. They had a fifth choice when they were turned over to the CFI.

During the entire period they were in the custody of the CFI they were able to ask for repatriation at any time. Others had an opportunity during the explanations. Many had still another opportunity during screenings by the CFI. Now they had their seventh choice—and stood firm.

When the twenty-two thousand marched out of Freedom Camp on that frosty morning, they presented a Nationalist Chinese and a Republic of Korea flag to the men of the U. S. First Marine Division who were there to welcome them—and to come to their rescue had the communists gone through with their kidnapping plot.

They also distributed, to the cheering thousands of U. N. troops all along their line of march from the edge of the DZ to the Port of Inchon, a mimeographed one-page leaflet in English—every compound had a mimeograph machine, stencils and paper for reproduction of their educational materials. At the top of the leaflet was their foursquare slogan, "Oppose Communism, Resist Russia," with the symbolic sun of the Republic of China and Rose of Sharon of the Republic of Korea; at the bottom, the torch of liberty and freedom, which they had made their personal symbol.

The English of the leaflet was not too expert, but it brought a lump to the throat of every United Nations soldier who read it, from one of the original leaflets or in the press. This version is a retranslation from the original Chinese, so that its heartfelt message may not be impaired by its erratic English:

"20th Jan. 54.

"Dear, honorable U. N. Fighters:

"When the Red bandits commenced an unprovoked assault against the territory of the Republic of Korea, all of you heroes left your homes voluntarily to participate in a just war, and didn't spare self-sacrifice to halt the aggression of the Reds in hot fighting. For this action you have earned the respect of all

296

of the people of the world, and we too respect your resolute will to preserve world peace.

"We owe you a debt of gratitude because you fought for more than nineteen months for us alone. But we will not forget it and we will remember it in our hearts when we're in the anti-Red battle. All we have to give is our lives, and to thank you we will give them to destroy the world aggressor.

"Now the war in Korea has stopped, and we have been liberated because the United Nations came to our defense. We hope we will meet again in the anti-Red firing line, to struggle for happiness and for humanity.

"Our dear, honorable heroes, now our country-brothers live under the tyranny of the Reds, so we have to leave now because we want to relieve our country-brothers. We will see you again in the anti-Red battle!

"God bless you and help you fight victoriously all the time.
                    "All the Anti-Red Prisoners."

When the Chinese anti-Reds reached Taiwan, the Nationalist Government organized five-man teams of ex-prisoners of war and sent them to the four corners of the free world—Southeast Asia, Japan, North and South America and Europe—to tell of their struggle against communism. The team which came to Japan brought another letter, to the men and women of the United Nations Command who had worked in the rehabilitation project.

"We wish to express our heartfelt gratitude to you," the letter said. "When we underwent the bitter life of imprisonment, you taught us, despite all hardships, how to read and write, carpentry and blacksmithing; you provided us with newspapers, radio broadcasts and movies in order to comfort us when we were lonely; and you invited many instructors and experts to explain to us the principles of democracy.

"During those three long years, you were our teachers and companions. You encouraged and comforted us, enabled us to gain knowledge and skill in handicrafts. You were most concerned about us when we were transferred to the demilitarized zone. Now we have returned to Taiwan victoriously. Representing the 14,343 anti-communist brothers, we wish to pay you our highest respects.

"We have shaken ourselves free from the yoke of the communists and returned to our fatherland. But we could not forget that Russian imperialism and its running dogs—Chu-Mao—are persecuting our countrymen on the mainland and paving the way to the enslavement of humanity. We hope that you will help us tell the world our experiences so that others shall not be cheated and trapped by the communists.

"We don't understand why some statesmen still fall for communist peace propaganda. If the communist bandits were sincere in their desire for peace, why were we forced to go to Korea to fight? We have families on the China mainland; nevertheless, we, 14,343 anti-communist brothers, have risked our lives and chosen to return to Taiwan, our free fatherland. The Chu-Mao bandits are still killing our people in order to maintain their dictatorial rule. They are our deadly enemies. Taiwan has become the lighthouse of freedom of the Chinese people on the mainland. And President Chiang is their beloved leader. We, here, appeal to the Free World to strengthen its unity and to cooperate with Free China in the sacred battle of anti-aggression and anti-slavery.

"We again pay our respects to you for your untiring efforts in teaching us. We shall never cease to feel grateful for your help.

"Representatives of the 14,343 Anti-Communist Brothers."

35

Pavlovian Strategy Can Be Undone

It is easy to condemn the Koreans, the Americans and the Briton who cast their lot with communism. But to the UNC representatives who saw in the "explanations" what three or four or five hours of brainwashing can do to men who were forewarned of it and forearmed against it, the wonder was that there were not more when the brainwashers had five days, weeks or months to do their devilish work.

Edward Hunter gives an excellent general picture of the process in his splendid books, *Brainwashing in Red China* and its sequel, *Brainwashing*. A concise, scientific description is given by Dr. Joost A. M. Meerlo, who points at the same time to the most probable reason so few UNC troops were subverted in Korea.

Dr. Meerlo, former chief of the psychological department of the Army of the Netherlands and now a member of the faculty of Columbia University, wrote on the subject "Pavlovian Theory as a Weapon of Menticide" in the May 1954 issue of the *American Journal of Psychiatry*.

". . . Pavlovian strategy," Dr. Meerlo writes in part, "arouses

. . . a 'confusion neurosis'—a general feeling of irreality. It leads gradually to complete mental submission and willingness to play any role.

"Military officials are inclined to interpret some actions of prisoners of war as 'treason' or, more mildly, as 'unforgivable weakness.' Psychiatrically speaking, however, such a breakdown can happen to nearly everybody, though the limit of endurance varies with individuals. In everybody lives the inner traitor who gives in, and there is no law prescribing that all people shall be heroes."

But, says Dr. Meerlo, "Pavlovian strategy can be undone . . .

"Experience has proven that people subjected to totalitarian hypnosis are far from being taken in completely by the propaganda barrage to which they are incessantly exposed. Under the appearance of unanimity, people are emboldened to feel revolt and resentment. There is only one form of systematic immunization against the totalitarian attack on human convictions. That is a deeply founded conviction of democratic freedom, a deep faith in the steadily growing system of checks and balances, of laws and rights made to canalize the outburst of human hunger for power. . . .

"It is interesting to read the Soviet attack on the academician T. S. Beritashivili, who recanted later, but who originally tried to prove that there is 'psychonervous activity' beyond the pure reflex pattern in which the reflex-pattern is not valid. His colleagues censured him for being so dualistic and not historic-materialistic.

"Even in animals we have found by experience that goal-directedness spoiled the Pavlovian experiment. When, during an experiment, the beloved owner entered the room, all the conditioned signs were suddenly lost. As we experienced so simply in the physiology laboratory, love and laughter break through every rigid conditioning. That the dog's spontaneous affection for his owner ruins the mechanical calculation of the very investigator never came to the attention of the mechanically thinking students of Pavlov."

Even a prompt disclaimer here and now that this writer is not comparing the United Nations and Chinese and Korean anti-communist heroes who came home to freedom to dogs will not prevent communist propagandists from so charging, and further charging that Wall Street and Presidents Chiang and Rhee are their "owners." But quotation of the foregoing paragraph is necessary to drive home Dr. Meerlo's point in conjunction with the United Nations prisoners of war in Korea who successfully resisted brainwashing in the POW camps, and the Chinese and Korean anti-communist heroes who resisted it as successfully in the "explanations."

They were goal-directed.

Communist propaganda to the contrary notwithstanding, life is pretty good in free Australia, Belgium, Canada, Colombia, Ethiopia, France, Great Britain, Greece, Luxembourg, the Netherlands, New Zealand, the Philippines, South Africa, Thailand, Turkey and the U. S. A. Life hadn't been bad between wars in Free China. While only one of all of the Chinese anti-communist heroes was a Formosan and not too many of the Korean anti-communist heroes had known the Republic of Korea between the time of its establishment and the North Korean invasion, life in Red China and Red Korea was so bad that they were heading sight unseen for Free China and the Republic of Korea.

Love of home and freedom triumphed over communist brainwashing, as they will always triumph.

In the final test, free world ideas and ideals worsted communist brainwashing by a score of one thousand to one. Laughter, just as it helped the Korean anti-communist heroes who wore masks to the explanations, also provided an assist. One of the heaviest campaigns directed against the U. S. prisoners of war in North Korea was that designed to first convince them of U. S. use of germ warfare, then secure "confessions" from them of having participated in its use. When "window," the long thin strips of aluminum foil dropped by UNC planes to foil enemy radar, fell on one POW camp housing U. S. personnel, they told their communist guards that this was indeed a U. S. germ warfare device—for spreading rabies. Sacrificing some of their small and precious store of soap, they solemnly chewed this along with strips of the foil. When they foamed at the mouth, their guards fled in terror while they roared with laughter.

In another camp, the U. S. prisoners of war varied the monotony of simply killing the rats which abounded there by trapping them, branding them with a "US," and presenting them to their guards as "germ warfare evidence."

When one considers the total numbers of Koreans, Americans and Britons who fell into communist hands in the Korean conflict, the number of non-repatriates is a testimonial not to the efficacy but to the almost total failure of brainwashing. When one considers in addition the complete total of 88,000

Koreans and Chinese who chose freedom at the first opportunity after escaping from communist control, it is small wonder that the tune from the Kremlin, between conditioned-reflex blasts of belligerence, periodically harps on peaceful coexistence.

General Mark W. Clark, Commander-in-Chief of the United Nations Command, stood steadfast in defense of the principle of non-forcible repatriation, as had General Matthew B. Ridgway, his predecessor. His successor as CINCUNC, General John E. Hull, was equally firm and forthright. In his statement on Freedom Day, January 23, 1954, welcoming the anticommunist heroes to the free world, General Hull summed up the situation most trenchantly.

"The 22,000 men who have today regained civilian status and freedom," he said, "have triumphed in the final battle of the Korean conflict. They fought on for six long months after an armistice was signed, six months which encompassed a move back to their old battlefield, relinquishment of friendly United Nations protection, a cold Korean winter, Communist explanations and broadcasts, and blandishments of Communist agents who had surrendered to penetrate their ranks. They stand as living symbols, providing hope of freedom to the millions who still suffer under Communist oppression.

"This day begins a new epoch in the determined effort of the Free World to resist Communist encroachment on the lives and lands of free people. Today the principle of non-forcible repatriation for which the United Nations has fought so long has been firmly established. From this day on, all soldiers of every Communist army may know of a certainty that they may seek and find sanctuary in the Free World.

"That nearly half of the Korean and three-fourths of the Chinese prisoners of war in the Korean conflict declared that they would forcibly resist repatriation is highly significant. When they made their choice, the practical alternative of freedom in the Republic of China and the Republic of Korea, which now rewards them for their valiant stand against communism, had not been established. Yet their hatred of communism, having experienced it, was so great that even with no certain alternative they forswore their homes.

"To these men who so courageously have resisted both Communist blandishments and Communist threats, the Free World offers not only asylum, but welcome. Their example may well be a beacon to guide others now suffering under Communist tyranny to the sanctuary of freedom and human dignity."

The last of the anti-communist heroes freed, barely in time to catch the last LST to Taipei's port of Keelung, were the seven Chinese "murderers" from Compound 28. A Chinese-speaking American attorney furnished by the United Nations Command as their counsel, Allan R. Morrison, defended them brilliantly with the assistance of Richard E. O'Brien, in what was probably the first international court martial for "murder" with no corpse and with communist agents as witnesses. The latter parrotted their set stories, but were helpless when questions were asked for which they had not been drilled in the answers. The Northern Command met this situation by simply refusing to permit them to reappear as witnesses, and the CFI court martial had no choice but to discharge them.

305

The seven Compound B leaders sat for a studio photograph when they reached Taipei; this picture is reproduced in the photograph section of this book. Can you picture them as murderers, or, even more horrendous, as cannibals, as charged by the communists whom they defeated in this last little side-struggle of the conflict in Korea?

36

The Victory Behind Barbed Wire

The United States Senate ratified the 1949 Geneva Conventions for the protection of war victims in July, 1955. At that time they had been ratified or acceded to by forty-eight nations, including all of the Iron Curtain countries excepting North Korea and Red China. In presenting the report of the Committee on Foreign Relations, Senator Mansfield of Montana included the following statement:

"During the Korean armistice negotiations the most contested legal issue was whether the parties were obliged to compel prisoners to be repatriated against their will, or whether the detaining power could in its discretion grant asylum to any prisoner who desired it. The United Nations Command maintained the position that all prisoners who wished to be repatriated were entitled to repatriation, but that international law did not require force to be used if they were unwilling to return. The Communists asserted that forced repatriation was prescribed under the principle of Article 118 of the 1949 convention on prisoners of war. That article provides in part:

" 'Prisoners of war shall be released and repatriated without delay after the cessation of active hostilities.'

"In the United Nations General Assembly in the fall of 1952, during debates on the Korean armistice negotiations, the Soviet bloc sought to maintain the thesis that the principles of Articles 118 and 7 (which prohibits renunciation of rights by a prisoner) did not encompass a grant of asylum to prisoners of war. The exchanges, in which our own Government took a leading part, developed that the practice of many nations, including the practice of the Soviet Government, was authority for granting asylum to prisoners of war; that at Geneva, in 1949, the negotiators proceeded upon the premise that the doctrine of asylum was applicable; and that they did not intend to overturn customary law in this respect. Both General Assembly Resolution 610 (VII) and the eventual armistice agreement in Korea permitted the individual prisoner of war a free choice between return and asylum, under safeguards of impartial supervision. The fact that it is an 'unrestricted opportunity of repatriation,' and not an absolute obligation or predetermined fate of repatriation which the prisoner is given under Article 118, was similarly recognized by the General Assembly in Resolution 427 (V) of December 14, 1950, and reaffirmed in Resolution 741 (VIII) of December 7, 1953.

"Members of the committee, exploring the problem of involuntary repatriation with the executive branch, were informed at the hearing that the United States official position continues to be that maintained in Korea and overwhelmingly supported in the resolution of the General Assembly, and that Article 118 does nothing to change accepted principles of international law under which asylum is applicable to prisoners of war.

"The committee unqualifiedly concurs. It finds nothing in the Geneva conventions of 1949 which will compel the United States forcibly to repatriate prisoners of war who fear political persecution, personal injury, or death should they return to their homeland. That article, being intended for the benefit and well-being of prisoners, will permit the United States to continue the policy of nonforceable repatriation, while at the same time leaving it free, where necessary, to refuse requests for asylum. The interpretation which has thus prevailed gives due weight to the word 'release' in Article 118, is faithful to precedent and legislative history, and is fully consistent with the great humanitarian purposes which underlie all four of the conventions."

Non-forcible repatriation is thus firmly established as U. S. and U. N. policy, but it may be expected in the future that it will be accepted by the U. S. S. R. and the satellites only when it runs in their favor. It is inevitably repugnant, too, to many free world military men.

The anti-communist heroes, in a press statement which they also turned out on their mimeograph machines on Freedom Day, praised General Thimayya for the wisdom he had shown in the discharge of his difficult duty. "We believe that the Indian officers and men," they said, "who have learned a profound lesson on the choice between freedom and slavery during the 120 days in the demilitarized zone in Korea, will bring that lesson back to New Delhi and to Mr. Nehru. We shall feel happy if the free world gains a new friendly force through their reports."

Yet even General Thimayya felt obliged, once his mission had been discharged, to dissent from this principle. He expressed the view that this concept would offer soldiers the opportunity to rationalize acts of cowardice on the battlefield on ideological grounds—notwithstanding the fact that it took more bravery in Korea to surrender than to remain under communist control—and despite the fact that it was an Indian resolution in the U. N. General Assembly which offered a formula giving virtual recognition to the principle of non-forcible repatriation, clothed in the face-saving term "non-direct repatriation."

United Nations and United States leaders hailed the application of the principle as a triumph of the ideals of the free world, and the Swiss senior delegate to the NNRC recommended that a conference be convened to rewrite the Geneva Convention to spell out clearly recognition of the principle of voluntary repatriation. But in view of the implications of this principle for the communist world, agreement on its explicit inclusion in a new Geneva Convention is most unlikely.

In fact, in view of the callous communist disregard for all aspects of the Geneva Conventions as they now stand with respect to the treatment of prisoners of war, it is apparent that any future conflict between the free and communist worlds, should the communists be so rash as to provoke one, will again be fought with the free world making every effort to adhere to humanitarian principles, and the communists ignoring them.

310

A very special set of circumstances operated with respect to the anti-communist heroes in the Korean conflict. Just as the prisoners of war in communist hands had their seventeen homelands on which to focus their goal-directedness, the Chinese and Korean prisoners of war in UN hands had Formosa and the Republic of Korea as spiritual homes about which their hopes and prayers might center. Such a situation may not obtain in a future conflict between the free world and communism.

One of the immense threats of the sprawling Eurasian communist complex in a global war is that communism, in an effort to reduce the danger of mass defection of its troops by units as well as individuals, may employ European troops in Southeast Asia, and Asian troops in Europe.

Parents and armies all over the world have learned by experience that it is wise to send their children to college and their inductees to basic training camps as far away from their homes as possible, to secure increased attention to studies and minimize the temptation to go absent without leave. In the same way, even an anti-communist Vietnamese might be discouraged from surrendering to the free world in Norway, and an anti-communist Albanian from surrendering in Vietnam.

If South Vietnam remains outside the communist orbit as South Korea has, the Vietnamese would have a spiritual home, a goal to which to direct his hopes. But what of the Albanian, whose only hope could be that the war would result in the liberation of his homeland so that he might return to a free Albania? In addition to China, Korea and Vietnam, only Germany lies astride the Iron Curtain.

There is a simple solution to this dilemma, one which will at the same time rally a maximum of "communist" personnel as individuals and units to the banners of the free world, guarantee them asylum and sanctuary, minimize the mass manpower advantages of the communist world, and provide for the anti-communist heroes of the next conflict a spiritual home and goal to which they may direct themselves.

In any future conflict with communism, free world national and international policy should declare that only those individuals who are captured in the traditional sense will be considered and classified as prisoners of war. Persons seeking asylum would not be considered as having "fallen into the power of the enemy," and they would never acquire prisoner of war status.

All individuals, once freed from communist control, should be screened immediately, to determine their category. To absolve the free world belligerents from charges of "terrorization" and "persecution" such as the communists levelled at the UNC in Korea, a neutral body such as the International Committee of the Red Cross might sit in on or actually conduct such screenings.

These screenings would produce personnel of two categories; traditional prisoners of war who would choose repatriation to communist control at the conclusion of the conflict and anti-communists seeking asylum and sanctuary. The prisoners of war in the traditional sense would be so classified immediately and interned in prisoner of war camps.

The anti-communists should be organized immediately in Free Albanian Brigades, Free Bulgarian Divisions, Free Czechoslovakian Corps, until there were eventually Free Armenian, Byelorussian, Estonian, Georgian, Great Russian, Hungarian, Karelian, Latvian, Lithuanian, Polish, Romanian and Ukrainian Armies on the Free World side.

Ample precedent exists in recent history on both sides of the Iron Curtain for the non-classification as prisoners of war of individuals changing sides in a conflict: the Czech prisoners in World War I, the French offering initial resistance to allied landings in Africa during World War II, and the Chinese Nationalists press-ganged into the Chinese communist forces in 1948-49.

If governments-in-exile were recognized by the free world high command, an ideal psychological factor would arise, replacing the stigma of desertion or defection with the patriotic matrix of "escaping from oppression" and "joining the forces of liberation." Existing governments-in-exile could be reinforced by outstanding patriots from the ranks of these escapees, and parallel governments should be organized where they do not already exist.

Provisional units should be activated among nationals of countries which do not have sufficient personnel at the onset of hostilities to organize battalions and regiments of their own, and from among disabled anti-communists unfit for further active military service, to guard the communist prisoners of war, freeing further free world troops for combat duty. Fully forewarned, such guards would obviate the possibility of Koje-style agitation and riots.

There would be communist infiltration, dogged and determined, of course. But the agents who were not discovered in the original screening would have only to open their mouths for the first time in their military units to be revealed for what they were, and delivered to POW compounds. Many of them, just as in Korea, might decide to throw in their lot with the free world rather than to carry out their communist assignments.

And the free brigades, divisions and corps would grow apace. "We believe," the Chinese anti-communist heroes in Korea said in their Freedom Day manifesto, "if there had been troops of the Republic of China at the Korean front at the time of fighting, defection en masse from the communist side would have been in regiments and divisions."

Army units would not be the only ones to come over. Aircraft and naval crews would seek sanctuary. Communist power would crumble on land, at sea and in the air.

"Until the end of the fighting," the *Christian Century* editorialized on Korea, "these surrenders showed that the communists could not trust their soldiers. This fact will have to be taken into account by the communists before they renew their aggression here or elsewhere.

"If, beginning in Korea, the tide which has been sweeping across Asia starts to recede, it is highly probable that future historians will locate this decisive conflict on no battlefield, but in the victory which was won behind the barbed wire. . . . But it is hardly likely that this will happen unless the people of the United Nations, and particularly of the United States, realize the meaning of what has happened and build it into their policy."

If this is done, the free world will win again and for all time, and by a margin of far more than one thousand to one.

Appendix A — Demographic Data

Statistics on the Chinese and North Korean POWs in Korea are of necessity based on the 50,000 anti-communist soldiers. The 38,000 anti-communist Korean civilian internees were excluded from surveys of the military population of Korea for obvious reasons, and the communist minority could not be relied upon for accurate answers. Actually, the communist minority was surprisingly cooperative in many aspects of the rehabilitation program, up to the time of the Red-instigated riots in April of 1952. But from that time on they felt obliged to be recalcitrant and increasingly non-cooperative, an attitude which finally culminated in their hysterical disrobing when they were eventually repatriated.

Many of the repatriates were unquestionably as anti-communist as the non-repatriates. Despite their hatred of communism, they were going home, to families, wives, children, their native villages. But having been taken prisoner, being suspect of having surrendered, having been out of communist control, they knew that they were under a communist cloud. The best protection was a militant show of communism which increased with every step back toward communist control.

But since the sample which was surveyable was so large, the findings unquestionably apply to the whole of the prisoners of war. As one would expect, the bulk of both the Chinese and the North

Korean POWs were from 18 to 35 years old—91.1% of the Chinese, 86% of the Koreans. A detailed breakdown by age groups reveals significant differences, however.

Age Range	Chinese		North Koreans	
	Number of POWs	Per cent of POWs	Number of POWs	Per cent of POWs
Under 15	0	0.0	4	.01
15-17	30	0.2	21	0.06
18-25	6,239	43.7	14,702	42.45
26-35	6,767	47.4	15,089	43.57
36-45	1,148	8.1	4,383	12.65
Over 45	81	0.6	436	1.26

The average age of the Chinese POW was 27.4 years; of the Korean, 28.11. The significantly larger proportion of Koreans over the generally accepted military age—13.91% as against 8.7% for the Red Chinese—is one more indication, added to the testimony of the North Koreans themselves, that the bulk of the North Korean troops were swept up in the spring and summer of 1950, from fields, schools, mines and factories, and employed, to use a favorite communist phrase, as cannon fodder.

A complete breakdown on the Chinese POWs who chose to return to Red China is not available, but partial figures show an interesting divergence, again, between the Red Chinese and the confirmed communist North Koreans. While only 17.3% of the total Chinese POW population voted to return to Red China, 43% of those over 45 years of age decided to return to communist rule, but hardly any of those under 18 chose to return. There is an interesting parallel here with the Hungarian revolt, in which youth—the "new Communist men"—took a leading part.

On the other hand, a survey of 32,000 North Korean POWs showed that, although an average of 34% desired repatriation to Red rule, and 59% of those over 45 wished to be repatriated, 54% of those under 18 formed the next highest percentage group who

316

wished to return to their homes. Family ties, purportedly even stronger among Chinese than Koreans, operated with respect to the older age groups of both, but not at all with respect to the younger Chinese.

Before any profound conclusions are drawn in this respect, it might be well to point out that there were not more than two-score Chinese POWs under 18, and the American camp commanders and their staffs, feeling that they had no more place in a prisoner of war compound than in an army, gave them jobs as house-boys and mess attendants.

In such jobs, it was rare for them to have an opportunity to participate in any part of the rehabilitation program other than the after-hours recreational features such as moving pictures and radio re-broadcasts. They did have at hand, however, American magazines and books, and they saw the English-language movies in the messes after the evening meal. With a far better opportunity than their elders to learn and use English, they often progressed to additional duty as interpreters and even as instructors. It was this group which, when the terms of reference of the armistice agreement with respect to the POWs were publicized, was most keenly disappointed to find that they could not go to the United States. The U. S., to them, most definitely was not a "neutral nation."

There appeared to be no connection between the age of Chinese POWs and the rate at which they surrendered to U. N. forces. But there was a definite connection between surrender and ex-membership in the Chinese Nationalist Army (CNA)—soldiers first impressed into the communist forces and then "volunteered" for service in Korea. No over-all survey was ever made of the proportion of ex-Nationalist soldiers among the Chinese POWs, but individual surveys of representative samples gave results ranging from 43% to 66%.

The explanation which the Chinese POWs themselves gave for this unexpectedly high proportion of former Nationalist troops was that these troops were generally considered unreliable from the communist viewpoint, and consequently expendable. They were being employed as cannon fodder just as the untrained Koreans had been. At any rate, the younger ex-CNAs, those under the average age, surrendered to the U. N. forces at nearly twice as great a rate as the other Chinese troops. Those over the average age surrendered at very nearly the same rate, whether or not they had been in Chiang Kai-shek's forces. Since motivation for surrender among the Chinese was very largely the hope that they would be able to fight on the other side, either for the U. N. or for Nationalist China, there are two explanations for this. One is the very normal decrease in appetite for warfare—for personal participation in it, at any rate—with advancing age. The other is that the communist faith in developing the "new Communist man" among communist youth is unfounded.

Statistics on Korean surrenders seemed to bear this out, for the ratio of surrenders among the younger group to that among the older was approximately 4 to 3. Ex-ROKA soldiers among the younger group should have been considered unreliable from the communist viewpoint, for among the ROK Army men captured by the communists, impressed into the North Korean Army, then regained by the U. N. forces, 97% surrendered.

Two-thirds of the Chinese POWs were single, 31% were married, and 5% widowed, divorced, or separated. A majority of the Korean POWs were married, 60.9%; 38.1% were single, and only 1% widowed or divorced. In both groups, it was those who were widowed, divorced, or separated who most readily chose repatriation; those who were married or single opposed or chose repatriation in almost exactly the same proportion.

Although of the Chinese POWs who were married 17% had children and 74% still had living parents—an even more important consideration to a Chinese—this made relatively little difference in their attitude toward repatriation.

318

When the Indian Custodial Forces and the Indian component of the Neutral Nations "Repatriation" Commission (NNRC) arrived in Korea following the armistice, the most inexplicable thing to them about the situation with respect to the anti-communist prisoners of war was their unwillingness to return to their homes and families. The Indians had been subjected to an intensive barrage of communist propaganda to the effect that the U. S. was "forcibly detaining" the remaining anti-communist prisoners of war. When this line was defeated by the promptness and cheerfulness with which the United Nations Command handed over the prisoners to the NNRC, the propaganda line was shifted and stepped up. Now it was "Chiang and Rhee agents" among the prisoners who were supposedly terrorizing them into refusing repatriation. The communists were still unable to explain how a man or group of men could be terrorized into remaining in terrorist hands, when all he had to do to be repatriated was to raise his hand. Nor did they estimate how many "agents" it would take to detain forcibly up to five hundred men in a compound, or explain how these "Chiang and Rhee agents" had penetrated the so-called North Korean People's Army and Chinese People's Volunteers.

When the communists finally summoned enough courage to begin belatedly the explanations to the prisoners of war and it became apparent to the Indian officers that the only "agents" among the prisoners were a handful of communists who had penetrated the prisoner of war camps, the Indians still could not understand how the great majority of the men could resist the appeal of home and family. As the explanations continued in a communist attempt to save face, and the men kept on pouring out their hatred and contempt of communism, the Indians began to learn what the Americans had already found out from the prisoners of war—that life under communism can be so abhorrent that no sacrifice is too great to escape it.

One important difference develops when one compares the marital status of the Chinese who surrendered with that of those who were captured. Forty-one per cent of the Chinese who surrendered were married, and only 17% of those who were captured were married. Further, 21% of those surrendering reported having children while only 10% of those captured had children.

The only possible explanation of this is that the experience of these men under communism made them assess their chance of returning to parents, wives and children as better via Taiwan and a liberating Nationalist Army than by direct repatriation. They fully realized that the penalty for escaping from the communist system, if only briefly, could be death if they were lucky, a slave labor camp if they were unlucky.

There was a strong presumption, too, that they no longer had families. To discourage surrender, both the Communist Chinese and North Koreans carried out and widely publicized a policy of shooting the families of defectors.

When the opportunity for repatriation came in 1953, the great majority of Chinese soldiers had been away from home for at least five years, several of them years of intense communist propaganda against the Chinese family concept and in favor of replacing it with a stronger concept of loyalty to the "People's Liberation Army" as an adjunct of the communist state. The political officers in each unit of the "volunteers," which were but thinly disguised units of the communist Army, had as their primary objective the tearing down of the individual soldier's obeisance to his family and replacing it with squad, platoon, and company loyalty.

Another factor which militated against a choice of repatriation on the part of married Chinese soldiers was the Red marriage law, propagated in May, 1950, just before the Korean aggression began.

Religion is usually the first target of attack in a communist consolidation campaign, but in China the communists recognized the Chinese family system as a greater obstacle to the acceptance of communism than the philosophical Chinese religions, none of which

320

precluded acceptance of still another religion, even communism. Their marriage law had two objectives, to weaken the family system and ostensibly to raise the status of women, thereby gaining for the extension of communist ideology some support from a "have-not" portion of the people.

The principal feature of the marriage law as far as the reluctant dragoons of the CCF (Communist Chinese Forces) were concerned was its provision for quick, cheap, and easy divorce. If a soldier's wife had not been in correspondence with her husband for two years, she could apply to the nearest magistrate and in a matter of minutes and for the equivalent of fifty cents get a divorce. Then she could marry the prosperous communist cadre, exempt from conscription because of his party position, who had put her up to it.

Leaves and furloughs were as few and far between as mail calls in the "people's volunteers," which is to say non-existent, and CCF soldiers were particularly vulnerable to the feminine weakness for a man around the house. Worst of all, they had no way of knowing just what the situation at home was—whether they were still married, divorced, widowed or cuckolded.

United Nations Command psychological warfare made much of this, particularly after October, 1952, when the Chinese troops had been in Korea for the necessary two years under the law. They were so vulnerable to radio broadcasts on this theme that Peiping was forced to institute a daily series of half-hour suppertime programs, relayed by two Manchurian stations, telling them how happy they really should be about the situation back home. Not only that, but an Article 49 to the marriage law was promulgated and thoroughly publicized to the troops. This article specified that if the husband in a divorce action were a soldier, his wife could not divest herself of him even if she had not been in correspondence with him for two years, without his express permission. Since mail continued to come only to men who were officers, communists or—even better —both, Peiping's efforts hurt far more than they helped.

Just as interesting is the relation of their educational level to their choice of repatriation. Among the Chinese with one to nine years of education, there was no discernible difference from level to level; well above 80% wanted no part of communism. Only 68.1% of those with 10 to 12 years of education were anti-communist, however, and a bare 38.7% of those with over 12 years. The samples in the upper educational brackets were small, however, since both of these groups together comprised only 1.1% of the total Chinese prisoner of war population. Any deduction that the communists appeal more to Chinese intellectuals than to farmers or laborers, therefore, would be dangerous.

It would be particularly dangerous in view of comparison with the North Korean prisoners of war. Among more than 32,000 North Koreans surveyed in this connection, 10,000 chose repatriation. Those with no education went communist in the greatest proportion, 41.5%; those with more than 12 years of schooling in the smallest proportion, 4.2%. The complete breakdown follows:

Educational Level	Number of POWs	Number of Returnees	Per cent of Returnees
None	1,883	781	41.5
1-3 years	11,825	4,813	40.7
4-6 years	14,448	4,427	30.6
7-9 years	2,837	717	25.3
10-12 years	1,105	225	20.4
Over 12 years	95	4	4.2
	32,193	10,967	34.1 (average)

Additionally, special and separate studies of Chinese and Koreans alike disclosed that prisoners of war with over six years of education surrendered to U. N. forces more readily than those with less education.

When the Chinese prisoners of war are broken down by percentage of non-repatriates for each occupation, there can be no doubt that the greater number of Chinese intellectuals, if afforded the opportunity, would choose freedom. The largest occupational

322

group among the Chinese, former farmers, comprised 40.5% of the total number of prisoners. The next largest were professional soldiers, 36.9%, but it is likely that these too were principally from the farming class and because of their youth had had no other employment in their lives except soldiering. Next came commerce, with 9%; students, 4.5%; unskilled labor, 4.4%; skilled labor, 2.2%; professional men, 1%; and civil servants, 0.4%.

The percentage of each of these categories to choose to return to communism shows quite definitely who may expect to profit most under communism—and how few of even those who might profit most want to take the chance. In this survey, no distinction was made between skilled and unskilled labor. But only 24.4% of the professional soldiers chose communism, 16.1% of the laborers, 11.5% of the farmers and 4.7% classed as "miscellaneous." Of merchants, students, professional men, and civil servants, out of more than 14,000 prisoners of war not a single man of these asked to return to Red China.

In similarly classifying the Korean prisoners by civilian occupation, the distinction between a professional soldier and a conscripted farmer or student was made plain, and only 1.4% of the North Koreans represented themselves as professional military men. The complete table is as follows:

Occupation	Number of POWs	Per cent of POWs
Agriculture	23,144	66.8
Student	3,720	10.7
Unskilled laborer	2,809	8.1
Commerce	1,655	4.8
Skilled laborer	1,479	4.3
Civil servant	527	1.5
Military	470	1.4
Miscellaneous	417	1.2
Professional	279	0.8
No occupation	135	0.4
	34,635	100.0

In relation of occupation to anti-communism, the North Koreans broke down as follows:

Occupation	Anti-communists (%)	Communists (%)
Military	44.8	55.2
None	54.5	45.5
Professional	54.8	45.2
Unskilled labor	63.4	36.6
Agriculture	66.3	33.7
Skilled labor	69.1	30.9
Student	69.2	30.8
Miscellaneous	73.6	26.4
Government worker	82.3	17.7
Commerce	84.4	15.6
Average	65.9	34.1

Appendix B—List of Instructional Units, Books and Pamphlets Used in the Rehabilitation Project

INSTRUCTIONAL UNITS

Note: The makeshift materials used in the pilot project, of which records were lost in the second communist occupation of Seoul by the Chinese "Volunteers," made up "Series I."

SERIES II

1. Let's Look at Our Home
2. Let's Make Our Home Better
3. These Are Our Neighbors
4. Our Friends, the Policemen and Firemen
5. Our Schools and Our Teachers
6. Having a Good Time With Others
7. Safeguarding Our Health
8. Our Community and Ourselves
9. How We Make a Living
10. Our Very Own Land
11. Working Together
12. Ourselves and Our Province
13. Ourselves and Our National Government
14. Ourselves and the World

SERIES III

1. The Individual in Free Nations and in Communist Nations
2. Family Life in Free Nations and in Communist Nations
3. The Basic Freedoms Under Democracy and Under Communism
4. The Law and the Police in Free Nations and in Communist Nations
5. Education in Free Nations and in Communist Nations
6. (not issued)
7. The Individual and Public Health in Free Nations and in Communist Nations
8. (not issued)
9. Making a Living in Free Nations and in Communist Nations
10. The Farmer in Free Nations and in Communist Nations
11. The Urban Worker in Free Nations and Communist Nations

SERIES IV

1. The Individual and His Family in the United States
2. The American Family and Home
3. Maintaining Public Safety, Health, Welfare and Recreation in the U. S. (The Good Neighbor Spirit in America)
4. Education Is for All in the U. S.
5. The Law and the Police in the U. S.
6. Recreation and Leisure Time in America
7. How the People in the U. S. Govern Themselves
8. The People of the U. S. Work for World Peace

SPECIAL PAMPHLETS

The Foundation of Our Liberties
A Study of the United Nations
Healthful Recreation and Games (Vols. I, II, III)
Rules of Procedure for Meetings
"Animal Farm," by George Orwell

326

"1984," by George Orwell
Democratic Local Government
Public Health and Sanitation
*James Yen Thousand Character Lesson (Vols. I-IV incl.)
The British Political System and Its Use in Associated Countries
Sweden and the Swedes
The People of Switzerland
*Communism and the San Min Chu I
Communism in Russia
*Inside Communist China—Political and Social Life
*Inside Communist China—How the People Live
Communism and Fascism
What Is Totalitarianism?
What Is Imperialism?
*China and Her Neighbors
*Sino-American Relations
*China and the West
*Sino-Russian Relations
*China's History: The Republic
*A Short History of the Chinese Empire
*History of China (Vols. I, II)
*Literature of China (Vols. I, II)
World Development
*Friendship Between the Soviet Union and China
Songs of the United Nations
The Family in a Democracy
The Diary of a Prisoner of War
Economic Life in a Democracy
Developing a Democratic System of Education
Becoming a Member of the Family of Free Nations
Soviet Imperialism Plunders Asia (Parts I, II)
*Reconstruction of China

* Chinese only

Basic Documents of the United Nations
**The War Against Tuberculosis in Korea
The Story of the Truce Talks
The United Nations Civil Assistance Command, Korea
Songs of Many Lands

AGRICULTURAL SERIES

Improved Agricultural Technique
How to Grow Rice and Fish
How to Grow Vegetables
Poultry and Livestock
Soils and Fertilizers

** Korean only

Appendix C—Titles of Feature Films Selected for the Program of Education and Recreation for POWs

---

Columbia:
  You Can't Take It With You
  Mr. Deeds Goes To Town
20th Century-Fox:
  Young Mr. Lincoln
  Story of Alexander Graham Bell
  Chicken Every Sunday
  Miracle on 34th Street
MGM:
  Life Begins for Andy Hardy
  Our Vines Have Tender Grapes
  Young Tom Edison
  Mutiny On The Bounty
  Adventures of Huckleberry Finn
R.K.O.:
  Farmer's Daughter
  I Remember Mama
  Pride of the Yankees
Warners:
  Johnny Belinda
  Life of Emile Zola
United Artists:
  Carnegie Hall
  High Noon
  Stage Coach

UNC
No.	Title
1.	Electricity and the Land
2.	Border Without Bayonets
3.	English Criminal Justice
4.	Freedom of the Press
5.	U. S. Community and Its Citizens
6.	White Collar Worker
7.	Auto Worker in Detroit
8.	World Food Problem
9.	American Working Women
10.	Journey Into Medicine
11.	Water, Friend or Foe
12.	Winged Scourge
13.	How Disease Travels
14.	Insects as Carriers of Disease
15.	Public Sanitation *
16.	Defensive Footwork in Basketball
17.	Ball Handling in Basketball
18.	Shooting in Basketball
19.	Catching in Baseball
20.	Hitting in Baseball
21.	Dashes, Hurdles and Relays

* Japanese film.

329

UNC
No.   Title

22. Jumps and Pole Vault
23. Throwing in Baseball
24. Adult Education
25. Air Progress
26. Art in Haiti
27. As Russia Sees It
28. Assignment Tomorrow
29. Atlantic Pact
30. Bearing in a Modern World
31. Berlin Powder Keg
32. Better Tomorrow
33. Blue Ribbon
34. Bryn Mawr
35. California Junior Symphony
36. High Over the Border
37. A Child Went Forth
38. Community Workshop
39. Library of Congress
40. Factory Worker Turns
      Farmer
41. How To Conduct a Meeting
42. Using Parliamentary Proce-
      dures *
43. World Wide Communism
44. Facts About 16mm Film
45. Facts About 16mm Projection
46. UN Army Commander
47. Democracy's Diary
48. Searchlight on the Nation
49. San Francisco Conference
50. The Photographer
51. Meet Your Federal Govern-
      ment
52. Make Way for Youth
53. Land of Enchantment
54. Our American Heritage
55. Sport's Golden Age
56. Men of Gloucester

UNC
No.   Title

57. Inauguration of President
      Truman
58. Story That Couldn't Be
      Printed
59. Smoke Eaters
60. Lobster Town
61. Han Kul Typewriter
62. Teacher's Task
63. Cleveland, USA
64. Youth in Camps
65. White House
66. The Family
67. Life With Junior
68. A Day At School
69. New England
70. Johnny Jones
71. UN And World Disputes
72. Edith Sampson
73. Truman's San Francisco
74. Acheson's Speech
75. World of Friendship
76. Clear Track Ahead
77. Brothers in Arms
78. Capital Story
79. Community Advisory Service
80. Community Chest
81. Country Store
82. County Agent
83. Creative Leisure
84. Democracy in Action
85. Danish Hospital Ship Returns
      to Her Own Country
86. Eisenhower
87. Everyman's Empire
88. Everyone's School
89. First Steps
90. Cattle and the Corn Belt
91. Cleaning Brings Health
92. County Government

* Japanese film.

UNC
No.   Title

93. Cummington Story
94. Defense Against Invasion
95. Design for Learning
96. Eyes of Tomorrow
97. Foreign Sports
98. Freedom to Learn
99. Forgotten Victory
100. Gift of T'sai Lun
101. Girard College
102. Governor Dewey's Visit to Korea
103. Green Mountain Land
104. Guardian of the Wild
105. In Defense of Peace
106. Harvest for Tomorrow
107. Henry Brown, Farmer
108. Home on the Range
109. Hookworm
110. Hoover Dam
111. Hydro-Electricity
112. Independence Day in Korea
113. International House
114. International Ice Patrol
115. Lincoln's Speech at Gettysburg
116. Living in a Metropolis
117. The Lumber States
118. Korea On the March
119. Korea Today
120. Living Silver
121. Men of Goodwill
122. Maine Harbor Town
123. Museum of Science and Industry
124. New York's Finest
125. Nation's Capital
126. New Neighbors
127. (none)
128. North Atlantic Treaty

UNC
No.   Title

129. Northwest U. S. A.
130. One Year in Korea **
131. Partnership for Peace
132. Peanuts, a Valuable Crop
133. People's Response
134. The Policeman
135. Postwar Farms
136. Progressive Education
137. Panorama
138. Poultry Raising
139. Public Opinion
140. San Francisco
141. Rural Co-op
142. The School
143. Screen Report
144. Shipbuilders of Essex
145. Soil and Water Conservation
146. Starting Line
147. Streptomycin
148. Sweden Looks Ahead
149. Switzerland
150. Story of Two Cities
151. Steel Town
152. Tanglewood Music School
153. They Do Come Back
154. This Is New York
155. This Is Recovery
156. This Is Tomorrow
157. Top Soil
158. Toscanini
159. Town Solves a Problem
160. Traffic Safety
161. Transportation in the U. S.
162. The Town
163. Trees to Tame the Wind
164. Truman's Address to Congress
165. Tuesday in November
166. Tennessee Valley Authority

** USIA film.

UNC
No. *Title*
167. Tuberculosis
168. Tulsa, U.S.A.
169. U.C.L.A.
170. UN Aids Republic of Korea
171. UN Answers Aggression
172. UN At Work
173. Under Western Skies
174. Union Town
175. U. S. Elects Truman
176. Village Storekeeper
177. Water for Dry Land
178. We See Them Through
179. Western Stock Buyer
180. What Is Disease?
181. When Good Neighbors Get Together
182. Women and the Community
183. Aesop's Fables
184. The American Cop
185. American Folk Festival, No. 1
    No. 2
186. American Housing Problem
187. President Truman Calls Up-on the Nation
188. American Stock Raising
189. American National Parks
190. Australian National Capital
191. Boys Clubs in America
192. Briefs from America
193. Britain Speaks
194. Bus Driver
195. CARE Story
196. Charter of the UN
197. Citizen's Public Hall
198. Cook Island Oranges
199. County Fair
200. Cowboy Festival
201. Defeat Tuberculosis

UNC
No. *Title*
202. Design for the Future
203. The Doctor
204. English Coal Mining
205. Exploring the Mysteries of New Zealand
206. Fight For Better Schools
207. The Fireman
208. Floating Theatre
209. Folk Songs of the South
210. Glimpses of America, #19
211. Government, the Public Serv-ant
212. Great Lakes
213. How Laws Are Made
214. Industrial Safety Devices
215. International Arts Festival
216. It Happened in Our Town
217. Job in a Million
218. Junior Red Cross
219. Latest From America
220. Let's Play Baseball
221. Local Drama
222. Los Angeles
223. Louisiana Story, #1
    #2
224. The Mailman
225. Men of Tomorrow
226. Men of Tomorrow
227. Men Who Fish *
228. Mexico
229. Model Health Center
230. Modern Medicine
231. Mountains and Seas of Scot-land
232. Music in America
233. Nanook of the North
234. New England Farmer
235. New South
236. New West

* Japanese film.

UNC
No. Title

237. New York Fire Department
238. Gillette College
239. Our Eating Life
240. The Pale Horseman
241. People's Charter
242. Productivity, Key to Plenty
243. Progress of Japanese Women
244. Rediscovery of America
245. Redwood Saga
246. Right for the Worker
247. Rodent Control
248. Seeds of Destiny
249. Sketches of Britain
250. Sports Review, #15
251. Beautiful Dreamer
252. Come Where My Love Lies Dreaming
253. Jeannie with the Light Brown Hair
254. Nellie was a Lady
255. Oh, Susanna
256. Story of a Local Newspaper
257. Story of the YWCA
258. Texas
259. Around Arkansas
260. Themes from America, #11
261. Themes from New Zealand, #30
262. They Walk Again
263. This Land Is Mine *
264. Topics of America
265. Topics of New Zealand, #16
266. Toronto Symphony, No. 1
                        No. 2
267. Treasure House
268. Truck Farm
269. Under the UN Flag
270. UN Finds a Home
271. UN Screen Magazine

UNC
No. Title

272. UN Week Festival, #9
273. Republic of Uruguay
274. Views of America, No. 1
275. Views of America, No. 2
276. White Carnival
277. Why Labor Unions
278. Winter Sports
279. World Series of 1949
280. New England Calling
281. President Truman's Korea Speech
282. Ohio Town
283. Audio-Visual Aids to Learning
284. Discussion Techniques *
285. Agricultural Home Project *
286. Burrough's Newsboy Foundation
287. Erosion
288. Building of Boys
289. Basic English, #1
290. Basic English, #2
291. Basic English, #3
292. Basic English, #4
293. Basic English, #5
294. Basic English, #6
295. Preface to a Life
296. Feeling of Hostility
297. Angry Boy
298. Meeting Emotional Need in Childhood
299. This Is Robert, Part I
300. This Is Robert, Part II
301. Beans, Food for the World
302. Big Lie, The
303. Bridging the Golden Gate
304. Youth Guidance
305. Will for Peace
306. Earthquake in Ecuador

* Japanese film.

333

UNC
No.   *Title*
307. Adobe Village
308. Fight for Freedom
309. American Country Postman
310. University of the World
311. Boy Named Alan
312. World in a Schoolroom
313. Atomic Power
314. Bent with the Years *
315. Fishing Co-operatives *
316. ECOSOC and Its Sub-Agencies
317. Norway—Farmer-Fisherman
318. Sea, My Native Land
319. Telephone Hour, The
320. Town Meeting of the World
321. Better Rural Homes *
322. For Bright Home Life *
323. Social Change in a Democracy
324. American Museum of Natural History
325. American Woman Speaks
326. Switzerland Today
327. Crime of Korea
328. UN 5th Anniversary
329. Where's the Fire

* Japanese film
** USIA film

UNC
No.   *Title*
330. Eternal Fight
331. Highlights of 1952 **
332. Partners for Freedom **
333. Public Opinion and Political Action **
334. Education for Peace **
335. One Year in Korea (130)**
336. POW Exchange **
337. Ward of Affection **
338. Fire Fighters
339. Why Korea?
340. Library Without Bars *
341. New Eyes, New Ears *
342. Home Care of Tuberculosis
343. Vacation Sports
344. Themes from Britain
345. Labor Union
346. Topics of Britain
347. Seas and Mountains of Scotland
348. Footsteps to the Future
349. Growing Children
350. Baseball Swing King
351. This Is the Story of Country People
352. Preparation of Teachers
353. Tommy's Day

334

Appendix D—N.N.R.C. Secretariat, Panmunjom

RULES OF PROCEDURE GOVERNING
EXPLANATIONS & INTERVIEWS

I. GENERAL PROVISIONS

1. Any act of force or threat of force to prevent or to effect repatriation of prisoners of war is prohibited.
2. No prisoner of war shall commit an act of violence against another prisoner of war.
3. Any action infringing upon the rights of prisoners of war under the Terms of Reference of the Commission is prohibited.
4. Any acts of prisoners of war which have the effect of derogating from or obstructing the authority of the Commission to exercise its legitimate functions and responsibilities are prohibited.
5. Any act on the part of prisoners of war impeding the work of EXPLANATIONS & INTERVIEWS is prohibited.
6. As soon as the custody of prisoners of war has been assumed by the N.N.R.C., through the Custodian Force, India, the Commission shall ensure that the prisoners of war are acquainted with the provisions contained in the preceding paragraphs 1-5.

7. Explanations and interviews can be given to groups of or individual prisoners of war as requested by the explaining representatives of the nation to which the prisoners of war belong. Every one of the prisoners of war shall attend the explanations and interviews.

8. Several explanations and interviews to the same group of prisoners of war or the same individual prisoner are permissible within the time prescribed in Article 8 of the Terms of Reference of the Commission.

9. Prisoners may apply for repatriation at any time and at any place. The N.N.R.C. shall ensure that every prisoner of war has an opportunity to do so without interference.

10. At the time of the explanation, there shall be present the N.N.R.C. or its subordinate body, along with one representative each of the two sides to observe the operation and one representative of the detaining side.

11. A sufficient number of subordinate bodies not exceeding 35, composed of one representative from each member nation on the N.N.R.C., shall be established to attend all the work of explanations and interviews and to determine the validity of applications for repatriation.

12. The explaining representative shall have the right to distribute to the prisoners of war written explanations in accordance with the provision of Article 8 of the Terms of Reference, having duly been examined by the Commission or its subordinate body.

13. At no time during the explanations and interviews shall the observer of either side be permitted to interfere with the work of explanation, their sole function being to observe.

14. The representative of the detaining side shall not participate in the work of explanation or interfere with it in any way. He may, however, bring to the notice of the chairman of the N.N.R.C. or its subordinate body at the end of each explana-

tory session, any matter which may be construed as violating the Terms of Reference.

15. In the process of explanations and interviews, interpretation to N.N.R.C. representatives present shall, without obstructing the work of explanations and interviews, be concurrent and shall not interrupt the explanation and interview work.

16. The explaining representatives may ask the prisoner of war any relevant questions provided the latter is warned of his right that he need not answer the questions if he thinks or the N.N.R.C. or its subordinate body thinks that the answer to the questions may be used to threaten or coerce him directly or indirectly.

17. If in the opinion of a member of a subordinate body, in charge of the supervision of explanations, an explainer infringes upon the Terms of Reference or the present rules, or also in any case of disturbance or any major incident, the session shall be immediately suspended; the subordinate body will then without delay examine the situation brought about by such an incident and state upon the conditions under which the session shall be resumed and/or report the case to the Commission.

II. ARRANGEMENTS AND FACILITIES

18. The sites for explanations and interviews, whether to individuals or to groups, shall be so constructed as to ensure that the work of explanations and interviews be free from any interference or obstruction.

19. Facilities shall also be provided for the conduct of the work of explanations and interviews to sick, wounded and injured prisoners of war.

20. Prisoners who have applied for repatriation, those who have been given explanation in accordance with para 7 above but have not submitted their applications for repatriation and those

337

who have neither been given explanation nor applied for repatriation shall be kept separated in custody.

21. Each enclosure for the conduct of individual or group explanations shall have two exits to be used separately by the prisoners of war; one for those who apply for repatriation and the other for those who do not.

22. The work of explanation shall be carried out each day of the week, except Sundays, from 0730 hours to 1630 hours with a lunch interval of one hour.

23. The explaining representatives of the nations to which the prisoners of war belong shall forward to the Secretariat of the N.N.R.C. plans one day in advance from day to day regarding the method of explaining work. They should reach the Secretariat not later than 1000 hours on the day previous to the date on which the plan is to be put into operation.

Index

339

345

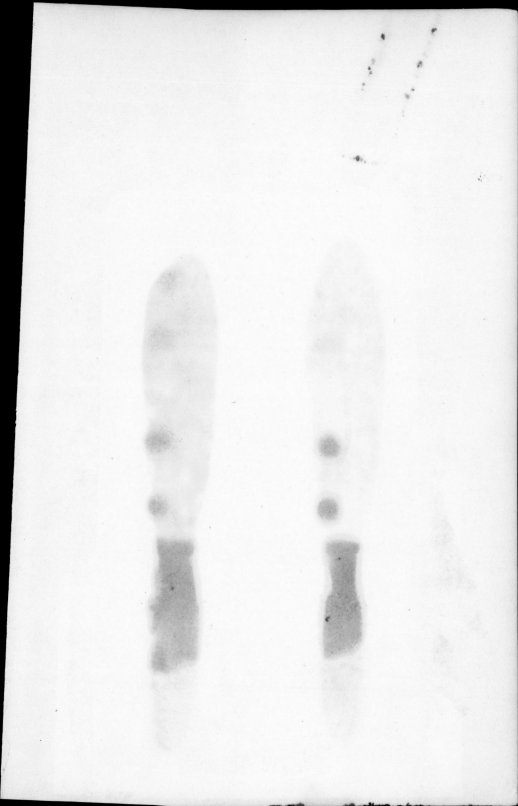

DATE DUE	
ILL 1/3/95	